CW00644420

FINANCIAL ACCOUNTING

Anthony Guter graduated in economics from Cambridge University. During his training he took second place in the Intermediate Examination of the Institute of Chartered Accountants in England and Wales. Since qualifying he was three years with a leading firm of Chartered Accountants and is currently Group Financial Accountant at the European HQ of an international engineering corporation.

Michael Guter is a Certified and Cost & Management Accountant who followed a successful commercial career for many years. In 1971 he began lecturing in Accountancy, thus fulfilling a long-held ambition to teach.

TEACH YOURSELF BOOKS

FINANCIAL ACCOUNTING

A. Guter, MA, FCA

and

M. Guter, FCCA, ACMA

Principal Lecturer in Accounting
Harrow College of Higher Education

Editorial Adviser
Ronald Chappell,
Dean of the Faculty of Social Sciences,
Harrow College of Higher Education

TEACH YOURSELF BOOKS
Hodder and Stoughton

First impression 1978
2nd edition 1981

Copyright © 1978, 1981
A. and M. Guter

British Library C.I.P.
Guter, A.
 Financial accounting.—2nd ed.—(Teach
 yourself books).
 1. Accounting
 I. Title   II. Guter, M.
 657′.48   HF5635

ISBN 0–340–26566–3

Printed and bound in Great Britain for Hodder
and Stoughton Paperbacks, a division of Hodder
and Stoughton Ltd, Mill Road, Dunton Green,
Sevenoaks, Kent
(Editorial Office: 47 Bedford Square, London
WC1 3DP) by Richard Clay (The Chaucer Press),
Ltd., Bungay, Suffolk

Contents

Acknowledgements

We are grateful to the following companies for the use of extracts from their annual accounts: Courtaulds Ltd; The Delta Metal Company Ltd; John Lewis Partnership Ltd; Ocean Transport and Trading Ltd; Pilkington Brothers Ltd; Ruberoid Ltd; Scottish and Newcastle Breweries Ltd; and to the following organisations for the use of examination questions: Association of Certified Accountants; Institute of Bankers; Institute of Chartered Accountants in England and Wales; Institute of Chartered Secretaries and Administrators.

We thank Ronald Chappell, Dean of the Faculty of Social Sciences at Harrow College of Higher Education, for assistance in planning the book, Margaret Pankhurst, senior lecturer in accounting at Harrow College of Higher Education, for helpful comments on the manuscript and Ruth Kimber of Hodder and Stoughton for her help and patience at all times. For any errors that remain we accept responsibility, and would welcome comments, and if necessary, corrections from readers for inclusion in future editions.

Abbreviations

The following abbreviations have been used throughout the book in the interests of clarity and space:

ACCA	Association of Certified Accountants
ICA	Institute of Chartered Accountants in England and Wales
ASC	Accounting Standards Committee
IASC	International accounting standards committee
ED	Exposure draft
IED	International exposure draft
SSAP	Statement of standard accounting practice
IAS	International accounting standard
FAS	Financial accounting standard
CC	Current cost
CCA	Current cost accounting
CPP	Current purchasing power
HC	Historical cost
NRV	Net realisable value
RC	Replacement cost

Preface

Financial accounting is a rapidly changing subject. For some years the accountancy profession has been examining the principles underlying the preparation and presentation of financial reports, using a theoretical approach to review traditional methods, and establishing accounting standards intended to provide uniformity of practice throughout the world. It is essential for anyone concerned with financial accounting—whether as accountant, student, businessman or investor—to follow these changes and to understand why they are occurring, their effects on traditional accounting, and the problems they bring in their wake.

This book presents a general view of modern financial accounting in the United Kingdom. Although emphasis is placed on the accounts of limited companies, the principles may be applied to all forms of financial reporting. Part 1 of the book surveys the field, explaining the theory on which practices are based and outlining the current influences on financial accounting. Part 2 deals with the problem areas of accounting, where the advent of accounting standards is not sufficient to remove the need for judgement.

One such problem—accounting for inflation—requires a separate part to itself (Part 3). The book explains the need for inflation accounting and examines the new UK accounting standard '*SSAP 16 Current Cost Accounting*'.

Many companies own shares in other companies and it is important that their financial accounts correctly reflect the consequences of such investments. Part 4 expounds the standard approach to group accounts.

The legal and professional requirements affecting published accounts are summarised in Part 5. In part 6 the interpretation and uses of financial accounts are considered.

Financial accounting is still developing and it is appropriate to conclude by reviewing the path future developments may take.

The book is intended to cover the syllabi for the financial accounting papers in the examinations of The Institute of Chartered Accountants (PE 1/PE 2), The Association of Certified Accountants (PE sections 1 and 2, the Certified Diploma in Accounting and Finance), The Institute of Cost and Management Accounts (Professional stage 2), The Institute of Bankers (Part 2) and similar bodies. A selection of questions from recent examinations is given in an Appendix.

In addition to students, the book is relevant to the needs of the businessman, manager or general reader who requires an up-to-date survey of the practices and problems of published financial accounting. It is complemented by, and intended to be a companion to, other books on accountancy in the Teach Yourself Series, including those on Bookkeeping, Cost Accounting and Management Accounting.

The reader is also urged to obtain copies of the published accounts of public limited companies, many of whom are pleased to supply copies on request.

PART 1

The Background to Financial Accounting in the UK

1

Introduction to Financial Accounting

1. Introduction to Financial Accounting

Each year every limited company and State enterprise is required by law to prepare accounts. A great many unincorporated firms and sole traders do so voluntarily and many clubs and associations do so because their by-laws require it. Such accounts show the results of the transactions made during the year and summarise the financial position at the end of it. They are used by shareholders and members to see what has happened to their money, by the State to determine tax liabilities, by creditors to see if their debt is safe, by the Press to inform the public what has gone on, by potential buyers of the business—the list of users and uses of accounts has grown significantly since the Companies Act of 1844 made it compulsory for newly formed joint stock companies to present a balance sheet annually to their shareholders.

It is the responsibility of the financial accountant to prepare and explain such accounts and this book will examine the theory and practice of financial accounting as it exists in the United Kingdom today. There will be little discussion of double-entry bookkeeping; the student of accountancy will already be familiar with bookkeeping methods, and the non-accountant reader will be able to understand this book without such knowledge. The bookkeeper records entries; the accountant's task is to decide which figures will fairly reflect the truth and be in accord with the law and with current professional standards. This demands both knowledge and personal judgement and today is performed amidst a high and increasing volume of legislation, pronouncements by the professional bodies, and greater interest than ever before in the standards of financial reporting.

1.1 The scope of financial accounting

The work of the financial accountant falls into two parts:

(a) The analysis of the transactions of the business over the past accounting period, in order to ascertain the figures to be reported on as profit or income. This requires the application of accounting theory to the transactions, and the ability to look beyond the figures recorded by the bookkeeping system to the true financial position of the business. The financial accountant must decide what information is needed to prepare the accounts and must ensure that he has it.

(b) The preparation of the information in a form suitable for publication. Financial accounts are prepared for the use of people outside the business, whose knowledge of what has happened during the past accounting period must be assumed to be nil. The accounts must be clear and comprehensible. When legal requirements apply, as with the Companies Acts or Friendly Societies Act, the accounts must be drawn up to comply with those requirements.

Financial accounts contain a profit and loss account (or income statement) showing the result of the transactions of the past period, a balance sheet showing the assets and liabilities of the enterprise at the end of that period, and supplementary information designed to give the reader a fuller picture of activities and prospects. Some large public companies include reports on each of their activities, products and achievements in their published accounts. Other organisations may wish to provide only the minimum information required by law, in order to maintain the maximum secrecy about their affairs. Small companies and most partnerships and sole traders like to preserve their privacy, and usually decide on 'minimum disclosure'.

The financial accountant is normally fully occupied with preparing the information that will satisfy the minimum requirements; as will be seen there are a great many of these and for most limited companies a 'minimum' set of accounts will be a complex document of many pages.

Whatever else may be included, the profit and loss account and the balance sheet remain the heart of the annual report.

For most organisations the most important figure produced by the financial accountant is the amount of profit for the year. The theory of profit and of how accounting can best compute profit is the foundation of accounting as an academic subject, and any claim that accountancy may have to being scientific lies primarily in its ability to produce a cogent and clear approach to the subject-matter of financial statements.

2

Time, Profit and Capital

2.1 Accounting and time

One of the earliest forms of accounting was developed to show merchants whether their ventures had been successful. Records were kept of the cash receipts and payments resulting from each venture. Subtraction of the latter from the former at the conclusion of the venture gave the profit. The two key elements in this simple scheme were:

(a) The accounts were drawn up on completion of the venture, not after an arbitrary period of time (such as the modern accounting year).
(b) The income and expenses were the cash receipts and payments and the final profit was a sum of cash held by the merchant. Profit was therefore certain and tangible.

In an industrial economy such an elementary approach to accounting will not do. Investors require regular information about the progress of their investments to enable them to decide whether to take any action, such as investing further or withdrawing. To wait for the life of an enterprise to finish before adding up the cash proceeds is clearly absurd. Indeed, the assumption normally made when a business is started is that its life will be infinite, or at any rate will continue for the foreseeable future. As well as investors, others also want to know what progress a business is making. Some of the users of accounts have been listed in Chapter 1. Their need for regular accounts on an annual basis (if not more frequently—*e.g.* the stock exchange requires quoted companies to prepare biannual reports) means that businesses must prepare accounts while transactions continue and the future may be uncertain. At the end of any year during its life, a typical business will consist of a group of assets and liabilities—property, machinery, stocks, sums owed to it and sums it owes, in addition to any cash it possesses. If we could wait until the end of its life the assets would be sold and the liabilities paid off leaving a cash residue. But we cannot wait, and therefore a way must be found to measure the assets and liabilities each year in such a way that the profit for that year can be determined. The concept of profit for a year seems easy to understand, but is in reality difficult to define concisely, and much of the work of the accountant lies in interpreting its meaning.

Time presents many problems in accountancy. When annual accounts are prepared, we are, in effect, arbitrarily slicing into segments something that is really continuous. Unlike the merchant who merely had to count the cash at the termination of a venture, we have to value the assets and liabilities of a business at the end of each accounting period. Such a valuation is necessarily influenced by our view of the future. Many techniques have been developed to assist in this process, but it should be emphasised that, because the future is uncertain, accountancy can only give approximate answers.

2.2 Profit theory

It is the task of the financial accountant to measure profits as they arise. Given the difficulty of trying to assess profits for an arbitrary period, it is necessary to use a workable and comprehensive theory to provide for whatever problems may have to be tackled. Without theory, we can only resort to a series of practical rules which have to be developed piecemeal and which sooner or later are bound to produce contradictory results. The reader will find some evidence for this in the post-war development of the historical cost convention, which will be mentioned in the next and in many later sections of the book.

It is a paradox of accountancy that its central theoretical pillar—profit theory—was developed not by accountants but by economists. It is no longer true to say that accountants neglect the essentials of their subject; the changes in recent

years in teaching and research into accountancy are tantamount to a revolution in accountancy thought which is
transforming the intellectual basis of the profession. (One of
the signs is the increasing proportion of university graduates
entering the profession.) However, we must still start our
discussion of profit theory with the standard approach
developed by economists who have for many years tried to
define the idea of income (profit is a category of income,
being the income earned by a business enterprise).

The usual starting point is the comment of the economist
Sir John Hicks, first published in 1939[1]: 'The purpose of
income calculations is to give people an indication of the
amount they can consume without impoverishing themselves.' Following this idea through, it would seem that we
ought to define a man's income as the 'maximum value that
he can consume during a week which will leave him as well-
off at the end of the week as he was at the beginning'.

If we substitute 'company' or 'business' for 'man', and
'accounting period' for 'week', we have a workable concept.
It is, however, still hopelessly imprecise, since it presents us
with a proposition about the state of mind of the recipient
of income—'well-off' can only mean how 'well-off' a person
thinks he is. We have to make two assumptions before we
can move from the psychological to the accounting approach:

1. That we can measure 'well-offness' in terms of money and
   ignore any other factor that might affect well-being. A
   bonus of £100 together with a letter of appreciation from
   the management to an employee might make that
   employee happier than if he simply received £100. However, accountants must ignore the satisfaction received
   from the letter. Such satisfactions cannot be exchanged in
   our economy and cannot easily be compared in different
   people (if at all). Money is that which can be exchanged
   and is used throughout our society to measure wealth. If
   we can legitimately assign a money value to something it
   can be accounted for; if not, we must ignore it.
2. That we can measure how 'well off' the business is at the
   start and at the end of the period. Unless we are able to

---

[1] J. R. Hicks *Value and Capital* (Oxford, at the Clarendon Press, 1939).

do this, we do not know whether the business is as well off at the end of the period as it was at the beginning. We are still, however, left with the problem of deciding the basis to use in the actual valuation of assets and liabilities.

2.3 Profit and capital

Moving on from the second assumption above, we can express the concepts of profit and 'well-offness' in a series of equations.

The amount by which assets (A) exceed liabilities (L) is the value of the business to the owners and represents the investment made by them. In a limited company this amount is known as the shareholders' interest, but in general it is known as capital (C). Capital in this sense means more than the legal definition which will be encountered when company law is discussed. Here it means the value of a business to the owners, and it may have been built up by direct investment by the owners or by the retention of past profits, or both.

Thus at the start of an accounting period we have:

$$C_0 = A_0 - L_0 \quad\text{... (1)}$$

Let us now suppose that the business is trading profitably, that all profit is retained in the business, and that no additional capital is brought in (*e.g.* there is no issue of shares or injection of money by a new partner). When the business is valued at the end of the period it will therefore show a new value of net assets, thus:

$$C_1 = A_1 - L_1 \quad\text{... (2)}$$

We can now apply Hick's definition. For the business to be as well off at the end of the year as it was at the beginning, net assets equal to C_0 must be retained but any surplus can be taken out of the business without harming it. Thus the profit is represented by the increase in capital. Hence:

$$\text{profit} = C_1 - C_0 \quad\text{.. (3)}$$

or

$$\text{profit} = (A_1 - A_0) - (L_1 - L_0) \quad\text{...................... (4)}$$

Equation (4) says that profit is the increase in net assets over the period, and this will be the definition used throughout.

Traditionally net assets have been measured at the original cost to the business, regardless of subsequent changes in prices. This, the 'historic cost' convention, has always been the basis of bookkeeping systems. Any increase in the value of net assets, measured at historic cost, is profit. In times of changing prices and/or changing price levels, historic costs cease to be directly related to the market value of net assets employed in a business (this is considered further in Chapter 4). Alternative conventions have been proposed to measure the effects of inflation in accounts, and one of these—current cost accounting—is, in the UK, to replace historic cost accounting in the near future.

3

Theory and Practice

Chapter 2 set out the theoretical approach to profit. It is the task of the accountant to devise methods of measurement and valuation which will make workable the concept of 'well-off' upon which profit theory is based: the theme of the book is how theory is applied in practice.

This chapter examines the influences upon accounting and the environment within which financial accounting is carried on. Accountancy is a developing subject, and the pace of change has accelerated in recent years. As a result of the programmes of research now being undertaken, changes may be just as far-reaching in the future. An understanding of the forces shaping accounting is therefore essential in order to grasp what financial accounting is trying to do, and why.

3.1 The bookkeeping system

Accounting must start with a system that records, classifies and summarises transactions. It is not possible to pluck meaningful figures from the air. A set of accounts is the result of a bookkeeping system—whether operated by clerks writing up handwritten ledgers, using accounting machines or operating electronic data-processing equipment—and deficiencies in the system will inevitably produce inadequate accounts.

Although detailed prescriptions for an efficient book-keeping system are outside the scope of this book, the information necessary to produce financial accounts should be collected through the normal bookkeeping system, even if it has no direct relevance to the day-to-day functions of

such a system (paying creditors, recording sales and collect-
ing cash due, paying wages *etc.*). The accountant should have
the annual financial accounts in mind when planning the
work of the accounts department (although it may be
necessary to use most of its resources on the day-to-day
functions). For example, the valuation of stock is a difficult
yearly chore for many businesses. The task can be simplified
if stock records are kept throughout the year, but this will
require all purchases and sales to be recorded in stock
records as well as in purchases and sales journals or day-
books. Although it can mean extra work for the accounts
staff, the accuracy of the financial accounts is likely to be
improved. (For limited companies there is a special incentive
in that the more accurate the accounting system, the less the
audit work likely to be thought necessary by their auditors,
and the lower the audit fee.)

By the end of the accounting period the bookkeeping
system will have produced a classified group of figures
which relate to that period. Typically, this will be in trial
balance form, and arithmetically correct. The major responsibility of the financial accountant is exercised at this
stage. He must ensure that the figures correctly show the
profit for the period and the state of affairs (*i.e.* the assets
and liabilities) at the end of the period. Thus developments
that affect the business but which could not have been
picked up by the bookkeeping system must be incorporated
by the financial accountant. Income earned or expenditure
incurred before the period end, but not recorded in the
books, are examples of such developments. Some decisions
are left to the accountant as a matter of course (*e.g.* estimat-
ing the profits on long-term contracts which may need a
specialist knowledge of the amount of work to be done and
the costs likely to be incurred). Some decisions rest upon the
application of accounting theory and also on deliberate
policy decisions (*e.g.* the treatment of research and development expenditure which may materially affect the reported
profits).

The 'trial balance' figures will be altered as a result of
these decisions to include all relevant information. It is then
necessary for the accountant to present the figures in a
suitable form, and this requires up-to-date knowledge

of the law and the current rules for preparing financial accounts.

When examining trial balance figures for conversion into annual accounts, the financial accountant is not forced to rely on his own inspiration. In the first instance there is the traditional approach to accounting, based on many years of practice, which contains a set of working rules which are usually applicable to all types of business. These rules are described here as conventional accounting.

3.2 Conventional accounting

Conventional accounting embodies a common-sense approach to accounting problems. It is typified by the rule that used to be applied to long-term contracts—that the profit was to be calculated by a formula such as the following:

$$\text{profit} = \frac{amount\ of\ work\ done}{\text{total amount of work on the contract}} \times$$
$$\frac{cash\ received\ to\ date}{\text{invoiced work to date}} \times \frac{\text{total expected}}{\text{profit}} \times \tfrac{2}{3}$$

Such a formula was a prudent attempt to relate profit to work done, but it was put forward as correct because it was a practical, time-honoured rule and not because it was an attempt to match profit with the effort undertaken to earn it. The latter, the theoretical approach, would discard the elements of cash received and the reduction of the profit recognised to two-thirds, as practices applicable only in certain situations and not in others. (The section on stocks in Chapter 7 discusses the problem in more detail.)

The practices of conventional accounting were sometimes glorified as 'principles' of accounting. It was taken for granted that accounts had to be in terms of money; assets deemed to have lost value were to be written down immediately and the loss taken to the profit and loss account, but assets whose value had increased were still to be accounted for at cost. (This convention, 'prudence', has been partly undermined by the theoretical reappraisal of accounts carried out in the 1960s and 1970s.)

The influence of conventional accounting is still very strong. It is used whenever a modern approach has not yet been created and is often found to be satisfactory even when the modern approach is forthcoming. A most peculiar characteristic used to be that, while in normal bookkeeping debits are posted to the left and credits to the right, in the balance sheet assets (debit items) were shown on the right and liabilities (credit items) on the left. Here the modern approach has triumphed and vertical balance sheets have become the accepted form of presentation.

3.3 Accounting theory and standards

Because conventional practices have come to be regarded as inadequate, the profession has embarked upon a programme which will transform financial accounting. Accountancy used to be almost entirely a practical subject, taught to students in the same way that craft apprentices were taught—on the job. Each generation therefore learned to do what the previous generation had done. Academic training was scorned; research into accountancy was unknown.

Today the profession is rapidly moving towards accepting only university graduates and well-qualified school-leavers as its new recruits. Accountancy is taught in many universities and polytechnics. There has been significant research into accounting theory both in the United Kingdom and outside, and there are now accounting standards which apply theory to specific problems and indicate the desired solution. Increasingly, the accountant no longer has to memorise a set of practical rules but must study and understand a theoretical basis and a set of principles derived from that basis. The discipline is striding towards academic respectability and to what some would regard as the ultimate accolade of being called a science.

The move towards accounting standards did not happen simply because theory was developed. Unease about the state of accountancy had spread in the 1960s. It was becoming apparent that accountants were capable of producing a wide range of profit figures to explain identical transactions, since the 'principles' of conventional accounting allowed great latitude in the interpretation of transactions. Unscrupulous directors of companies could 'choose' their own profit figure for a particular year by changing the accounting practice adopted and pretending there had been no change. (For example, by including overheads in stock valuation, a company can raise its profits compared to what would have been reported before the change.) A key event in the build-up of pressure on accountants to tighten up their practices was the merger of the General Electric Company Ltd. and Associated Electrical Industries Ltd. in 1967. Before the merger, in an effort to persuade shareholders to reject GEC's offer, the directors of AEI issued a profit forecast of £10 million. However, the offer was accepted. After the results of AEI had been examined by GEC's accountants, a £4 million loss was announced—for the same period as the forecast. Poor forecasting was only part of the difference—the rest lay with different accounting rules.

In 1969 the accountancy profession announced its intention to reform itself. The Accounting Standards Steering Committee, the name being later shortened to Accounting Standards Committee (ASC), was formed by the Institute of Chartered Accountants in England and Wales. The membership now consists of the three Institutes of Chartered Accountants in the UK, the Association of Certified Accountants, the Institute of Cost and Management Accountants and the Chartered Institute of Public Finance and Accountancy. The ASC has announced a programme of work which will introduce accounting standards to cover all areas in which existing practical rules are deemed inadequate. The rules are replaced by 'Standard Accounting Practice' which applies to all accounts intended to give a 'True and Fair view'.

It is the responsibility of all members of the professional bodies to apply standard accounting practice where it is relevant. If it is not applied, the fact must be stated and the reason explained in the accounts. The rule applies to accountants whether preparing or auditing accounts. Disciplinary action may be taken by the appropriate professional bodies in cases of noncompliance.

A proposed standard is first issued to the profession and public in the form of an Exposure Draft (ED). At this stage it represents what is thought to be the best practice and after comments and criticisms have been studied, the ED will emerge as a Statement of Standard Accounting Practice (SSAP) and will be binding from the date mentioned in the SSAP.

Apart from ED 3, all exposure drafts have become or appear likely to become SSAPs, but many have been altered in the light of criticism; indeed criticism has even served to have SSAPs altered. In 1976 the starting date from which SSAP 11 was to become binding was postponed because the tide of public criticism had become too great to be ignored. The response to ED 14 was such that a second attempt was made in ED 17. SSAP 7, on inflation accounting, was felt to be so controversial that it was dubbed 'Provisional', to be applied at the discretion of a company's directors.

These apparent setbacks are not as important as they may seem. The concept of accounting standards is itself regarded uneasily by many members of the professions who feel that they stifle individual initiative. In the longer run, however, as the new generation of accountants comes to dominate the profession, it is certain that standards covering all the problem areas in accounting will have been issued and agreed.

The UK is in any case joined by many other advanced countries in the creation of standards. In the United States both the profession and the Government have bodies examining and pronouncing on accounting matters. In 1973 the International Accounting Standards Committee (IASC) was formed by ten industrial countries, including the UK, to produce standards that each member country would apply. The long-term aim of the IASC is to achieve similarity of accounting practice across the world, rendering accounts of companies in different countries comparable with each other (which they are not at present). Many countries have subsequently joined the IASC, including some who lack strong professions capable of producing their own standards and who therefore seek to apply the international standards directly. The purpose of the IASC is not to override member countries but to find points of agreement, and so far it has upheld UK practice.

3.4 Accounting and stewardship

Accounting standards and the quest for theory did not grow
in a vacuum. Powerful practical influences have always
shaped accounting and the most important is that derived
from the use of accounts to discharge the obligations of
stewardship. A short historical digression will bring the
matter into perspective.

Financial accounting can be traced back to medieval
practices. Stewards were employed by Lords to administer
their estates and affairs and were entrusted with money and
with the assets of the estates. At regular intervals a steward
would be required to produce figures which showed how he
had conducted the affairs of the estate. The formal examination (usually oral) of such figures was the origin of auditing,
and their preparation the origin of financial accounting.
These accounts might have been used to help in the more
efficient administration of the estate, but their primary
function was to support the claims of the steward that he
had acted honestly.

During the eighteenth and nineteenth centuries the
concept of stewardship was transformed. At this time the
process of industrialisation was encouraging the growth of
business organisations, and the limited company or corporation was found to be the most useful type of such organisation. A century of suspicion of limited companies followed
the collapse of the South Sea Company in 1720 and it was
difficult for individuals to form themselves into a company
until the 1844 Companies Act. With this act, which accom-
panied the rapid expansion of railways and railway companies, it became common for wealthy individuals wishing to
earn profits from business to pool their funds in a company
and to entrust the running of the business to elected directors.
New Companies Acts made the creation of limited companies easier and such companies became the dominant
form of industrial organisation by the end of the century. In
the twentieth century they have come to be the major source
of industrial output in the UK and throughout the non-
Communist world.

A limited company possesses two special features which
emphasise the need for accounting. These are:

1. The *limited liability* of the individual shareholder (not the
   company itself): once a shareholder has paid for his
   shares he has no further liability should the company fail.
   A creditor of the company can only look to the assets of
   the company itself for repayment, not to the personal
   assets of the shareholders. (In sharp contrast are the
   Bankruptcy Laws which allow virtually all of the private
   assets of an individual owner to be reckoned part of the
   trading assets should an enterprise collapse.) Shareholders
   (in relation to their ownership of shares in a limited
   company) are given a privilege denied to the remainder of
   society.
2. The *divergence between shareholders and directors*: shareholders cannot always all be directors. In small family
   companies it is comparatively easy for every shareholder
   to join in the management of the business, but larger
   companies, with many thousands of shareholders, would
   be quite unmanageable if every shareholder tried to have
   a say. Instead directors are elected to run the business on
   behalf of the shareholders, and it is not even necessary
   in law for such directors to own shares in the company
   (although many companies specify share ownership by
   directors as one of their Articles of Association). There is
   an ever-present danger in such companies—and in smaller
   ones with shareholders who take little part in the management—that the directors will use their power for their
   own ends because the shareholders have no way of
   challenging them.

Both of these features involve questions of stewardship—
the first the use by shareholders of the right of limited
liability, the second the use by directors of the assets of the
shareholders. The solution to the problems that could be
caused by abuse of stewardship is seen in the establishment
of a framework of law regulating companies, the law being
enforced by making companies accountable to their shareholders and also to society. A company must by law prepare
annual accounts which are issued to each shareholder and
deposited with the Registrar of Companies, who makes his
copy available for public inspection.

However, it would be pointless to require companies to

publish accounts if there were no independent check upon their accuracy. Since 1844 the principle of the audit has been connected with company accounts and since 1948 every limited company has been required to present a profit and loss account and balance sheet to its members, which must be audited by professionally qualified accountants. There are detailed requirements for what must be disclosed in the accounts (see Chapter 19) and an overriding obligation placed upon the auditor to report to the shareholders whether in his opinion the accounts comply with the provisions of the Companies Act and whether they show a true and fair view.

The law has never defined a 'true and fair' view, though the phrase has been used for over a century. It has been left to the accountancy profession to decide. A series of court cases has produced some enlightenment, but judges can only interpret the law and without a legal formula were forced to resort to the professional experts—the auditors themselves. The profession did not attempt to lay down rules which would define what was 'true and fair' but left the matter to the individual members, perpetuating the 'conventional' accounting described earlier. However, from 1944 the ICA began to issue accounting recommendations to assist its members and we now have accounting standards which are authoritative rulings on what practice is deemed to be true and fair.

It is instructive to note that the history of accounting in the United States has been similar, except that US accounts are required to be 'in accordance with generally accepted accounting principles'. As with the ASC in the UK, the American Financial Accounting Standards Board issues statements outlining what are considered to be generally accepted accounting principles.

If an auditor of a limited company in the UK feels that accounts do not comply with accounting standards and cannot support the policy of the company, he is required to 'qualify' his audit report (which is printed as part of the accounts) on the grounds that a true and fair view is not being shown. Thus do the theoretical and practical approaches meet.

3.5 Further current influences on accounting

In addition to these general requirements, other factors are at work. Financial accounts are the principal public source of information about limited companies. They have begun to be regarded as a major instrument of control over companies, in an extension of the concept of 'accounting for stewardship' introduced in the nineteenth century.

There have been a number of cases of the abuse of power by directors of companies in post-war years. These were sometimes announced by boardroom disputes, or revealed in the wake of financial collapse. Each new scandal strengthens the call for greater openness in company accounts. The hope is that it will be harder for directors to act fraudulently or negligently if the accounts are both wider-reaching and more detailed than before. The Companies Act, 1967 contained a number of new provisions requiring greater disclosure and the Companies Acts, 1976 and 1980 tightened the rules affecting directors. The emphasis has shifted to redefining the duties of directors and giving greater power to auditors to carry out their work; but disclosure in the accounts is still seen as a key feature in regulating companies.

Many of the reforms contained in recent or proposed company legislation are 'fire brigade' responses. They are brought out to prevent the future recurrence of a particular problem that has flared up into public notice and which can be blamed on insufficiently stringent legal or professional requirements. Such reforms do not seek to change the overall structure of law but to adjust it in those places where it appears weak. In contrast, the accountancy profession has begun to examine the structure of financial accounting and reporting as a whole, starting from first principles and building up to a detailed conclusion, the aim being to discover what kind of accounts are needed. A major development in the process of reappraisal was signalled by the publication, in August 1975, of a discussion paper entitled 'The Corporate Report', which was produced by an ICA working party whose terms of reference were to study the scope and aims of published financial statements. The paper starts with the question: who uses accounts and what do the users really want to see in them? From there,

existing accounts are assessed and it is concluded that they
are inadequate to meet users' needs. Recommendations are
made to the effect that these needs can be satisfied by
retaining regular financial statements and adding new
statements to the existing profit and loss account and
balance sheet. The total information thus provided should be
adequate to satisfy users. The criticism of existing financial
accounts and the proposals for reform made by the working
party are discussed in detail in Chapter 24.

3.6 Inflation

At the same time as the working party was examining the
basis of accounts, a Government Committee of Enquiry
headed by Francis Sandilands was examining proposals for
accounting methods which would show the effects of inflation. Inflation, a phenomenon experienced in many parts of
the world since the Second World War, was recognised as a
major distortion to conventional accounting. The pace of
inflation had quickened in the late 1960s and pressure for
amendments to conventional accounting grew. The Sandilands Committee found that since conventional accounts
were so seriously distorted by inflation, it was necessary to
examine the entire structure of accounting.[1] The committee
therefore considered what accounts were used for and what
they should show, and its report, published in 1975, reached
almost identical conclusions to those in the Corporate
Report. The proposals made by the Sandilands Committee
were accepted by the Government and, with reservations,
by the profession, and after some difficulties with the first
exposure draft, SSAP 16 *Current Cost Accounting* was
published in 1980.

SSAP 16 marks a major shift in accounting, from the time
honoured practices of the past hundred years to newer
concepts based on accounting theory. But the debate about
the most useful forms of financial accounting has continued
and is certain to go on influencing accounting practice.

[1] *Report of the Inflation Accounting Committee* (HMSO, 1975).

PART 2

Principles and Problems
in Financial Accounting

4

Principles of Profit Measurement

The definition of profit in Chapter 2 is no more than a starting point. In practice it is not possible merely to record and classify transactions in order to produce financial accounts. We need to employ a variety of principles in dealing with raw accounting data in order to produce coherent, clear and theoretically satisfactory results. This chapter examines the chief principles used by accountants in the industrialised Western economies.

4.1 Terminology

Theory is comparatively new to accountancy. Each contributor to the subject is to some extent free to use terms such as 'axiom', 'principle', 'concept', 'assumption' and 'convention' when discussing the generally accepted theoretical and practical rules governing accountancy. The rules classified under a particular heading by one writer may be given a different name by another; furthermore the list of rules itself might vary. Thus while the ASC distinguished four 'fundamental accounting concepts' in SSAP 2, the IASC chose three of the four to be 'fundamental accounting assumptions' and classified the fourth as a 'consideration'. Such free use of terms creates confusion. In this book the following terms are used with the meanings assigned, and although they correspond closely to general usage, the reader should check precisely what meaning is given to them when they are encountered in other works.

Axioms are the ideas which are the starting points for the preparation of accounts. Usually they are thought to be so obvious that they are ignored. Three axioms, 'entity', 'accounting period' and 'money measurement' are discussed.

Concepts are those rules found to be indispensable in practice in order to produce relevant information. Unlike the axioms they may be discarded if special circumstances warrant. The chief concepts are 'going concern', 'accruals', 'consistency' and 'prudence'.

Conventions are methods of measuring transactions, assets and liabilities in money terms. Three major conventions exist—'historical cost', 'current purchasing power' and 'current (or replacement) cost'. The historical cost convention has been the traditional method; the others are newer conventions developed to remove the distorting effects of inflation. Only one convention can be chosen as the method used to measure profits. In the absence of directions from the State or Professional bodies, a business must decide which convention is the most suitable.

4.2 Axioms

1. *Entity:* By entity is meant any organisation which, by virtue of separate legal or economic identity, can be thought of as distinct from the people who run it. Entities include limited companies, public corporations, partnerships, sole traders, associations, clubs, charities and the State. If an entity can be said to be better or worse off (in economic terms) at the end of a period than it was at the start, then accounts can be prepared measuring the change and measuring the state of affairs at the end of the period.

An entity is quite distinct from its owners. The purpose of accountancy is to show what has happened to the entity itself. Thus company accounts do not report on shareholders' well-being, and the accounts of a sole trader are restricted to business activities only and do not include the trader's personal assets or liabilities in measuring his state of affairs.[1]

The assumptions and conventions used in this book are those developed for business entities. They can nearly always be applied to other forms of organisation but should not be

---

[1] Except when bankrupt.

adopted uncritically. For example the 'going concern' concept has a particular meaning when used in business; it has less relevance to a private club where the members may be prepared to finance operations from their own incomes.

The entity axiom is based on real factors rather than legal fiction. Thus, although accounts are prepared for companies even when wholly owned by others, group accounts consolidating the results of an owned company with those of its owner are also prepared. These reflect the economic reality of the business entity, which in this case is the group of two (or more) companies.

2. *Money measurement:* In a monetary economy all transactions are expressed in money terms and wealth is measured in money. We therefore express all assets and liabilities in money values only, and where there are transactions in more than one currency, as in the case of firms with overseas interests, we convert the foreign values into those of the domestic economy. If money cannot be used as the yardstick, financial accounts cannot be prepared.

3. *Accounting period:* A time period must be chosen to which the accounts are to relate. This period can be the entire life of an entity or a lesser period. The vast majority of entities produce accounts covering periods of one year, and some businesses will often attempt to prepare accounts more frequently than that, because those who wish to use the accounts need them at shorter intervals.

The accounts must cover all the activities of the entity during the accounting period, and the financial state of the entity at the end of the period. The end of the period— the balance sheet date—is used as the 'cut-off' point in deciding in which period activities fall. However, it may be necessary on occasions to look beyond the balance sheet date in order to assess the true position at that date.

4.3 SSAP 2 and fundamental accounting concepts

SSAP 2, '*Disclosure of accounting policies*' issued in November 1971, is the cornerstone of the attempts now being made to achieve standardisation in accountancy practice. It is required reading for students of financial accounting. The influence of SSAP 2 is likely to be far-reaching, both in raising standards, and in changing the practices of many enterprises often insulated from developments in accountancy. The standard is binding upon *all* accounts intended to give a true and fair view, which are produced or audited by members of the professional bodies comprising the ASC.

SSAP 2 requires:

(*a*) That accounts are drawn up embodying what the statement calls 'fundamental accounting concepts'.
(*b*) That entities must decide how best to incorporate the concepts into their accounts. In applying the concepts, problems are encountered in a number of areas. SSAP 2 defines the methods used to deal with problems as 'accounting bases'. Examples of problem areas include turnover, depreciation, stock valuation, consolidations and deferred taxation. The entity must select the accounting base which, in the opinion of its management, is appropriate to its circumstances and best suited to present fairly its results and financial position. The specific accounting base chosen is an 'accounting policy'.
(*c*) That accounting policies followed for dealing with items judged material or critical in determining profit or loss for the year and in stating the financial position be disclosed as a note to the accounts. In addition, if assumptions which differ in material respects from the fundamental concepts are used, the facts should be disclosed and explained. In the absence of a statement to the contrary it is presumed that the fundamental concepts have been observed.

The effect of SSAP 2 is that all accounting practices must now be justified in the light of generally accepted principles, and explained to readers of the accounts. The fundamental concepts in the statement are:

1. *Going concern:* the entity will continue to operate in the foreseeable future. No provision has to be made now for losses caused by winding up, and there will be no forced business activities which would not normally be made,

such as the sale of a large part of the business in order to raise the finance to support the remainder. The 'going concern' concept is of special importance in that it must not be applied if a business is thought likely to collapse, or if a business is in difficulties which might have drastic effects on its future performance. However, the mere disclosure that the going concern basis is inapplicable can bring about the actual collapse of a business. Creditors will demand repayment of sums owing and future credit will be curtailed; employees will leave, customers will be worried about future supplies. Thus the very disclosure of problems can intensify these problems.

2. *Accruals* (also known as 'matching'): within the period selected for the accounts, all income and expenditure is dealt with in the accounts, regardless of whether actual receipts or payments have taken place. The profit and loss account should show the results of all transactions that have taken place in the period. The concept is the embodiment of the ideas advanced in Chapter 2 but is qualified in SSAP 2, in that if it conflicts with the prudence concept (see below) the prudence concept prevails. The accruals concept is the basis of many of the new accounting standards which deal with areas where problems of the allocation of income or expenditure to a particular period exist.

3. *Consistency:* once accounting policies are selected, they should be retained within each accounting period and in successive accounting periods. The reason for this is that continual chopping and changing would distort results and make an interpretation of the accounts and long-term trends very difficult. (Policies will obviously be changed if they become irrelevant in changing circumstances, but this will not often be the case in the vast majority of businesses.)

4. *Prudence:* revenue and profit are not anticipated until realised in the form of cash or assets reasonably certain to be turned into cash. However, losses are to be provided for as soon as thought reasonably likely to occur even if not certain.

The preferment of the prudence concept over the strict

theory as represented by the accruals concept is an indication of the ASC's wish to make SSAP 2 commercially acceptable, since a conservative approach to accounting has always been regarded as good business sense. The 'concept', however, is really a sound common-sense rule rather than a concept. It is notable that the 'fundamental accounting assumptions' listed by the International Accounting Standards Committee in their first Statement of International Accounting Standards, also called 'Disclosure of accounting policies', should include only the first three of those selected by SSAP 2. A second tier of useful 'considerations' is introduced by IAS 1. These are

1. *Prudence:* as in SSAP 2.
2. *Substance over form:* where reality conflicts with legal formality, reality should prevail.
3. *Materiality:* accounts should separately disclose all material items. The concept of materiality is necessary when preparing the accounts of most entities, where the correct stating of a few major items has much more value than the enumeration of infinite trivial ones. However, materiality does not mean 'large' but 'significant'. Most items thought to be material are usually large in relation to the the size of the entity, but an item may be material by its smallness, if normally it is large. For example, a business which did not depreciate plant and did not disclose the fact or the nil charge for depreciation, on the grounds that the item was too small to be material, would mislead users of its accounts, if it were generally accepted that depreciation should be provided on plant in that particular line of business.

The reader will find many references to materiality in this book. It is very hard to define, but like art, it is known when it is seen. Sometimes material is defined as that which influences the view given by accounts, so that an item which would not influence the view given by accounts can be considered immaterial to them. However, each reader of a set of accounts may interpret it in a different way and there are many borderline cases where the accountant must rely on his experience and judgement in deciding what is, and what is not, material.

4.4 Disclosure of accounting policies

SSAP 2 is ostensibly about disclosing the policies used in
preparing accounts. In fact there can be no disclosure unless
such policies actually exist. SSAP 2 has had the effect of
forcing businesses to decide what their policies are and to
make sure they are both applied and disclosed in the
accounts. Public companies have tended to show such
information anyway, but many other enterprises have never
reviewed or disclosed their policies and are finding that
SSAP 2 has caused changes in their practices.

It is the aim of the ASC to cut down on the choice of
accounting policies, and the other accounting standards deal
with the various areas of difficulty caused by the wide variety
of accounting bases available. However, it is stated in SSAP 2
that 'it has to be recognised that the complexity and diversity
of business renders total and rigid uniformity of bases
impracticable'.

Exhibits 1, 2 and 3, which follow, illustrate the modern
trend of disclosing the accounting policies in a single statement. They show the range of subjects and the typical
wording used by leading public companies.

EXHIBIT 1, from the Report and Accounts of The Delta
Metal Company Limited for the year ending 1 January 1977
shows the policies of a large international group making
finished engineering products and components, and semi-
manufactured products. EXHIBIT 2, from the Report and
Accounts of John Lewis Partnership Limited for the year
ending 29 January 1977 is representative of the policies used
by retailers. EXHIBIT 3, from the Annual Report and
Accounts of Ocean Transport and Trading Limited for the
year ending 31 December 1976 is more specialised, reflecting
the particular accounting problems concerned with dealing
with ships and voyages.

The reader should note the similarities of these exhibits—
each deals with depreciation, stocks and taxation, for
example—and their differences, reflecting the varying
nature of their businesses. Delta, whose activities involve
the extensive use of metals, isolate gains arising on changes
in metal prices from trading profits. John Lewis, who own
many retailing properties, note how they are valued. Ocean

does the same for its ships and acknowledges the special risks of shipping by noting how vessels are insured

EXHIBIT 1

The Delta Metal Company Limited

Report and Accounts for the year ended 1 January 1977
Accounting Policies

1 Associated companies
The group share of the profits less losses of associated companies attributable to the equity holding is included in the group profit and loss account (note 5).

The group defines associated companies as those in which the group has an equity interest of 20% or more and board representation, provided that regular management accounts are received (note 22).

---

2 Bank overdrafts
Bank overdrafts constitute an important part of the source of the capital employed by the group and are included in the balance sheet accordingly.

---

3 Depreciation
In the case of United Kingdom assets, depreciation is provided on the following straight line basis:

Plant and equipment	10%
Motor vehicles, trucks, etc.	25%
Furniture, fittings and office equipment	20%
Freehold land	Nil
Freehold buildings	2%
Leasehold property	Over the term of the lease

There are minor variations from the above rates in the case of some overseas subsidiary companies.

---

4 Goodwill
Net goodwill arising from acquisitions is written off (note 10).

---

5 Metal profits and losses
A substantial proportion of the group's manufacturing operations involves the use of copper, brass and other copper alloys and consequently profits and losses arise from price fluctuations

in respect of metal stocks, part of which are not covered by sales contracts. Such profits and losses are segregated from trading profits and dealt with by transfers to or from metal price contingency reserve. The metal price contingency reserve is available to offset metal stock losses which may arise in the future due to fluctuations in metal prices.

In the opinion of the directors these accounting procedures are appropriate in the particular circumstances which apply to the company's business and the profit and loss account is presented accordingly.

---

6 Foreign currency
The accounts of overseas group companies and overseas assets and liabilities held by UK group companies are converted into sterling at the rates ruling on the last day of the financial year. The effect of translating profits and net assets by reference to rates ruling at the year end as against rates ruling at the beginning of the year is shown in respect of:

(*a*) Overseas trading profits (note 2).
(*b*) Net assets.

---

7 Patents and trade marks
All expenses incurred in connection with patents and trade marks are written off as incurred.

---

8 Research and development
All research and development expenditure is written off as incurred.

---

9 Stocks and work-in-progress
Stocks and work-in-progress are valued at the total of the lower of cost and net realisable value of the separate items of stocks and work-in-progress or of groups of similar items.

The basis of valuation of stocks has been modified where necessary, in certain subsidiaries, to include overhead expenses as required by Statement of Standard Accounting Practice No. 9. The surplus arising on the change in accounting basis applying to the opening valuation of stocks and work-in-progress is treated as a prior year item, in accordance with Statement of Standard Accounting Practice No. 6 and opening reserves are restated accordingly (note 13). The change has had no material effect on the profits for the year.

---

10 Taxation

The taxation charge for the year includes adjustment of previous year's provisions (note 7).

Corporation tax deferred by relief for stock appreciation is included in deferred taxation at the rates applicable to the years in which the original liability arose (note 15).

Deferred taxation is provided in accordance with the suspended Statement of Accounting Practice No. 11 on the liability method, except that no provision has been made on surpluses on revaluations of properties and investments, for capital gains tax which might arise on future disposals (note 15). The opening reserves are restated to include as a prior year item the release of the opening capital gains tax provision (note 13).

EXHIBIT 2

John Lewis Partnership Limited

Notes on the accounts

Accounting policies

The consolidated profit and loss account and balance sheet include the accounts of the company and all subsidiaries.

Turnover is stated at the total amount receivable by the group for goods sold and services provided during the year, but excludes sales within the group. Goods sold on hire purchase are included in full but the profit is spread over the term of the contract.

Stock is stated at the lower of cost or net realisable value. Cost of manufactured stock includes an appropriate portion of overhead expenditure.

Properties are included at valuations made in 1965 and 1974 or at cost. The valuations were made on the basis that each property was regarded as available for existing use in the open market.

Surpluses arising on the revaluation of properties are credited to reserves.

No depreciation is charged on freehold or long leasehold land. Depreciation is calculated in equal annual instalments for all other assets at rates deemed appropriate to write off the assets over their useful lives.

The deferred tax provision includes taxation deferred as a result of capital allowances exceeding the depreciation charge in the accounts, taxation relief on increased stock values and the liability to taxation of capital gains which would arise if properties were to be sold at the amounts at which they have been revalued. The balances on the deferred taxation account are not revised on changes in rates of taxation.

EXHIBIT 3

Ocean Transport & Trading Limited

Annual Report and Accounts for the year ending 31 December 1976

Accounting policies

The accounting policies adopted by the Group are set out below and are consistent with those of the previous year.

Basis of consolidation

The Group accounts consolidate the audited accounts of the Company and its subsidiaries all of which prepare accounts at 31 December. The accounts of subsidiary companies acquired during the year are included in Group figures from the effective dates of acquisition.

Associated companies

The Group profit and loss account includes the Group's share of the results of its associated companies as shown by their audited accounts or unaudited management accounts for years ended not earlier than 30 November.

Trading results

Results of voyages completed during the year are included in trading profit. No amount is included in respect of voyages which had not been completed at the end of the year. Period time charters and non shipping activities are accounted for on an accrual basis.

Depreciation

Depreciation of the fleet is provided evenly over the expected useful lives of the ships in the trades operated by the Group, which are normally

Off-shore supply ships	10 years
Container ships	15 years
Ore/oil and chemical carriers	16 years
Product and dry bulk carriers	20 years
Cargo liners	20 or 24 years

Investment grants have been deducted from the costs of the relevant assets. Depreciation is based on the net costs of assets and after taking account of estimated residual values at current scrap prices. Dry bulk carriers are now depreciated over 20 years; up to 1975 they were depreciated over 16 years.

Depreciation is not normally charged in respect of the Group's freehold and long leasehold properties.

All other assets are depreciated evenly over their estimated useful lives.

Fleet insurance
Insurance of cargo liners is effected almost wholly within the Group. Other ships are insured mainly outside the Group.

Survey costs
The fleet is maintained generally on a continuous survey basis. In arriving at the trading profit, survey expenses are charged in the year in which they are incurred.

Investment income
Profits and losses arising on the sale of United Kingdom Government securities which, on purchase, were due for redemption within five years, are accounted as investment income.

Development expenditure
Expenditure on new projects is amortised by five equal annual instalments commencing in the year in which it is incurred.

The balance of any expenditure on projects not subsequently employed in the Group's trading activities is charged against trading profit when abandoned.

Foreign currencies
The costs of ships are expressed at the rates of exchange ruling when they were acquired. Other assets and liabilities arising in foreign currency are expressed at the rates of exchange ruling at the balance sheet date.

Profits or losses due to currency fluctuations, other than those arising on the settlement of day-to-day transactions, are shown as a separate item in the profit and loss account.

Stocks
Stocks are stated at the lower of cost and net realisable value.

Tax equalisation
Provision is made under the net deferral method to take account of the timing differences for accounting and taxation purposes of depreciation and other charges. Advance corporation tax payable on dividends is deducted from this provision. In the case of the parent company the excess of advance corporation tax over tax equalisation is separately shown in the balance sheet.

4.5 The historic cost convention

We have stated that money measurement is an axiom of accounting. The historical cost method of accounting has been the convention adopted for recording transactions, assets and liabilities for as long as accountancy has been practised in its modern form. The method involves using the money value of assets at the time of acquisition by the business as the value to be used in accounting for those assets. In other words, when preparing a balance sheet the basis of measurement of the value of an asset shown is its cost to the enterprise. Profit is calculated by subtracting from the proceeds of sales the cost of the goods sold, such cost being the cost when the goods were purchased or made. The method used to seem so obvious that discussion of it appeared pointless, but in practice it has ceased to be regarded by many accountants as the best way of achieving a 'true and fair' result.

4.6 Advantages of the historical cost convention

The advantages claimed by proponents of the convention are:

1. It is objective. Accounts show the actual money cost of assets, incurred in an outside transaction rather than an arbitrary valuation. The scope for manipulation is reduced to a minimum.
2. It is simple to operate. Accountancy is dependent upon the accurate collection of information by a bookkeeping system (or by a data-processing system if electronic methods are used). Without reliable inputs of information, accounting is a waste of time. The historical cost method makes bookkeeping straightforward, in that the entries in the books follow the money values on the prime documents (invoices, wages sheets *etc.*). Thus when wages are paid, the wages account is debited with the amount of the payment and the cash account is credited. There is no problem for the bookkeeper about which figure to use (apart from routine transfers of PAYE *etc.*). The payment can subsequently be traced to the profit and loss account, together with all other wages payments, and the amount in the profit and loss account will be the total of the cash sums paid or payable during the accounting period.

4.7 Disadvantages

Experience of the method has revealed the following weaknesses:

1. Lack of objectivity in some areas, such as
(*a*) *The valuation of some fixed assets:* historical cost in its pure form values land at cost, regardless of the date of purchase. This can lead to ridiculous understatement of its market value in the balance sheet. Many companies in the 1950s and 60s were taken over for the sake of their land, because shareholders did not realise its true worth (as this was not disclosed in the accounts) and were thus prepared to accept lower share prices. In consequence the takeover created big capital gains for the buyers. To prevent this, many firms now revalue such assets regularly and show them at that valuation in the accounts, raising the reserves (and henceforth the value of the shareholders' funds or owners' capital) by the same amount, less possible tax liabilities. This practice gives a truer and fairer view, but it allows for a subjective opinion in fixing the value (and in deciding how often to revalue).
(*b*) *The valuation of transactions which extend beyond the present accounting period:* as discussed in Chapter 2, we are forced to estimate the future as best we can in order to value uncompleted transactions. Subjectivity cannot be avoided when choosing depreciation rates, accounting for profit on long-term contracts, or deciding the value of expenditure, on research for example, which may or may not bring in future benefits. In addition, application of the prudence concept requires that stocks be valued at no more than net realisable value if thought to be less than cost. Again this can only be an estimate.
2. Inconsistencies of approach. While stocks are written down if necessary, to provide for losses as soon as possible, unrealised profits are not recorded until realised. (The meaning of realisation is explored in the next chapter.) This treatment applies to assets, unless revalued, but such revaluations are normally confined to land and buildings.
3. In matching historical costs against current sales, which is

the way in which profits are calculated under this method, we are ignoring the possible movement in prices of inputs, which means that the real cost of sales to the business is not correctly stated. For example, a unit of a stock bought at the start of a month costs a business £10. It is sold for £20 at the end of the month, but by then the cost has risen to £15 on the open market (so that if the business had bought and sold on the same day it would have paid £15). The historical cost method records a profit of £(20 – 10) = £10. Yet the value of the good to the business when sold was at least £15. The problem of current cost as against historical cost affects both stock and fixed assets. The latter may be depreciated on its historical cost producing depreciation charges which are too low if the cost of assets is rising—or too high if costs are falling.

4. In addition to movements in specific price levels, there may be movements in the general level of prices. As prices rise, so the value of money falls. A profit of £100 in 1965 bought goods that would have cost £235 if bought in 1975. To show a 1975 profit of £235 as being 'more' than the 1965 figure is to mislead the users of accounts. If indeed historic cost profits in 1975 were £200 against a 1965 level of £100, the shareholders would be worse off with the 1975 results than they were ten years before.

5. The conventional balance sheet records the assets and liabilities of the entity, measured at cost, less any amounts written off for depreciation *etc*. The balance sheet shows mainly what has happened to the sums of money invested in the business and is a valuable aid to the examination of the stewardship of directors or management. But the balance sheet does not measure the market value of the net assets. The reader cannot judge the performance of the management in using the resources entrusted to it, because the value of those resources is not disclosed. Furthermore it is difficult for the investor to judge the value of his investment.

Example 1
A property company is formed with £1 million of share-holders' funds and invests the sum in an office block.

Twenty years later it receives annual rents of £500,000. The accounts, prepared under the historical cost convention, will show a return of 50% on the capital of the business, and an asset still apparently worth £1 million (assuming no depreciation). Obviously the market value of the block is greater than £1 million and hence the return on capital employed is less than 50%. Yet unless a revaluation takes place, the accounts will continue to value the block at cost.

As pointed out in criticism 1, revaluations do take place, particularly for property. But if the performance of a business is to be judged correctly, all assets should be valued in a way which reflects inflation, and not merely when it is blatantly obvious, as in the case of property.

The effect of these criticisms has been to shake the confidence of the accountancy profession, the business world and the Government in the historical cost convention. However, as inflation accounting still has to be widely used, historical cost principles are applied in the following two chapters, in which profit theory is applied to practical problems of the measurement of transactions and of assets and liabilities.

5

The Elements of the Profit and Loss Account

5.1 Trading profit

The accruals concept is the starting point for the treatment
of trading transactions. That concept requires income and
expenditure to be allocated to the time periods in which they
arise. It is fundamental that the allocation is made upon the
correct theoretical grounds and not to suit the vagaries of a
particular accounting system; indeed, one of the consequences of the full adoption of the concept is that accounting systems may have to be overhauled to ensure that they
record the information necessary to produce accounts that
comply with it and thus with SSAP 2.

The allocation of income and expenditure to the appropriate time period is a three-part exercise which involves:

1. Deciding what income arises in the accounting period;
2. Relating to that income all the expenditure necessary to
   earn it;
3. Examining all other expenditure incurred in the period
   which may have to be charged against income now if it
   will not lead to the creation of income in the future
   against which it would otherwise be charged.

5.2 The allocation of income

Income can be broadly defined as a flow of resources into an
entity. That flow is measured by the money value of the
transactions which create it—the sale of goods or services,
the receipt of interest or rent—and given that income-
creating transactions are going on continually, the problem
is to decide at what point a transaction creates income, so

that completed transactions can be separated from those still to be completed (which therefore are regarded as creating income in the future but not in the present accounting period). This is a practical business problem. In a society where purchasers were not legally bound to pay for goods until, say, three months after they were handed over, the sale could not be said to be made until that point, and the transaction would not therefore be recognised as a sale until then. In the Western world the law recognises a binding sale at a much earlier point, normally when there is an offer and acceptance of a sale, and business practice, though tending to be more conservative, also looks to the time when the transaction is made and not when it is completed by the payment of the amount due by the buyer. There is, however, a most important proviso—that payment *will* ultimately be made. Since the entire point of making any sale is to receive payment, a transaction that merely creates a debt which will not be paid cannot be regarded as a source of income. Indeed, while on theoretical grounds the completion of the production of goods could be said to create income, in the sense that the goods are bound to be sold in some future time period, business sense insists that no income is recognised until two conditions are met:

(a) *The income must be earned:* the activity which will generate a sale must have been completed. The point at which an activity is complete varies from business to business. For example, in the retail trade, merely putting goods in a shop window is not enough—a customer must be found ready to pay.

(b) *The income must be realised:* an event must have occurred which significantly increases the likelihood of conversion into cash.

Realisation is of major importance in determining the recognition of income. As already stated, it is not necessary for payment to have been received, but it is necessary to be reasonably confident that payment will be received. Until that is the case, it is not regarded as prudent to recognise income on any transaction. Thus, goods in the shop window continue to be valued at cost until they are sold to a customer who either pays or agrees to pay in the future; after that, even if the goods remain on the premises, they will be regarded as the property of the customer (unless the business has special rules of its own) and will not be included in the net assets of the business, being replaced by the debt due from the customer (or the cash paid).

An important corollary is that all transactions where realisation has taken place must be included in the income of the present period. It is normal for businesses to carry out special 'cut-off' tests at the end of their accounting year to ensure that all transactions that have been realised are recorded. For example, sales may not be accounted for in the books until the invoice is made out, but this may be several weeks after delivery. If delivery is on the basis of a firm order, so that the movement of the goods outward is the true point of sale, the business must ensure that all deliveries up to the year end are included in the figure of sales for that year. This is a good example of the need to check the accounting system to obtain all the required information: the system would record the sales relating to deliveries for the few weeks before the year end, and hence the profit on the sales, in the following accounting period and the matching concept would not be followed.

5.3 The choice of accounting base

Each business must apply both the general concepts of accounting and the specific conditions of earning and realisation to its particular trading circumstances in order to formulate an appropriate accounting policy. In the case of a manufacturing enterprise producing against firm orders, the following are all theoretical possibilities as a base for the accounting policy towards turnover:

1. Receipt of the order;
2. Commencement of production against the order;
3. Completion of production;
4. Delivery to customer;
5. Invoicing the customer;
6. Receiving payment.

Applying the accruals concept we can say that the income

on the sale arises at some point between numbers 1 and 6 but we cannot be more precise. It is possible to argue a case for each stage as the appropriate point at which to draw the line. However, applying the conditions that income must be earned and realised to be recognised in accounts, we would dismiss points 1 and 2 on the grounds that nothing has been earned until the goods are made; we would dismiss 6 because if the customer is known to be reputable when the order is taken, the invoicing of the goods is tantamount to realisation (stock has been turned into a debt that is payable within a specified period). But whether stages 3, 4 or 5 are the appropriate points is much harder to say, since it depends upon the type of contract that governs the whole transaction. Usually delivery marks the stage when businessmen would say that realisation is certain, because until then there is no guarantee that the goods will be delivered (they might prove to be faulty or delays in delivery might lead to a repudiation of the order by the customer). For this reason delivery is very often the accounting base chosen as the accounting policy for turnover and profit. If, however, production was not carried out against an order, but goods were produced for retail sale, there could be no certainty of realisation until the point of sale in a shop and that would be the appropriate point to recognise the income.

In the case of long-term contracts more complicated rules apply. Sometimes work is invoiced and paid for as it is carried out; sometimes progress payments are made which are not directly related to the work done; and in both cases there is always the problem of uncertainty about the future since the income apparently earned and realised in one period may prove to be illusory in the future if things go wrong. This problem is considered further in Chapter 7.

5.4 The allocation of expenditure

Once the income for an accounting period has been determined, it is necessary to apply the accruals concept to expenditure and to ensure that all expenditure incurred in earning the income is charged against it in the same time period. Under the historical cost convention, expenditure is charged in the profit and loss account at the values at which it was originally incurred. Thus the cost of goods sold will be the amount of money paid for the goods by the business. This, and other types of expense classified as direct, such as wages, transport, packaging, tools consumed *etc.* are relatively easy to assign against income. For example, all of the wages paid to shop assistants in a year must have been incurred on selling goods during the year and could not be said to create sales in any other year.

However, many types of expense do not bear an obvious relation to income, either because they are indirect and accrue on a time basis (such as rent or rates which must be paid for whether or not any particular level of income is made) or because they may provide a benefit in future time periods and thus can be capitalised at the year end. 'Capitalisation' means that the amount of the expense not used up in the current period is treated as an asset and shown as such in the balance sheet. The most obvious example is the treatment of fixed assets (such as items of plant, machinery, property and fittings). Although such items are usually bought in one transaction and hence the cost (in terms of money being paid out) is borne in one accounting period, the benefits will be spread over the useful lives of the assets and therefore the cost should be spread out over these lives in due proportion. The methods of dealing with fixed assets and other forms of expenditure which can be capitalised are discussed in Chapters 8 and 9.

In addition to capitalising expenditure which relates to future income, the accountant must scrutinise the balance sheet each year to ensure that amounts brought forward and shown as assets really are going to provide future benefits. Thus, if in the past plant has been bought which is now known to be obsolete, it must be regarded as worthless (or at least worth only scrap value) and the consequent loss in value must be charged as an expense in the accounts of the current period.

In practice, the accountant can check that all expenditure incurred in a year has been charged in that year by ensuring that every item in the balance sheet can be justifiably placed there. The accounting system will automatically treat every item of expenditure not capitalised as an expense. The stress placed upon the correct valuation of the assets and liabilities of a business can thus be seen to be just as much a stress on the proper ascertainment of income and expenditure.

5.5 Capital gains

Under the historical cost convention, the profit or loss on the sale of an asset is the sale proceeds less original cost. Although businesses exist primarily in order to trade, they may also sell non-trading assets from time to time: property may be disposed of when a business moves to a new site; motor cars are usually changed every few years; shares or stock held as an investment may be sold to realise cash when other sources of finance are not sufficient. These are all examples of capital transactions (*i.e.* dealings in the capital assets of the business as distinct from the trading assets). It is important that the profits or losses on such sales are disclosed separately in the profit and loss account (unless too small to be significant) because they represent a different class of income to trading income. A business can expect to trade indefinitely as long as a market for its products exists. It continually replaces the goods it sells. But businesses selling their capital assets are in different circumstances. They make a profit (or loss) primarily because the price of the assets has risen since they were bought, not because they have earned a genuine profit through their efforts which can be made again and again. Once a capital asset is sold it is lost to the business unless replaced, but if replaced it will almost certainly have to be replaced at the same price or in the same price range as the asset sold. Thus if a factory on a piece of freehold land bought twenty years ago for £10,000 is sold for £100,000 it is probable that the business will have to buy another factory in order to carry on production, and it will cost it in the region of £100,000 and not £10,000, to buy the new factory. The historical cost convention which would show a gain of £90,000 is therefore misleading in such cases; the accounts must be framed to show which sales of capital assets denote true profits (*i.e.* assets which are not necessary for the maintenance of the business) and which sales must not be regarded as sources of profit because all proceeds from them must be retained in the business. (The alternative definition of profits in Chapter 2 was the amount that can be taken out of a business and still leave the owners as well-off.) Traditionally 'reserve accounting' was the method employed to deal with capital transactions, and the profits made through capital gains were not disclosed in the profit and loss account at all, unless it was thought reasonable for the profit to be distributed. Reserve accounting meant that the reserves were directly credited with the profit on capital transactions (or debited with the loss), so that the balance sheet was accurate but the profit and loss account was restricted to detailing trading transactions. It was also normal for capital gains to be transferred to a special capital reserve which would be shown in the accounts as a separate item from the revenue reserves. The interpretation of a capital reserve is that the amounts it represents cannot be regarded as profits as long as the business is a going concern; but should the business be wound up, the owners receive the sums shown in the account (assuming that the assets are realised for book values on winding up).

One further problem with capital gains concerns revaluations. Under the historical cost convention an asset should be shown at its cost, less any amounts written off for depreciation. But many long-lived assets such as land and buildings usually are worth far more than their cost, and from time to time businesses may revalue such assets, restating them in the accounts at the current market value and hence increasing the net assets of the business. The amount of the revaluation will be credited to a capital reserve. However, the gain is not realised if the assets are never sold. Therefore, while the current value of fixed assets probably shows a truer and fairer view of their worth to the business than their historic cost, such revaluations, when unrealised, must be kept distinct from any figure of profit. This is the reason behind the exception made for unrealised surpluses or losses on the revaluation of fixed assets in SSAP 6, which is discussed below. The question of revaluations and the effect on depreciation is discussed further in Chapter 7.

5.6 Extraordinary items and SSAP 6

From time to time in the life of most businesses something unusual occurs which affects the profits in a particular year but is not likely to happen again and is not regarded as a normal transaction. For example, part of the business may be sold off and a profit recorded over the net book value of the net assets sold. Such sales cannot be frequent or the business would cease to exist.

For many years there was no agreement as to how such an item should be regarded. Some businesses would deal with items regarded as non-trading through the reserves, while others would disclose them in the profit and loss account. This may appear to be a mere question of bookkeeping, but it has wider implications. Great importance is placed on the profit figure as the prime indicator of performance, and it is of little use if that figure is distorted by extraordinary items. Equally such items are important in themselves and may affect the financial position of the business. They should therefore be brought to the attention of the users of the accounts and not hidden away in the note dealing with changes in reserves. This was the reasoning behind SSAP 6, which deals both with extraordinary items and with prior years' adjustments.

5.7 The definition of an extraordinary item

SSAP 6 is a controversial standard and argument has focused on the difficulties of deciding exactly what is and what is not 'extraordinary'. The definition in the standard is that an extraordinary item derives from events or transactions outside the ordinary activities of the business; it is material but is not expected to recur frequently or regularly. But in practice it is not always obvious whether or not a particular item derives from ordinary activities, or whether or not it might recur. There may also be 'public relations' considerations. A bad loss on a contract might make the trading profits look poor. But if it can be shown separately as an extraordinary item the figure for profits will be unaffected. Conversely, the management may wish to include extraordinary gains within the profit figure so as to make the trading performance seem more impressive. The accountant must be aware of such 'window-dressing' activities. The purpose of SSAP 6 is to have all extraordinary items dealt with in a consistent and fair way and to eliminate this area of discretionary accounting.

But what is meant by extraordinary? The standard suggests as examples the profits or losses arising on the following:

1. The discontinuance of a significant part of the business;
2. The sale of an investment not acquired with the intention of resale;
3. The writing off of intangibles such as goodwill because of unusual events or developments in the period;
4. The appropriation of assets.

Defined as ordinary (no matter how large in relation to profits) are: abnormal charges for bad debts, the writing off of stocks and research and development expenditure, provisions for losses on long-term contracts and most adjustments of prior years tax provisions.

The American Accounting Principles Board reached a different conclusion in their Opinion no. 30 on extraordinary items. The conditions allowing an item to be treated as extraordinary are much more tightly drawn; in particular, the disposal of part of the business is not seen as extraordinary.

The problem with the definition given in SSAP 6 is that it does not define what an ordinary item is, and it therefore gives no general guidance on when an item is outside normal activities. As for examples in the standard, they are not as obviously extraordinary as they might seem. As noted above, the Americans reject the idea that changing the business itself is outside normal activities. In the case of goodwill, or the sale of an investment, such items are acquired in the normal course of business and will usually be closely connected to business activities that affect their value following acquisition. When the intangibles written off are such items as pre-incorporation expenses, it is even harder to regard them as extraordinary, since they are fundamental to the normal business activities.

One of the knottier problems is associated with the gains or losses on exchanging foreign currencies. SSAP 6 skated over the matter but more guidance was offered in an amendment to the standard in the form of ED 16 (the first time a standard has been amended after coming into effect). The suggested rule (for the time being) in ED 16 was that exchange differences relating to extraordinary transactions were themselves extraordinary; otherwise they were part of normal trading activities. However, an accounting standard on currency translation problems is to be published in the near future, and the present situation is outlined in Chapter 11.

As already explained, unrealised surpluses on the revaluation of fixed assets were not to be treated as extraordinary items but are to be adjusted directly in the reserves. Surprisingly SSAP 6 contains no discussion justifying this exception.

5.8 The presentation of extraordinary items

SSAP 6 requires that the profit and loss account should show a profit or loss after extraordinary items, reflecting all profits or losses recognised in the year (other than prior years' adjustments—see p. 62) and unrealised surpluses on the revaluation of fixed assets which should be credited direct to reserves). Items of abnormal size or incidence which are derived from the ordinary activities of the business should be included in arriving at the profit for the year before taxation and extraordinary items, and their nature and size disclosed. Extraordinary items (less attributable taxation) should be shown separately in the profit and loss account for the year after the results derived from ordinary activities, and their nature and size disclosed.

Example 1 illustrates the application of the standard. Note that the sale of plant is not treated as extraordinary, but is disclosed in a note to the profit and loss account as being an item which, though derived from the normal activities of the business, is of abnormal size or incidence.

Example 1

Gumbey Ltd. has the following results in the year to 31 December 1978:

	£
Trading profits	500,000
Profit on sale of plant	10,000
Goodwill written off	(20,000)
Realisation of investments held for long term	30,000
	520,000
Corporation tax (of which £5,000 refers to realisation of investment)	(220,000)
Dividends	(100,000)
Retained profit	200,000

Presented in accordance with SSAP 6 the profit and loss account would appear thus:

Gumbey Ltd

Profit and loss account for year ending 31 December 1978

	Note	£
Trading profit	1	510,000
Taxation		215,000
Profit after tax before extraordinary items		295,000
Extraordinary items	2	5,000
Profit attributable to members of Gumbey Ltd.		300,000
Dividends		100,000
Retained profit for year		200,000

Notes to profit and loss account

1. Trading profit is stated after crediting:

	£
Profit on sale of plant	10,000

2. Extraordinary items (net of tax):

	£
Realisation of long term investments	25,000
Goodwill written off	(20,000)
	5,000

5.9 Prior year adjustments

An important exception (to the treatment of extraordinary items) recognised in SSAP 6 is an extraordinary item in the form of a prior year adjustment. Such an adjustment is an acknowledgement that last year's accounts were incorrect and that this year's figures have to be adjusted to restore the position. Such adjustments may arise for several reasons, not all of which are necessarily extraordinary. These reasons are:

1. When estimated figures can be corrected in the light of experience: *e.g.* tax provisions made when the accounts had yet to be agreed with the Inland Revenue, or provisions against bad debts which proved inadequate. Such adjustments occur all the time and are inevitable. Many figures must be shown in accounts which can only be based on estimates—the further away from the year end the more accurate the accounts become, but obviously the greater the gap between the year end and the date of publication, the less relevant will the accounts be, and a balance must be struck. Because these adjustments are therefore inherent in the nature of accounting, they are not considered extraordinary and should be incorporated in the figure of profit before extraordinary items.

2. A fundamental error may have been made in the previous year: such an error destroys the usefulness of the previous accounts because it can now be seen that they do not show a true and fair view. It is therefore appropriate to make a prior year's adjustment (the method is shown at the end of this section).

3. An accounting policy has changed: this will be the usual reason for making a prior year's adjustment. The concept of consistency means that such changes should be made only when it is clear that the change is necessary to present a true and fair view. The policies should not be changed simply to present better-looking results. But if the policy is changed then the previous year's accounts will need restatement to comply with the policy. If this is not done not only will they not be consistent with those of the present year but all the burden of the adjustment will fall upon the reserves of the present year. For example, if a

business that previously valued its stock at marginal cost now follows SSAP 9 and includes an appropriate proportion of overheads in the valuation, the past year's stock figure will need to be recalculated as if this year's policy had been in operation then. Otherwise this year's stock will include a proportion of fixed overheads, the stock figure brought forward will not, and the profits for the year will be overstated.

When a prior year adjustment is effected, the net effect on the reserves must also be incorporated in the accounts (if we raise last year's stock value we must raise the reserves by the same amount). SSAP 6 requires the change in the reserves to be shown, if practicable, in a separate statement of retained profits so that the distinction between the profits of the year and the changes in the profits of last year is perfectly clear.

5.10 The presentation of prior year adjustments

The standard format of the profit and loss account adds together ordinary profits, extraordinary items and such capital gains as are disclosed through the profit and loss account, and deducts taxation, to reach a figure of profit available for distribution. Dividends or distributions of profit are subtracted and the resulting figure is the retained profit for the year. Following the profit and loss account, SSAP 6 requires a statement of retained profits. Any prior year adjustments will be shown as amendments to the original figure of reserves brought forward in the present year and also that of the previous year; the profit for both years is then correct and any residual difference, representing what the profits for the years before the penultimate should have been, is charged against the opening reserves for the penultimate year. The retained profit for the year is added and the retained profits carried forward, equal to the figure of retained reserves in the balance sheet, will be the final figure in the statement. The Appendix of SSAP 6, which shows the recommended layout and explains the way the prior year adjustment is calculated is reproduced below.

Appendix

*This appendix is illustrative only and does not form part
of the Statement of Standard Accounting Practice.*

*Example of a statement of profit and loss for the year
and a statement of retained profits/reserves*

Statement of Profit and Loss for the Year Ended 31 December 1974

	1974		1973	
	£000	£ 000	£000	£ 000
Turnover		183,000		158,000
Operating profit after charging or including:		19,400		18,100
Depreciation	⌈4,100⌉		⌈4,000⌉	
Exceptional loss on major contract (see note 2)	1,000		—	
Other items	⌊ 325⌋		⌊ 310⌋	
Other income:				
Investment income		300		500
Profit before taxation and extraordinary items		19,700		18,600
Taxation		9,850		8,835
Profit before extraordinary items		9,850		9,765
Extraordinary items *less taxation* (see note 3)		835		850
Profit after extraordinary items		9,015		8,915
Dividends		4,410		4,200
Retained profit		4,605		4,715

Statement of Retained Profits/Reserves

Retained profit for the year		4,605		4,715
Retained profits/reserves at beginning of year:				
as previously reported	48,890		44,000	
Prior year adjustment (see note 1)	450		275	
As restated		48,440		43,725
Retained profits/reserves at end of year		53,045		48,440

Notes
1. The policy followed in accounting for research and development
expenditure, which in prior years was written off over a period of

four years, was changed during the year ended 31 December 1974 and such expenditure is now written off in the year in which it is incurred. It is considered that the new policy will give a fairer presentation of the results and the financial position of the company. Research and development expenditure carried forward at 31 December 1973 (less attributable taxation £340,000) amounted to £450,000. In restating the results for 1973 on the basis of the new policy, the charge for research and development in that year has been increased by £175,000 out of the expenditure carried forward at the end of 1973. The remainder, £275,000 relating to 1972 and earlier years has been charged against retained profits at the beginning of 1973.

2. Items within the normal activities of the company which require disclosure on account of their abnormal size and incidence.
3. Description of actual items.

5.11 The distribution of profit

One further concept is of great importance in interpreting profits. This is the question of whether or not a profit is 'distributable'. Originally company law allowed all profits to be distributed (in other words, paid out by way of dividend to the shareholder); the only requirement was that share capital must never be paid out.[1] This requirement still holds in law, but business practice has refined the approach to distributability and goes further than the law in restricting what can be paid out of profits. In deciding what is distributable two criteria should be borne in mind:

(a) Is the profit realised? Operating profits must be realised —a trading profit is not recognised until realisation has taken place. But accounts can include unrealised capital gains and also unrealised extraordinary items (for example the gain on holding foreign assets following a devaluation of the pound). Although it is necessary to include such items in the accounts in order to present a true and fair view and to comply with the accruals concept, business sense insists that unrealised profits must not be regarded as distributable because of the risk that, after the money has been paid out of the business, the apparent profits may disappear upon realisation and the business may be left having effectively distributed its capital. This is not merely a theoretical possibility, nor does it argue excessive and unnecessary caution, as many

---

[1] Except in the event of a winding-up.

investors in property companies discovered when the property market collapsed in 1973.

(b) Even if the profit is realised, will payment of the profit outside the business reduce the real capital? The example given earlier of the factory costing a tenth of its sale value is relevant here. The business may have made a money gain but if that money is essential to the business it is illusory to regard it as profit. Systems of replacement cost or current cost accounting have been developed to deal with this problem. These systems start with the concept that profit is not made until the business has charged as an expense the cost of replacing the assets used up, not the historical cost of those assets. The approach has become widely known through the pressing need for inflation accounting; it is the basis of the present proposals to adjust accounts for inflation but it is relevant even if there is no general inflation; prices can still rise in some sectors of the economy, creating apparent profits.

The idea of classifying realised profits as undistributable (because the real capital of the business will be eroded if they are distributed) marks the awareness by businessmen and accountants of the distorting effects of inflation on accounts. Classifying such profits as undistributable warned the owners of businesses that although they could insist in law on receiving profits as dividends, they would be most unwise to do so if they wished to maintain their businesses at their existing size. Inflation accounting does the same job, but on all transactions. It therefore offers a general solution to the problem while previously only capital gains tended to be examined critically.

In the past, profits regarded as undistributable were transferred to capital reserves. Today the distinction between capital and revenue reserves is often blurred and companies may maintain just one account for all reserves with a note to the balance sheet showing the movements in the year. Provided that the dividend each year is paid out of the distributable profits for that year, there is no danger of a distribution of capital; but if it were proposed to pay a dividend out of reserves brought forward, it would be necessary to show that the dividend was covered by distributable profits brought forward, otherwise the whole point of classifying profits in this way would be lost.

Summary

Starting with the concept that profits equal the increase in net assets, we have classified the transactions that create profits into three types: trading, capital and extraordinary. All trading transactions must be realised if profit is to be recognised, but capital and extraordinary profits may be unrealised. It is essential for all material items to be disclosed in the profit and loss account so that the performance of the business can be understood, and it is also essential that management classify profits as distributable or undistributable: all unrealised profits are undistributable and certain realised transactions may also create undistributable profits. The categories of profits are tabulated overleaf.

The reader should note that the concept of distributability as applied in this chapter represents an attempt to amend a basic fault in the historical cost convention. If accounts are prepared under a general system of inflation accounting all profits calculated may be distributed without eroding the capital of the business.

One additional point to note is that 'profits' should not be confused with 'cash'. A business may have earned profits which are distributable but may have no cash and cannot therefore pay a dividend. Conversely, owning plenty of cash does not entitle a business to distribute more than its total distributable reserves. The question of which profits are available for distribution is a matter of accounting principles: the question of *when* the profit should be distributed depends upon the availability of liquid resources and the business's need to expand its capital by retaining profits indefinitely.

The Classification of Transactions under the Historical Cost Convention

Example of transaction giving rise to profit or loss	Classification of profit or loss arising	Should the profit be eligible for distribution?
1. Sale of goods and services	Trading (or operating) profit	Yes
2. Sale of part of a business which is not contributing to current income	Realised extraordinary item	Yes (proceeds are not essential to the maintenance of the business)
3. Sale of part of a business which is contributing to current income	Realised extraordinary item	No (proceeds must be reinvested to maintain the business)
4. Revaluation of foreign-held assets following a devaluation of the domestic currency	Unrealised extraordinary item	No (unrealised)
5. Sale of plant not contributing to current income	Realised capital gain	Yes (as 2)
6. Sale of plant contributing to current income	Realised capital gain	No (as 3)
7. Revaluation of property	Unrealised capital gain	No (unrealised)

6

The Approach to the Balance Sheet

The purpose of the balance sheet is to show the financial
state of the enterprise reported upon. At one extreme the
balance sheet can be no more than a list of the balances
remaining in the books after all items of income and
expenditure have been transferred to the profit and loss
account; at the other, it can virtually constitute an independent valuation of the net assets of the business. Under the
historical cost convention it has elements of both approaches, with greater emphasis on showing what has happened to the funds invested in the business than in valuing
the assets acquired with those funds. The current cost convention proposed in SSAP 16 shifts the emphasis towards
valuation, losing the link with the funds introduced in the
past.

The remaining chapters in this part of the book deal with
the application of the historical cost convention to the major
areas of difficulty encountered when moving from a simple
'trial balance' balance sheet to a balance sheet suitable for
publication. Such areas are either covered by existing
accounting standards or are on the agendas of the ASC and
IASC.

The components of the typical balance sheet which present
no particular accounting problems are described in this
chapter.

6.1 The general layout

In order to highlight the salient features of a balance sheet
it is usual to group, under appropriate headings, fixed assets,
investments, current assets, current liabilities, long-term
liabilities and shareholders' or owners' interest. These

categories allow for an immediate appraisal of the sources and disposition of the finance employed in the enterprise.

It is now common for the 'vertical' layout to be used (see page 248 for an example) in which current liabilities are deducted from current assets to give net current assets. To this figure are added fixed assets and investments. The resulting total represents the long-term finance of the enterprise which is shown divided between external liabilities (long-term liabilities and deferred tax) and the shareholders' interests. The value of shareholders' interests is the residual figure, dependent upon the measurement of all other items.

The distinction between current and long-term is not always obvious, but the usual rule is to classify as current those items which are payable or receivable within twelve months from the balance sheet date. Adequate supporting information is of considerable value in cases of doubt; as balance sheets become more simplified with fewer details on the face of the accounts, the importance of the notes to the accounts grows.

6.2 Cash and overdrafts

There should be no difficulty in measuring the amount of cash and bank balances held, or overdrafts outstanding. These items are always classified as current. Although overdrafts may be held indefinitely, because the banks will renew them as long as they are satisfied with the customer's ability to repay, they are regarded as current liabilities because they are technically repayable on demand.

6.3 Debtors

The normal accounting system should be capable of recording all sums due, although 'cut-off' tests may be required at the year end to ensure that all transactions that took place at that time have been accounted for in the correct period. A review of the pattern of income and expenditure of the year may also be needed to account for prepayments and such special cases as interest receivable. From the total figure of debtors, debts considered to be irrecoverable must be extracted and written off to the profit and loss account. This applies to debts that appeared to be good at the year end but which subsequently were seen to be irrecoverable. Under the accruals concept it could be said that a bad debt should be recognised in the period that it is known to have become bad; but the prudence concept overrides the theoretical approach, and bad debts are charged to the earliest period available. Thus, if the year end is 31 December and a debt at that date was known to be bad in March of the following year, before the accounts had been completed, the debt would be written off as at 31 December.

A provision for doubtful debts, subtracted from the total of debtors, might also be appropriate where experience has shown that a certain percentage of debtors will default each year although it cannot be predicted which particular debtors will be bad. It is important to review such a provision in the light of experience each year, rather than to establish uncritically a provision fixed at, say, 2% of debtors which might become unrealistic as trading conditions change.

6.4 Creditors

The gross value of creditors will be determined in the same manner as for debtors, but there is no question of a deduction for non-payment. Under the going concern concept it is assumed that all liabilities will be met. The correct presentation of creditors is important in judging the liquidity position and sums not due for more than a year should be classified as deferred or long-term liabilities.

6.5 Taxation

Taxation must be divided into taxes on the income of the enterprise (corporation tax on companies), and taxes collected by the enterprise but paid by others, such as personal income tax on the earnings of employees deducted at source, and sales taxes paid by customers such as value added tax and excise duties. Taxes collected on behalf of the state are regarded as short-term liabilities and are included with the figure for creditors. The tax on the income or profits of the enterprise will be disclosed separately (see

SSAP 8 on page 244). The amount due for the current period has to be estimated, since it cannot be accurately determined until the accounts have been submitted to the Inland Revenue. Deferred tax, which is an accounting adjustment and not a sum actually payable, should be disclosed under a separate heading, grouped with long-term liabilities. The mechanics of tax computations are beyond the scope of this book. Deferred tax is discussed in Chapter 10.

6.6 Long-term liabilities

Loans, debentures and other forms of long-term finance supplied by external sources have a fixed monetary value and are disclosed at that value. It is arguable that the true value of such sums is the present value of the future payment, that is, the nominal amount discounted by the market rate of interest from the date of payment to the balance sheet date; however, this approach has not been used in historical cost accounting and is considered unsuitable for the first stage of the introduction of current cost accounting. Research into the valuation of long-term liabilities is proceeding.

6.7 Investments

Many organisations invest their funds in the securities of other organisations, either as temporary deposits or as permanent sources of income. Some enterprises specialise in dealing in the stocks and shares of others. When investments are held for short-term purposes, they should be valued at market value and treated as current assets. When held as permanent assets, it is customary to value them at the cost of acquisition, written down to market value when this is below the historical cost. Investments held for the long term should be classified separately.

The recommendations of SSAP 16 on current cost accounting are that investments should always be valued at market value, removing the illogicality of recognition of falls in market value below cost but no recognition of higher market values—an illogicality which exists in historical cost accounting.

When an investment comprises 20 % or more of the equity share capital of another company, or the shareholding is sufficient to give the investing company control, special procedures are used to value the investment in the accounts of the investing company. These procedures are the subject of Part 4.

6.8 SSAP 17 Accounting for post balance sheet events

Accounts usually contain some estimated figures. Thus, the value of assets may be based on a net realisable value which cannot be known for certain until realisation takes place; likewise, profit attributed to unfinished contracts cannot be known for certain until completion. In drawing up accounts to a particular date it may be useful to examine the results of activities in the period following (*i.e.* events occurring between the balance sheet date and the date on which the accounts are finalised for publication). For example, if a trade debtor is stated at £1,000 at the year end but two weeks later is known to be in liquidation with no funds available for unsecured creditors, it will be necessary to restate the debtor at £nil in the accounts and to charge £1,000 as a bad debt against the profits of that year.

A difficulty arises over subsequent events which are important but not directly related to the accounting period. It may be a matter of opinion whether such events should be reported in the accounts of the preceding period. On the one hand, a 'true and fair' view ought to mean disclosing everything of material effect; on the other, the accruals concept rules out events which do not relate to the period for which the accounts are prepared.

SSAP 17 classifies post balance sheet events as 'adjusting' or 'non-adjusting'. Adjusting events are directly related to the financial period that is being reported on, and may confirm the accuracy of the figures in the accounts or show them to be wrong. In the latter case, the accounts must be altered. There is no need to report adjusting events themselves unless they qualify as exceptional or extraordinary items. Examples of adjusting events are:

(*a*) A debt that becomes worthless after the balance sheet date (as discussed above);

(*b*) The declaration of a dividend for the year—final dividends are almost invariably declared after the year end;

(*c*) The sale of stocks, held at the balance sheet date, at prices lower than cost—the stocks would have to be valued at these prices in the balance sheet.

Non adjusting events relate to the periods subsequent to the balance sheet date and therefore do not affect the fairness of the accounts. However, if material, the notes to the accounts should disclose sufficient information so that the reader may not be misled about the current position of the business. Examples are

(*a*) The issue of shares;
(*b*) the acquisition of another business;
(*c*) a revaluation of property.

SSAP 17 also requires that 'window dressing' be treated as a non adjusting event, to be disclosed where material. Window dressing is defined as 'a transaction entered into before the year end, the substance of which was primarily to alter the appearance of the company's balance sheet'. It is the reversal or maturity of such a transaction that is classed as the post balance sheet event.

For example a bank can always raise the total of its assets by borrowing and lending, creating assets and liabilities simultaneously. Yet banks often advertise their results by calling attention to the size of their assets (and ignoring the liabilities). Any artificial loans made for this purpose, which were reversed soon after the balance sheet date, would require to be detailed in the notes. (If the loans did not fall to be repaid soon after the balance sheet date, the transaction would be unlikely to qualify as 'window dressing'; it would be far more likely to be a normal business transaction.)

There must come a point when accounts are finalised no matter what events might be about to occur, otherwise accounts might never be produced at all. SSAP 17 establishes the 'cut-off' date as the date the directors sign the accounts. After that there is an implicit duty on directors to inform shareholders about material post balance sheet events but through some other medium. Half yearly accounts, which are not required by UK law (although they are required by the Stock Exchange for listed companies) are often used for this purpose.

6.9 SSAP 18 Accounting for contingencies

Contingencies represent a form of post balance sheet event, but something which might happen rather than something that has actually occurred. The historical cost convention (and the EEC 4th directive) require provision to be made for future losses arising from current transactions while future gains are not accounted for (under the prudence concept and on grounds on non-realisation). But where there is uncertainty about the future and the size of any gain or loss can be only a guess, traditional accounting practice has formed no clear rules. SSAP 18 requires that all contingencies material to an appraisal of the position of a business be noted in the accounts. The date the accounts are approved by the directors should also be noted. This broadens the position of the Companies Act, 1967 which refers to the need to disclose contingent liabilities but does not mention gains. However, the question of what is a material contingency is likely to cause considerable debate, notably where the disclosure of a possible event will bring that event about.

7

Stocks and Work in Progress

7.1 The basic approach

During an accounting period a trading or manufacturing business is turning over its stock—using up existing stock, purchasing or making replacements, disposing of finished goods and ending the period with stocks on hand in various stages of production or processing which are to be sold in future accounting periods. The stocks form part of the assets of the business and the value placed upon the period-end stocks will therefore affect the profits for the period. The same is true of all other assets and liabilities, but under the historical cost convention stocks must be valued anew each time accounts are prepared. Unlike debtors or creditors, stocks have no fixed monetary value; furthermore, stocks are not usually dealt with in the formal accounting systems (while debtors for example are usually recorded and controlled in sales ledgers). The only way that a reliable stock valuation can be prepared, in the absence of sophisticated and well-tested stock records, is for the stocks to be counted and valued as near to the accounting period end as is practicable. The relative importance of stocks in the balance sheets of the majority of businesses reinforces the point.

The physical count of stocks is a matter of administration. Valuation is, however, a matter of greater theoretical difficulty. While it is comparatively easy to record that 85 Flange Nuts (left-hand) have been counted, it is harder to decide what value to put upon them. This section is devoted to the problem of the valuation of stocks of all kinds, including raw materials, work in progress and finished goods, and the special case of work in progress on long-term contracts.

The historical cost convention requires the matching of

income with expenditure based on actual costs. The theory of income developed in Chapter 5 concluded that trading income must be both earned and realised before it could be recognised in accounts. Realisation is the guiding factor to stock valuation: unless the business has already contracted to sell stocks on hand at the year end, the profit that will be ultimately received when the stocks are sold has not been realised. It may have been earned, or virtually earned, if the greater part of the normal activity needed to bring the stocks to a realisable state has already been undertaken (*e.g.* an importer might have brought goods into the country and warehoused them—the final step of selling them might represent only a minor part of the total activity). None the less, realisation is the governing factor: if the stock is on hand and not contracted for at the period-end, then it must be valued at the cost to the business and not at selling price.

The historical cost convention, through the prudence concept, does, however, insist that current assets be written down to net realisable value when lower than cost. The difference between cost and net realisable value will be recorded as a loss in the period in which it is recognised, not when the stocks are actually sold. This is a special case, for normally when stocks are held for resale, realisable values will exceed cost; valuation at cost will be the appropriate accounting base, and the need to write down stocks will not arise. When stocks are to be written down to net realisable value it is important that the choice of valuation bases be made against each unit or each category of stocks, rather than against the overall stocks. The following example demonstrates the reason.

Example 1

The following data relates to the stocks of Bert Ltd at the year end:

Category	Cost	Net realisable value	Value in accounts
	£000	£000	£000
A	50	70	50
B	105	120	105
C	80	50	50
D	200	230	200
E	60	40	40
	495	510	445

The cost for all stocks combined is less than the net realisable value. But for categories C and E net realisable value is lower than cost and should be used for accounting purposes. Separate comparison of values produces a cost figure significantly lower than the figure for cost of all stocks.

The types of stock encountered comprise:

(a) Raw materials which must be valued at cost of purchase;
(b) Work in progress, which must be valued at the cost of materials plus the cost of work carried out to bring the stock to its present state, and will include direct labour cost and indirect costs (overheads) attributable to production;
(c) Finished goods ready for sale, which are usually valued in the same way as work in progress, but with additional categories of overhead costs considered applicable;
(d) Long-term contract work in progress where, although the contract is not completed, the work which has been done entitles the contractor to a percentage of the final payment. In such cases the recording of profit on the work done is justifiable in theory and is usually recognised in practice.

The valuation procedures applicable to each category of stock are discussed in the next four sections. SSAP 9, '*Stocks and Work in Progress*', is summarised and discussed in the remaining sections.

7.2 Raw material stocks

The starting point is the theoretical postulate that the cost of raw materials is to be used to value them, but the theory does not say how cost is to be calculated. In practice there is a major difficulty. Stocks are usually bought throughout the year at varying prices and processed or handled within the organisation. Which costs can be identified in a warehouse, shop or factory full of goods at the year end thus depends on the accuracy of the accounting records and the simplifying assumptions that have to be made to prevent the valuation becoming a massive and time-consuming operation. Sometimes each item of stock can be traced back to the point of purchase—such as cars held in a dealer's showroom—but this is rare. Normally, purchased stocks are held without records for each separate item; even if the total cost of stocks held is recorded in the books, it is very common for businesses periodically to take a physical stock count and valuation as a way of checking on the accuracy of the recordkeeping. An assumption must be made about stocks deemed to have been issued, and about those left at the year end.

The usual method for dealing with raw materials or goods purchased for resale assumes that the stock is sold in the order in which it is bought—'first in, first out' (FIFO)—so that the stocks at the year end are identified with those purchased last. The stocks are thus valued at the prices of the most recent purchases, going backwards in time until the total quantity of the set of purchases examined equals the quantity on hand. The method is easy to operate, accords with a commonsense view of business and is acceptable to the Inland Revenue for tax purposes. When prices are rising it will value stock at the higher of the range of prices encountered during the year; conversely for a fall.

In contrast is the 'last in, first out' method (LIFO), which assumes that the latest batch of purchases go out first and the year end stock is the earliest set of deliveries. With this method, either very careful note of all stocks has to be taken, or the previous year's stock figure can be adjusted; an increase in stock is assumed to have come from the first deliveries of the year, and a decrease from goods sold at the end of the year. LIFO is not acceptable to the Inland Revenue in the UK, but is used widely in the USA where it is acceptable for tax purposes; it is also used by some UK firms for accounting, if not for tax reasons. It will usually show a reduced stock revaluation, compared with FIFO, in a time of rising prices (as now).

A compromise method acceptable to the Inland Revenue is 'average cost' (AVCO). This method requires the recording of each purchase and sale, with the stock priced as a weighted average of the purchases and revalued after each movement. This requires detailed recordkeeping for each receipt into and issue from stock.

Example 2

A retailing business has the following transactions in one of its stock lines. There were no stocks of this item at the start of the period.

Purchases

Date	Quantity	Price £	Value £
Jan. 1	50	5	250
Mar. 15	100	6	600
July 20	40	8	320
Sept. 10	50	10	500
	240		1670

Sales

Date	Quantity	Price	Value
Jan. 30	20	8	160
Mar. 30	100	10	1000
Aug. 11	60	10	600
Dec. 1	40	11	440
	220		2200
Closing stock	20		

The profit for the period is calculated by the usual formula:

	Sales		xx
	Opening stock	xx	
plus	Purchases	xx	
		xx	
less	Closing stock	xx	
=	Cost of sales		xx
	= Gross profit		X

We know all values except the closing stock. The three methods of calculation of the value of stock left after each sale, and hence of the cost of sales, give the results shown overleaf:

Cost of Sales

Date	FIFO Qty	FIFO Price £	FIFO Value £	AVCO Qty	AVCO Value £	LIFO Qty	LIFO Price £	LIFO Value £
Jan. 30	20	5	100	20	100	20	5	100
Mar. 30	30	5	150					
Mar. 30	70	6	420	100	577	100	6	600
Aug. 11	30	6	180			40	8	320
Aug. 11	30	8	240	60	422	20	5	100
Dec. 1	10	8	80	40	381	40	10	400
	30	10	300					
Total	220		1470	220	1480	220		1520
Stock C/F	20	10	200	20	190	10	5	50
						10	10	100
Total purchases	240		1670	240	1670	240		1670

Average Cost workings were as follows:

Sale on 30 March:
Stock comprises   30 at £5 = £150
100 at £6 = £600

130   £750

The sale is 100 units. The cost of sale is

$$\frac{100}{130} \times £750 = £577$$

and 30 units are carried forward worth £750 − £577 = £173

Sale on 11 August:
Stock now comprises 30 units b/f   £173
40 at £8   £320

70   £493

The sale is 60 units. The cost of sale is

$$\frac{60}{70} \times £493 = £422$$

and 10 units are carried forward worth £493 − £422 = £71

Sale on 1 December:
Stock now comprises 10 units b/f   £71
50 units at £10 £500

60   £571

The sale is 40 units. The cost of sale is

$$\frac{40}{60} \times £571 = £381$$

and 20 units are carried forward worth £571 − £381 = £190

It can be seen in this example that where prices are rising FIFO produces the highest, LIFO the lowest, and AVCO an intermediate figure 'for closing stock value'. The choice of method is significant and could be manipulated deliberately to affect profits. For this reason SSAP 9 suggests that LIFO is only to be used if it can be justified, since its assumption rarely accords with experience; FIFO and AVCO are regarded as satisfactory.

The question of which method to use may become less important when a change is made to current cost accounting since under this system stocks are to be valued at replacement cost and the cost of sales adjusted to take account of inflation (see Chapter 14).

7.3 Work in progress

The cost of raw material stocks is the cost of purchasing and acquiring those stocks (carriage *etc.*) and is wholly related to expenditure incurred outside the business. If stocks are subsequently processed, converted, adopted or worked on in any way, other expenses incurred within the business become relevant. Work in progress comprises stocks upon which expenditure has been incurred within the business (in addition to the costs of acquisition of raw materials) but which are not yet ready for sale. The problem is to decide which costs have been necessarily incurred in producing the work in progress, and which are not relevant to the production process.

Total production costs comprise those costs which are directly attributable to production and which vary directly with production (such as the cost of raw materials, production labour, bought-in components), and indirect costs, or overheads. There is no difficulty in measuring the direct cost elements of work in progress—invoices, stores requisitions and time sheets will normally provide the information.

Overheads may be classified as variable and fixed. Variable overheads include machine-depreciation, power consumed in production, the time of supervisory staff and foremen, and similar expenses which are indispensable to production but which cannot be directly attributed to particular items of work in progress. Fixed overheads are incurred regardless of the level of production, and include other factory expenses such as rent and rates, administration, selling and distribution expenses. Some of these expenses, while not varying with production are nonetheless essential. For example, factory rent and insurance will not normally alter during a year, no matter how much production is carried on. However, production could not take place without the factory. On the other hand, the volume of advertising will not affect production, only sales, and is not a cost attributable to production. The line must be drawn between necessary and unnecessary fixed overheads, but no hard-and-fast rule can be applied. Every business has its own special characteristics, and allocating fixed overheads between production costs and others is often an arbitrary process. If work in progress is to be valued at cost, a decision must be made as to which overheads are to be included in the valuation of work in progress. For example, work carried out by the accounts department in a business might assist both the production and selling divisions, but only that part of accounting work which assists production can be considered a production cost. A means must be found to apportion the costs of the department. Whether this is best done by estimates of the time spent on the work of various divisions, or by dividing accounts department costs by the ratio of production costs to total costs, or by some other method, depends upon individual circumstances.

There are differing views among accountants about the treatment of overheads in relation to stocks. Some, applying the theory of profit in full, would allocate a proportion of all production costs to work in progress, *i.e.* they would include all attributable overheads, whether variable or fixed. Others prefer the marginal costing approach, which values work in progress according to the extra production costs each unit incurs; those fixed overheads which do not change with the production of extra units would therefore be excluded from the stock valuation carried forward to the next period, and would be wholly written off in the year in which they were incurred. A justification advanced by advocates of the marginal cost approach is that once the marginal costs—raw materials, labour and variable production overheads (*e.g.* direct power)—have been incurred to make a product, those costs will not need to be incurred again. But if the product remains in stock, the fixed overheads incurred in the previous year will be incurred again in the following year; given that they are an expense of the business in that year, even if no production takes place, it is deemed imprudent to bring forward in stock values an element of the previous year's overheads as well.

Example 3

In Year 1 a business makes 1,000 items at a cost of £5 each for direct labour, materials, variable overheads *etc.*, and incurs fixed production overheads of £4,000. 700 are sold at £15 and 300 remain in stock at the year end and are sold at the same price in the following year, when no further production takes place. The overhead costing and marginal costing methods produce identical profits for the two years but different results between the years, thus:

Year 1	£	Overhead costing £	£	Marginal costing £
Sales		10,500		10,500
Total costs				
marginal	5,000		5,000	
overhead	4,000		4,000	
	9,000		9,000	
Less:				
Stock c/f	2,700		1,500	
		6,300		7,500
Profit Year 1		4,200		3,000

Note: Marginal cost of stock = £5 per unit
Overhead allocation = £4 per unit (£4000/1000 units)

Year 2	£	Overhead costing £	£	Marginal costing £
Sales		4,500		4,500
Total costs				
Stock c/f	2,700		1,500	
			4,000	
Overheads	4,000	6,700		5,500
Loss Year 2		2,200		1,000
Total profit Years 1 & 2		2,000		2,000

In this example (obviously oversimplified, since in practice a business ceasing production could cut some of its overheads fairly quickly) it can be argued that the marginal costing method presents a fairer view of the allocation of profits over the two years, taking a more conservative view than the overhead method and producing a less dramatic swing between the profits of Year 1 and the loss of Year 2. The desire to avoid undue fluctuations in reported profit figures is an important one in many industries and explains the reluctance of many businessmen to use full overhead costing methods to value stocks. However, when production is carried on normally from one year to the next, this method will not produce significantly different profits from the marginal costing method because although the former produces a higher closing stock value than the latter, which is deducted from the gross cost of sales, there will also be a higher opening stock value brought forward to be added to cost of sales.

However, the full overhead method shows a more accurate valuation of stock in the balance sheet, according to the general principles of profit theory, and for that reason it is required by SSAP 9 to be used in the valuation of work in progress and finished stocks.

A further problem arises when capacity is not fully utilised. It is common for many businesses to operate at less than full capacity (although in times of need the apparent 'full' capacity might easily be exceeded). In theory only the overheads necessary to production ought to be included in stock values. If a business operates at, say, 80% capacity, in a particular year, only 80% of the costs of rent of premises, rates, lighting *etc.* should be regarded as necessary. In practice it is difficult to decide in many cases what 'full' capacity and what the actual capacity achieved have been. An alternative is to use the concept of 'normal' capacity, so that if a business habitually operates at 80% of the apparent maximum production rate sustainable, only reductions in working below the 80% mark would require adjustments to the total of overheads eligible for inclusion in stock values. In such a case 'normal' replaces 'full' as the criterion. This is illustrated in Example 4.

Example 4
A business applying full overhead costing to the valuation of
work in progress has the following results for the year to
31 December.

Production of finished goods	133,000 units	
Work in progress at year end	8,000 units, half completed	
	4,000 units, three-quarters completed	

Direct costs—materials	£3	per unit
—labour	£10	per unit
Variable overheads	£900,000	
Fixed overheads—factory	£400,000	
—offices	£200,000	

10% of the office space is attributable to production. During
the year a two-month stoppage of production followed a
strike. Normal production was achieved in the remaining
period. Work in progress is to be valued at full overhead
cost.

Solution
The work in progress is equivalent to 7,000 completed units
—$(8,000 \times \frac{1}{2}) + (4,000 \times \frac{3}{4})$. The total production in the
year is equivalent to 140,000 units (133,000 + 7,000).
The prime costs (labour and materials) are £13 per unit.

Variable overheads are $\frac{£900,000}{140,000} = £5$ per unit.

Fixed overheads are not all attributable to production. The
factory costs and 10% of office overheads, which equals
£420,000, comprises 10 months of production and 2 months
idle. Thus attributable fixed overheads are £420,000 $\times \frac{10}{12} =$
£350,000.
The value of work in progress is therefore:

		£
Direct costs at £13 per unit	=	91,000
Variable overheads at £5 per unit	=	35,000
Fixed overheads comprise £350,000 $\times \frac{7,000}{140,000}$	=	17,500
Total cost of work in progress		£143,500

7.4 Finished goods

Finished goods comprise:

(a) Goods which have been manufactured and are now ready to be sold; and/or

(b) Goods bought from suppliers for resale without significant alterations.

In the case of manufacturers' finished goods, the methods used to value work in progress will be appropriate, except that certain overheads not deemed necessary to the production of work in progress may be necessary to the completion of production. For example, the cost of quality control or warehousing may be attributable to finished goods awaiting sale.

Retailers and wholesalers generally hold stocks for resale which have been acquired from suppliers, although some retailers manufacture their own stocks. It is usually impossible for stock records to be kept (except for such high-value items as motor vehicles) and the cost of stocks must therefore be estimated. Although the methods used to value raw materials can be employed, many retailers prefer to count their stocks, value them at selling price and deduct their usual gross margin to arrive at cost. Where stocks are turned over rapidly, this method is virtually the same as FIFO.

7.5 Long-term contract work in progress

There are some industries which undertake construction, production or development work for customers which extends over a long period of time. Builders may be engaged for years on the construction of housing estates or new office blocks; shipbuilders might be occupied for many months on particular vessels; power stations, chemical refineries and airports all take a long time to complete.

When such long-term contracts are in operation, it is customary for the contractor to invoice the customer regularly for work carried out, but for the actual sale of the completed job to be deferred until the work is complete. This means that the profit (if any) will not be recognised in the accounts until the job is complete. Until then, work done is valued at cost in the accounts of the contractor, and sums received on account are either deducted from it or credited to a (special) customer's account. Technically such payments are financial assistance to the contractor, rather than payments for the work carried out, since the sale is not deemed to be made until the end of the contract, at which point the payments on account can be credited to the customer's own account, which will have been debited with the invoice value of the contract.

The case for this prudent procedure is well founded on experience. Long-term contracts, particularly for construction or the development of new technology, are invariably fraught with problems. Even when work may have reached an advanced stage, it is often impossible to say whether a future difficulty might not upset the entire plan and lead to losses. Many small building firms become insolvent because profits are recognised in the accounts on uncompleted contracts, money is frittered away by the owners or management, and eventually, when the contracts are found to have been loss-making, the business has no funds with which to continue operations. And even on national projects using advanced management techniques controlled by experts, costs can rise beyond any predictions. The history of the Barbican development in the City of London and the Concorde project are salutary reminders of the risks inherent in certain types of long-term contracts.

In theory the ultra-conservative attitude is unjustifiable. Provided future losses are not expected, it is necessary to recognise profits as they are earned if the accruals concept is to be followed with consistency. Thus, if a contract is worth £100,000 and is expected to cost the contractor £80,000 to complete, it is legitimate to value the first £40,000 of costs as being worth £50,000 to the contractor, thereby bringing £50,000 of turnover and £10,000 of profit into account. Such a procedure depends on:

(*a*) Agreement by the customer that the work done is worth £50,000 (payment is not necessary, but acknowledgement of the liability by the customer is).
(*b*) A reasonable degree of probability that the estimates of

the costs and sale value of the remainder of the contract
are either unchanged or have at least not so altered as to
render the recognition of profit invalid. If a final loss is
foreseen it should be recognised at once, by charging the
amount of the loss against profits of the current year and
crediting the amount to a provision.

By making allowances for profit on long-term contracts as
the work is carried on, a business will avoid what can be
major distortions in the trends of reported profits. For
example, if profits are deferred until completion, a ship-
builder starting a contract for a ship which will take four
years to complete will show no profits for three years, and
all the profits on the contract in the fourth year. The
recognition of profit as it is earned and realised will spread
profits over the years and present a fairer view of the activities of the business.

The question of profit recognition on long-term contracts
reveals a conflict between the accruals and prudence concepts. SSAP 9 chooses the accruals concept and recommends
that work in progress on long-term contracts be stated
inclusive of attributable profits. This is an important
preferment of theory over practice, in the sense that theory
suggests the recognition of profits whilst practice has tended
to be wary of such recognition until contract completion.
But SSAP 9 does not insist on profit recognition in all cases
and businesses which regard the future as too uncertain to
warrant any recognition of profit until all risks are eliminated
can continue to value work in progress at cost.

7.6 SSAP 9 Stocks and Work in Progress

SSAP 9 distinguishes between stocks and work in progress,
and long-term contract work in progress. Accounting
requirements are:

1. *Stocks and work in progress:* The amount should be stated
   as the total of the lower of cost and net realisable value
   of the separate items of stock and work in progress of
   groups of similar items.
2. *Long-term contract work in progress:* The amount should

be stated as cost, plus any attributable profit, less any foreseeable losses on progress payments received and receivable. If anticipated losses exceed costs to date less progress payments, the excess should be shown separately as a provision. The total of cost of work in progress should be shown separately from progress payments.

These requirements are tighter than they seem, the key phrases used being carefully defined in the standard. The important definitions are:

Cost; Cost is that expenditure incurred in the normal course of business in bringing the product or service to its present location and condition. This expenditure includes costs of conversion.

Costs of conversion: these are costs

1. Specifically attributable to units of production *i.e.* direct labour expenses and sub-contract work;
2. Production overheads;
3. Any other overheads required to bring the product or service to its present location and condition.

Production overheads: these are overheads incurred in respect of materials, labour or services for production based on the normal level of activity. For this purpose overheads should be classified according to function—*e.g.* production, selling, administration—so as to ensure the inclusion in cost of conversion of those overheads (including depreciation) which relate to production, notwithstanding that these may accrue wholly or partly on a time basis.

Net realisable value: this is the actual or estimated selling price, less:

1. All further costs to completion;
2. All costs to be incurred in marketing, selling or distribution.

In an appendix to SSAP 9 it is argued that 'cost' means an approximation to actual cost, and that while FIFO and average cost methods do approximate in this way, LIFO (except in special circumstances) does not. However, the choice of costing method is not laid down as part of the standard accounting practice, and LIFO could be used provided the company could persuade its auditors that it was suitable in the particular circumstances.

The statement recognises the difficulties of deciding when profit can be prudently recognised on a long-term contract; (a long-term contract is defined as a contract where the substantial part of the work extends over a year—a rather clumsy definition since a six-month contract extending over the end of an accounting period, for which it might be thought some profit had been earned, would not qualify and the work in progress would have to be valued at cost). It stresses the importance of taking no profit until the end of the contract can reasonably be foreseen. For this reason 'attributable profit', which in theory should be the proportion of total work completed multiplied by the total foreseeable profit, can in practice be left to the management's discretion, since management alone can decide what it is prudent to take and whether there are snags ahead that ought to be surmounted first. Some check is provided, in that the accounting policies applied must be disclosed.

7.7 Exhibits

The following exhibits illustrate the accounting treatment and policies of two manufacturing companies. EXHIBIT 1 is taken from the accounts of Pilkington Brothers Limited for the year ended 31 March 1977, and typifies the approach of businesses with substantial stocks but comparatively little long-term contract work in progress. EXHIBIT 2 is from the accounts of Ruberoid Limited for the year ending 2 January 1977. The company has substantial, normally short-term, contract work in progress and does not recognise profits in such contracts until they are realised. However, it discloses the attributable profits in a note. Such additional disclosure neatly reconciles the requirements of the prudence and accruals concepts.

EXHIBIT 1

Pilkington Brothers Limited

Reports and Accounts for year ending 31 March 1977
Statement of Accounting Policies (extract)

(3) Stocks and work in progress
Stocks and work in progress are valued at the lower of cost and net realisable value. Cost includes all direct expenditure and works overhead expenditure incurred in bringing goods to their current state under normal operating conditions. The works overhead expenditure includes charges for depreciation, replacement and obsolescence of fixed assets but excludes research and development, distribution, selling, divisional and head office expenses.

Notes to the accounts (extract)

(11) Stocks and work in progress

	Group		Company	
	1977 £000	1976 £000	1977 £000	1976 £000
Raw materials	16,051	11,605	1,364	1,247
Stores	16,132	13,389	6,006	5,905
Work in progress	15,502	10,912	2,245	1,313
Finished goods	49,651	34,166	11,587	8,746
	97,336	70,072	21,202	17,211
Less progress payments on contract work in progress	7,374	4,748	—	—
	89,962	65,324	21,202	17,211

EXHIBIT 2

Ruberoid Limited

Annual Report for the year ending 2 January 1977
Note on Accounts (extracts)

(2) Turnover
Turnover represents sales to and work done for external customers.

(3) Profit deferred on uncompleted contracts
Contracts are included in turnover and trading profit when they are completed and evaluated. The excess of valuation over cost on

uncompleted contracts is regarded as deferred profit and carried forward.

During 1976 the amount of deferred profit carried forward decreased by £12,425, from £655,837 at 28 December 1975 to £643,412 at 22 January 1977.

The disclosure of the amount of deferred profit on uncompleted contracts is considered desirable because while contracts do not normally extend for a period exceeding a year, the incidence of completions can have a substantial effect on trading profit.

The basis of calculating trading profit remains unchanged from that adopted in previous years.

(16) Contract stocks and work in progress
Contract stocks and work in progress are valued at the lower of cost (including labour overheads) or net realisable value, reduced by a provision of £110,000 for unknown contingencies (1975–£90,000).

(17) Manufacturing stocks

	Group	
	2.1.77 £	28.12.75 £
Raw materials	545,249	424,759
Finished goods	1,061,944	650,787
Consumable stores, including maintenance stores and coal	397,318	261,058
	£2,004,511	£1,336,604

Stocks are valued at the lower of cost or net realisable value.
The cost of raw materials and consumable stores is normally ascertained on a FIFO basis.
The cost of finished goods is ascertained from standard costs incorporating production overheads.

8

Depreciation and the Valuation of Fixed Assets

Fixed assets are acquired and held to earn revenue, and are not for resale. The fixed assets category includes land and buildings, plant and machinery, furniture and fixtures, transport equipment and office equipment *etc*. Of these assets, normally only land and, perhaps, the buildings on the land will retain their physical characteristics indefinitely. Because they retain their value to the business during normal activity, and can be expected to do so in the distant future, there is no apparent cost associated with their employment in the business. In contrast, other types of asset are used up and eventually will be worthless. Each year therefore part of the value they represent to the business is lost and this is an expense to be charged against revenue. Because, under the historic cost convention, the value of an asset is taken to be its acquisition cost to the business, regardless of its market price subsequent to purchase, the loss of value through use must be calculated on that cost. At the end of its useful life the cost of the asset will have been allocated to the appropriate accounting periods, in accordance with the accruals concept.

8.1 Depreciation

The reduction in value of fixed assets, whether through time or use, is generally known as depreciation. The term is sometimes restricted to assets where use is the major factor causing loss of value, and the term 'amortisation' is used to describe the loss caused solely by time—typically in a lease where the benefit of the property on lease will end after a specified period of time. The problems in deciding how much depreciation to charge in a particular period are created by uncertainty as to:

(*a*) how much longer the asset will be used in the business; and

(*b*) whether there will be any residual value on disposal.

If, for example, it is known with certainty that an asset will last ten years and will then be worth nothing, it appears reasonable to charge a tenth of the cost as depreciation each year. The total depreciation charge to be spread over the lifetime of the asset will be cost less residual value. When the asset is finally disposed of, any difference between the written down value (cost less total depreciation to date) and residual value will be charged or credited in that year as a profit or loss on disposal. Thus, over the life of an asset, the total loss in value will be charged, and the more accurate the depreciation charge, the smaller the profit or loss on disposal. In order to calculate the depreciation charge accurately, the life of an asset and its residual value must be estimated and the appropriate method of charging depreciation must be selected at the time of acquisition and thereafter applied consistently.

It is because of the need to estimate in advance the depreciation of fixed assets, that controversy has arisen over the best method to use. A major criticism of conventional accounts has been that management can choose the depreciation method it prefers and that this can lead to distortion of profits. For example, a company wishing to show a higher profit than its accounts disclose at present could assume (for calculation of depreciation charges) that its assets were to have much longer lives than was actually intended and so reduce the depreciation charge accordingly. This would rebound when the assets were disposed of and major differences between the written down value and disposal value were charged to the profit and loss account in the year of disposal; this could not be foreseen by outsiders reading the 'doctored' accounts, unless they had special knowledge of the company and the industry. The disclosure of accounting policies for depreciation (SSAP 2) is one important safeguard against unrealistic depreciation rates. Another, is the implementation of standard accounting practice through

SSAP 12—*Accounting for Depreciation*, discussed in section 8.5.

8.2 Methods of calculating depreciation

There are three methods in common use:

(*a*) *Straight-line depreciation:* This is calculated by the formula: $\text{annual charge} = \dfrac{\text{Cost less residual value}}{\text{Estimated life in years}}$
and is applicable to leases, property (where the property is subject to reductions in value over time) and plant, machinery and equipment in general. It is the easiest method to explain and apply and the most widely used. In 1974/5, out of 257 major quoted companies disclosing their depreciation methods, 222 used the straight-line method.[1]

The straight-line method produces the same change each year and is sometimes referred to as the equal instalment method. It is therefore specially applicable to depreciation through time—for example, in the case of leases, or machinery where obsolescence will make it useless within a known time period, or such assets as motor vehicles which are regularly changed as a matter of policy, regardless of condition.

(*b*) *Reducing balance method:* The formula for this method is complex, being $D = 100 \left(1 - \sqrt[N]{\dfrac{S}{C}}\right)$, where D is the annual charge expressed as a percentage of written down value, C is the cost of the asset, S the residual value and N the time period over which the asset is to be held. The purpose of this method is to allocate depreciation more heavily in the early periods. The charge reduces in each period because the written down value reduces. A practical alternative to the use of the formula is to use a rate approximately double the straight-line rate based on acquisition cost. This will approximately reduce the written down value to zero over the life of the asset.

---

[1] *Survey of Published Accounts 1975* (Institute of Chartered Accountants in England & Wales, 1976).

Example 1: straight-line and reducing balance methods compared

An asset is acquired in Year 1 costing £1,000. It is estimated to have a useful life of eight years and scrap value of £200.

The straight-line charge will be $\dfrac{1,000 - 200}{8} = £100$ a year, which is 10% on acquisition cost. The reducing balance charge will be roughly double: $2 \times \left(\dfrac{100}{1,000}\right) \times 100\% = 20\%$

The yearly charges will be:

Year	Straight-line £	Reducing balance £	
1	100	200	
2	100	160	20% (1000–200)
3	100	128	20% (1000–360)
4	100	102	20% (1000–488)
5	100	82	20% (1000–590)
6	100	66	20% (1000–672)
7	100	52	20% (1000–738)
8	100	42	20% (1000–790)
	800	832	

The reducing balance method, while ultimately charging the same (or nearly the same) total depreciation as the straight-line method, spreads it in a different pattern. For some assets, notably motor cars, the loss of value is greatest in the early years and much less so towards the end of their lives, and in such cases the reducing balance method is more appropriate. Furthermore, as assets age, repairs and maintenance charges rise. Such charges, being necessary to maintain the assets in good physical shape, are costs which must be matched against revenue in the year they are incurred. One way of interpreting the total cost of an asset is the purchase price plus repairs throughout its life. The reducing balance method evens out such total cost charging high depreciation in the early years when repairs are low and vice versa.

(c) Usage method: The straight line and reducing balance

methods assume that depreciation is a function of time. In the case of certain types of machinery or in such specialised businesses as mining or oil drilling, the value of the assets employed falls as output is produced. An installation over an oilwell is likely to be useless once the well is dry. In such cases it is appropriate to relate the depreciation to output. An estimate of the total output is required when production commences, and depreciation each year will be $\dfrac{\text{output for the year}}{\text{total output expected}} \times$ cost of asset. Sometimes this is expressed in terms of working life. Thus, a machine with an estimated 1,000 useful hours of life can be depreciated according to the hours used in the accounting period.

(d) *Other methods:* Depreciation is a method of retaining funds in the business which would otherwise be regarded as distributable profit. It is arguable that these funds, invested either in the business or out of it, will earn a rate of return equal to the rate of return of the business or the investment made. In order to accumulate a total fund equalling the cost of the asset, money is regarded as being put aside each year by way of depreciation, which is then earning interest. The interest, whether actually earned on outside investments or notionally accounted for as profit made in the business, is added to the sums retained by depreciation. The total depreciation charge will therefore be less than under the methods discussed previously, since part of the fund will be interest.

There are various methods for incorporating the time value of money (*i.e.* its ability to earn interest) into depreciation calculations, including the sinking fund and annuity methods, in which the accounts show amounts generated by depreciation charges and invested outside the business as specific funds for the replacement of assets. These methods are not widely used in practice, one of the major problems being that rates of interest vary significantly between and during accounting periods, and such variations would force continual rechecking of calculations and changes in the annual depreciation charges. Such changes are undesirable; they make it difficult to tell what the 'true' charge is and what it might be in the future, and in any case they assume that the purpose of depreciation is to retain funds for the replacement of fixed assets. This is not so, although it used to be widely assumed that the depreciation would be sufficient to replace assets. It is now more clearly recognised that, under the historic cost convention, depreciation is merely the way in which the cost of an asset is apportioned fairly to those periods in which benefit is obtained from its use, so that when it ceases to be useful its book value will be equal to its residual value (which may be zero).

8.3 The replacement of fixed assets

If the price of an asset stayed constant and there was no technical change, the business replacing old with new would pay the same price for the new asset. The depreciation charges would have written down the old asset to its scrap value; that value plus the depreciation charges retained in the business would exactly purchase the replacement asset.

This attractively balanced model (which has little relationship to real life) is the one accountants have at the back of their minds when depreciation is equated with replacement. There is no obligation for a business to replace assets with identical assets; indeed, in a developing economy the latest models will be preferred to older types. Technical developments can make machinery obsolete before it is physically useless and can force management to revise their estimates of the useful lives of their existing plant. Thus, it is important to distinguish replacement from depreciation. If a business wishes to make allowance for replacement, this is a separate exercise, involving a decision about future operations and the future requirements of fixed assets. In contrast, depreciation is based on the historic cost, and expected useful life and scrap value of existing assets.

The ICA statement in 1945 on Depreciation of Fixed Assets (N 9) contained the following: 'Amounts set aside out of profits for obsolescence which cannot be foreseen or for a possible increase in the cost of replacement are matters of financial prudence. Neither can be estimated with any degree of accuracy. They are in the nature of reserves and should be treated as such in the accounts.'

This approach has been reaffirmed subsequently and the business which charges against profit an amount for replacement, over and above the normal depreciation charge, should treat the sum provided as a replacement reserve and part of shareholders' funds; the money or assets which it represents may never in fact be used for replacement of assets, and the fund is at all times distributable in law. Whether it is distributable under the going concern concept is debatable—a going concern must replace worn out or obsolete assets as they reach the end of their useful lives, or it will cease to be a going concern. Accounts prepared under this concept should therefore make it clear whether or not funds in a replacement reserve are considered essential (*i.e.* only distributable in the event of a winding up, or a reduction in the scale of activities of the business).

8.4 The revaluation of assets

In considering replacement, there is a twofold problem: will the new asset be physically larger or more technically advanced, requiring the outlay of greater funds than for the old asset, or will it simply be the same as before but more expensive? The experience of post-war years has been that assets almost invariably cost more on replacement than when first bought, a consequence of the inflation of this period. Not only does this present a problem for businesses in deciding whether to set aside funds for future replacement (there is no legal obligation to do so, although SSAP 16 requires disclosure of the amount needed to replace depreciating assets), but there is also the problem that if the cost of replacement assets is rising, the value of assets held at present in the business must also be rising above the book amount. In the case of such assets as plant or furniture, the market value is academic—the assets are usually held until they have only a scrap value. They may be worth more than their written down value, but under the historical cost convention, this is not relevant—by definition, fixed assets are acquired for retention, not resale.

However, land does not depreciate, unless used for mining or some other highly specialised activity involving the depletion of a natural resource. The weakness of the historical cost convention is that as inflation raises the value of land, so the accounts based on cost become less and less meaningful. There is scope for fierce controversy about the meaning of the convention in such a case: is it to be rigidly applied, or should the accounts bear some resemblance to market values. In any event, the pressures of the real world make it unwise to undervalue significant assets. As stated in Chapter 5, firms which maintained their property at cost in their accounts when property values were rising fast became the targets for takeover bids aimed, not at developing the business, but at breaking it up and selling the land to realise its full value. Such 'asset-stripping' has ceased to be socially acceptable, but it remains a threat to any business adhering rigidly to the historic cost convention.

The response by many companies has been to seek professional revaluation of their property, and to incorporate the revised value in the accounts. An increase in value is matched by a revaluation reserve which must be treated as a capital reserve—non-distributable except in the event of winding up, and possibly in the event of a sale. Some companies now revalue regularly; property companies do so every year. Revaluation is usually confined to property but it can be applied to any asset. The Companies Act 1967 introduced a clause requiring directors to report on the differences between book and market values of fixed assets but did not require such differences to be incorporated into the accounts.[1]

If assets on which depreciation is being charged are revalued, the amount charged must be reviewed. Depreciation is charged in order to allocate the cost of an asset over its useful life. If the cost of an asset has been retrospectively raised by a revaluation, it follows that the charge for depreciation, if unchanged, will cease to relate to the amount at which the asset is stated in the accounts.

There are three possible approaches:

(a) Maintain the depreciation rate unchanged;
(b) Raise the depreciation to write off the remaining part of the revalued amount; or

---

[1] For tax puposes in the UK, the maximum depreciation currently allowable is the historic cost.

(c) Raise depreciation as in (b) but also provide a charge for 'backlog' depreciation, *i.e.* that part already depreciated at what can now be seen to have been a low rate.

As an illustration, suppose an asset is bought for £100 and is expected to last ten years with no residual scrap value. The straight-line method of depreciation is chosen and the annual depreciation charge is therefore £10. After seven years, when the written down value is £30, the asset is revalued and the original cost deemed to be the equivalent of £200.

Under approach (b) the remaining value is three-tenths of £200 as three-tenths of its life remains. Future depreciation thus becomes £20 a year $\left(\dfrac{£60}{3 \text{ years}}\right)$. But this will produce total depreciation of $(7 \times £10) + (3 \times £20) = £130$, a shortfall of £70. Approach (c) would charge the additional £70 in the year of revaluation as backlog—an amount that would have been charged from the start if the final value could have been foreseen. The £70 is deducted from the revaluation reserve, rather than shown as a charge in the profit and loss account. A generally accepted solution to the problem of revaluation and depreciation has yet to be formulated, but because this is part of the general problem of accounting for inflation it is further considered in Chapter 14 where SSAP 16 requires approach (c).

8.5 SSAP 12 *Accounting for Depreciation*

This standard draft reinforces the basic approach of the historical cost convention, that depreciation is an allocation of the cost of assets having a finite useful life to the periods expected to benefit from them. If the estimate of the useful life changes, the remaining unamortised cost (*i.e.* written down value) should be charged to revenue over the life remaining. Once selected, methods of depreciation should not change unless a new method provides a fairer presentation of the financial position. If a revaluation takes place and the new value is incorporated into the accounts, the charge should be based on the revalued amount (supporting approaches (b) + (c) in the example above).

SSAP 12 has made changes to accepted practices in the
following areas:

1. It does not accept that depreciation is unnecessary on an
   asset whose market price exceeds the book value. The
   asset will either be held till its value is that of scrap only,
   or it may be sold before its life expires. In either case a
   depreciation charge and, if resale is contemplated,
   revaluation will be appropriate.
2. Land is not normally to be depreciated, except where
   social or economic factors have reduced or may reduce its
   value.
3. Buildings have a finite life and should be depreciated, and
   land and buildings should be treated separately. This is a
   clear challenge to existing practice, under which land and
   buildings are combined and not depreciated, on the
   grounds that the combined market value is always higher
   than book value. SSAP 12 suggests that where this has
   been the reason for no depreciation, a revaluation of land
   and of buildings is appropriate, and depreciation should
   then be charged on the revalued buildings. The first time
   that buildings are depreciated, the depreciation in respect
   of prior years will be a prior year adjustment, (backlog as
   in approach (c) above).

It is worth repeating what SSAP 12 itself emphasises, that
it deals with depreciation in the context of the historical cost
convention of accounting. There is no requirement to
revalue assets under this basis. It is a matter for commercial
judgement and a question of the interpretation of the 'true
and fair' view. Compliance with SSAP 12 will provide
compliance with the provisions of IAS 4 *Depreciation
Accounting*.

SSAP 12 gives a temporary exemption to property companies from depreciating their investments on the grounds
that as such property is held to be let, redeveloped or sold,
the properties do not normally depreciate in value. An
amendment to SSAP 12, ED 26, permits property companies
to value their investment properties at market value, not
historical cost.

9

The Valuation of Intangible Assets

The accruals concept requires that expenditure be matched against the income created through that expenditure. If expenditure will provide a benefit in a future period it is appropriate to carry it forward on the balance sheet as an asset and write it off against income in future periods. The previous chapter dealt with expenditure on tangible assets; this chapter considers intangibles—assets with no physical existence but without which the business would be worse off. There are several types of intangible asset and because of their diversity in nature and accounting treatment, they will be dealt with separately.

9.1 Research and development

In some industries, where technical advance is continuous, the survival of the competing businesses depends on each keeping abreast of the latest developments. In such industries as aerospace, pharmaceuticals, electronics and chemicals, substantial expenditure is incurred on research into new products, techniques and designs, together with perhaps even larger amounts on development (putting ideas into practice). Once a new product has been successfully marketed, it may continue to sell for many years by virtue of the research and development ('R & D') effort which has made it superior to competing products. In time new products will challenge it in the market place and the business now threatened will need to bring out newer products in its turn. During the period in which a particular product is successful, it is reasonable to equate its success with the previous R & D effort, and thus to capitalise R & D as incurred, to be charged against future income.

There are no traditional practices for R & D; it is only in recent years that such expenditures have become so large as to make the choice of accounting method important. Most UK companies have been very conservative and have written off all R & D as incurred, on the grounds that the future is too obscure for any value to be put upon it. In 1974/5, out of 139 companies disclosing their accounting policy for R & D, 130 wrote it off as incurred.[1]

Reflecting the strength of feeling in industry—as it seemed —the first exposure draft to deal with an intangible asset, which was ED 14 on R & D, recommended that all such expenditure be written off as incurred. This provoked a critical response by some firms, notably in the advanced technology industries mentioned above, who relied upon R & D efforts and who felt that their accounts would be seriously distorted without the option to capitalise R & D in certain circumstances. As a result a new draft, ED 17, was issued which defers to these opinions. ED 17 (later SSAP 13) refers to the conflict between the accruals and prudence concepts, the one being a theoretical justification for capitalising R & D and the other stating the practical case against. The compromise it produces is based on a detailed examination of the categories of R & D. These are said to be:

1. *Basic research:* Work carried out to add to the sum of knowledge without necessarily leading to technical advances or improvements in products. Although much technical progress can be traced back to pure research, the links are often tenuous and there is no way that a commercial value can be placed on such work until it has been developed.

2. *Applied research:* The activity of turning the fruits of pure research into know-how.

3. *Development:* Work on creating a product or process using the knowledge generated by research. Development is the category which the ASC in ED 14 had suggested could, in theory, be capitalised, but they felt that in practice the line between development and research was so hazy and the difficulties of identifying positive benefits

---

[1] *Survey of Published Accounts 1975, op. cit.*

from development so great, that in order to achieve consistency of practice, all development should be written off as incurred in addition to research.

9.2 SSAP 13 Accounting for Research and Development

The compromise reached in this standard (which follows ED 17) was that while all expenditure classified either as basic or applied research should be written off as incurred, development expenditure could be deferred, to be offset against future revenue. The conditions for development to qualify as an asset at the year end are:

1. That it should be a clearly defined project on which development expenditure is proceeding;
2. That such expenditure is clearly indentifiable;
3. That the outcome of the project has been assessed with reasonable certainty as to
   (*a*) technical feasibility;
   (*b*) commercial success
4. That if further development costs are to be incurred, the total revenues from the project will cover all known costs;
5. That adequate resources exist to enable the project to be completed and to provide for any consequential increases in working capital.

Given these conditions, development expenditure may be deferred to the extent that its recovery can reasonably be regarded as assured. A review of all such expenditure should be carried out each year and if the conditions no longer hold, the expenditure should be written off immediately.

The movements on deferred expenditure accounts and the balances at the beginning and end of the period are to be disclosed separately in the accounts, as well as the accounting policy followed.

9.3 Criticisms of SSAP 13

SSAP 13 satisfied management in the few industries where development expenditure is so large in relation to the profits of any one year that they felt serious distortions would occur if they could not defer such expenditure when it was appropriate to do so. However, the standard has been criticised thus:

1. It allows an element of subjectivity—management has to decide which projects are going to be successful and which not—whereas ED 14 cut out all subjective estimates by its single rule that all R & D was to be written off in the year of expenditure. However, many other problems of valuation require a subjective approach, *e.g.* deciding on the life of fixed assets, and there is no reason to treat R & D in a different way simply because it is intangible.

2. While SSAP 13 requires the total amount deferred to be shown, there is no provision for disclosing the total of R & D expenditure in a year. In the case of high-technology industries this information is of great interest to users of the accounts.

3. No time limit is set on carrying development expenditure forward. Some projects are so successful that, had development expenditure been capitalised, it would still be regarded as an asset because substantial future revenues can still be confidently predicted. The ball-point pen, Polaroid camera, electronic calculator, cassette tape are all examples of long-lived products based on successful development. A time limit for deferring development expenditure, say of five years, would provide a reasonable framework for most projects and achieve consistency, although there are exceptions to every rule. For example, British Aircraft Corporation Ltd stated in their 1970 accounts that the development expenditure on the 111 airliner was being written off over the first 200 to be sold. This took about seven years to achieve.

9.4 Patents, trademarks and know-how

A patent protects the developer of a new product by granting sixteen years of sole legal rights for the exploitation of the product. It is reasonable to write off the costs associated with a patent, including the development and the legal fees, over the full time period allowed, unless the product ceases to be valuable before the expiration of the period.

Once registered, a trade mark lasts indefinitely; it may cost virtually nothing to create, but another enterprise might pay substantially to take over a well-known trademark. In that case the cost of the trademark could remain on the books of the purchaser as an asset for as long as the firm derives an advantage from its use.

Know-how is a loose term for a production method or new technique which is sold by one firm to another because the seller is unable to exploit it as effectively as the buyer. There is no generally accepted method of accounting for know-how but as the Inland Revenue allow amortisation over six years on the straight-line method for tax purposes, this is a useful starting point. But there is no obligation for the accounting treatment to be the same as the tax treatment, and a more satisfactory approach to know-how would be to treat it as development expenditure to be related to specific projects.

9.5 Goodwill

Goodwill is the difference between the value of a business as a going concern, and the sum of the values of the assets of that business taken individually. The accounting treatment of goodwill created on the purchase of a subsidiary is dealt with in Chapter 16. This section considers the theory of goodwill in such cases, as well as its application to partnerships and takeovers of unincorporated businesses.

Why should a business be worth more than the sum of its assets? A business, a going concern, has already been established and is capable of earning future income beyond the income derived from selling the assets piecemeal and investing the proceeds in the money market. Evidence for this may be found in the results of the business, but the past is not relevant to whether goodwill exists or not. It applies solely to the future and if the future outlook is bad then any goodwill there might have been in the past will disappear.

9.6 Types of goodwill

Within the overall category it is important to distinguish the following types of goodwill:

1. *The surplus of market over book values.* Under the historical cost convention it is inevitable that, in a period of general inflation, the market value of assets will exceed their book value. Therefore when a business is valued, it is likely that the value will exceed book values. This is not really goodwill but arises because historical cost accounting does not claim to show market values. The most satisfactory treatment is to revalue all assets upon a takeover or a change of ownership (whether or not such revaluations are subsequently incorporated into the accounts) so that the true goodwill can be isolated.

2. *Genuine goodwill.* The market value of the business over the market value of its assets.

3. *Cost of control.* In order to take over a business it may be necessary to pay more than the apparent market value in order to secure control—this will be a poor investment in a highly competitive market, but if buying the business means removing an important competitor, the benefit will exist for the current business of the buyer. For example, two grocery shops in one street might each be making a trading loss. It could be worthwhile for the owner of one to buy out the other, even paying for 'goodwill', in order to close down one shop, sell it and remove a source of competition. There is no accepted treatment for 'cost of control' goodwill, and it is not normally distinguished from genuine goodwill; but the benefit derived from it is different in character from genuine goodwill. Unlike the latter, created by the efforts of the owners or managers of the business and itself replaced over time by goodwill built up by the new management, goodwill in the form of cost of control payments may give a lasting benefit (if a takeover permanently wipes out competition) or may be valueless within a short time (if fresh competition appears).

9.7 Accounting for goodwill

There is no provision in the presently accepted concepts of accounting for businesses to incorporate in their accounts goodwill created by continuing owners. This would contradict the principle of historical cost accounting—where is the cost of the goodwill?—and would open up problems of subjective estimation and possible manipulation of accounts.

When a business changes hands, however, or when a partnership alters, the correct valuation of goodwill becomes essential. A new partner or owner buys a business for its current value—essentially the net present value of the future streams of income that the business will provide—and the historical cost accounts will only provide part of the information required to make such a valuation. If, say, an outgoing partner did not have his share in the partnership valued on the basis of the market value of the partnership, *i.e.* historical cost accounting value plus goodwill, he would receive less than his entitlement for his share of the business. Indeed, partnership accounts are principally concerned with showing the correct shares of the partners at all times, and this requires the valuation of goodwill on every change. Similarly when a limited company acquires another it will pay the market price based on the future earning potential, regardless of the historical cost accounts. At that point goodwill (or its negative form) will have been valued. In group accounts this can henceforth be shown as an asset of the group, or it can be deducted from group reserves. But the figure itself cannot subsequently be increased, even if it is manifest that the takeover has greatly increased the earning power of the acquired company. To this extent the principles of the historical cost convention hold. Goodwill can be incorporated into the accounts when an event occurs which changes the ownership—either a takeover or an adjustment of partners' accounts to reflect the market value of the partnership at the time of the change. But if goodwill is brought into accounts in the absence of such an event, the accounts can only be regarded as not conforming with generally accepted principles.

There has often been disagreement between accountants on how to deal with goodwill. Treatments include: (*a*) preserving goodwill as an asset, unchanging in amount; (*b*) treating it as a fixed asset and depreciating over a suitable period; (*c*) deducting it from reserves (but not writing it off through the profit and loss account); and (*d*) writing it off to the profit and loss account immediately on acquisition. There are many other variants. Progress towards an accounting standard has been slow but two important developments have been the EEC Fourth and (proposed) Seventh directives on Company Law (discussed in Chapter 19); and an ASC discussion paper issued in 1980 as a prelude to an accounting standard. Called *Accounting for Goodwill* it recommends accounting practice (*b*) above (which conforms to the EEC directives). This paper was produced by a panel who have circulated it to generate discussion and it does not bind the ASC to its conclusion.

The EEC Fourth directive deals with the accounts of companies (not group accounts) and requires that purchased goodwill be written off either in five years or over a longer period if allowed by the law of the country concerned. The Seventh directive on group accounts is likely to require the same treatment for goodwill on consolidation.

The ASC discussion paper supports this treatment, although it recommends that the UK take the option of allowing a longer period for the amortisation of goodwill. Goodwill is seen as an asset, acquired with the other assets of a business, even though it is intangible. It should be measured by comparing the *fair value* of the net assets of the acquired business with the purchase consideration. (Fair value means the current open market value and not necessarily the historical cost of the assets. But because the assets form part of a genuine market transaction, the cost of the assets to the buyer is what matters.) The panel regard purchased goodwill (where the assets of a business are acquired for a sum different to the total of their respective fair values) as identical in kind to goodwill on consolidation (where the shares of a business are acquired for an amount different to the fair value of the net assets attributable to the shares). Furthermore, negative goodwill is to be treated in the same way—measured as the deficiency of the purchase consideration over the fair value of the assets, and written back to the profit and loss account over a suitable period.

The justification for treating goodwill as a depreciating asset (and negative goodwill as a depreciating liability) is that goodwill is a genuine asset, acquired as part of a business. But for whatever reason it exists, it is continually altering as the business develops. Its value at the time of takeover reflects the way the business was run in the past.

Thus new 'internally generated' goodwill created by the new management supersedes the previous goodwill (which was explicitly valued at the time of takeover). But internal goodwill cannot be measured under either the historical or current cost conventions. The paper recognises that it is inconsistent to value acquired goodwill and to ignore internally generated goodwill but sees no alternative given the present accounting conventions.

The paper proposes that goodwill be written off over a period calculated as $2\frac{1}{2}$ times the price–earnings ratio of the investment. The mathematical proof of the validity of this formula is beyond the scope of this book but is set out in the paper. Briefly, the aim is to relate the goodwill to the profits of the business acquired. Whatever the price paid for the business, the acquiring business may be assumed to be aiming to earn a stream of profits into the future which will yield it a suitable rate of return.

It can be shown that 90 % of the net present value of any future stream of profits will be recovered within 2·3–3 times the price–earnings ratio of the investment. Thus if the fair value of the net assets of a business is £40,000 and the distributable profits in the next year (taken as indicative of future profits) are £5,000 the P/E ratio at the time of takeover is 8 and any goodwill arising should be written off over not more than twenty years.

In abnormal circumstances P/E ratios may be high. To prevent goodwill being written off over extremely long periods, an upper limit of forty years is proposed (the US standard on goodwill also sets 40 years as the maximum life).

The EEC Fourth directive requires that goodwill be shown as a fixed asset in the balance sheet. The discussion paper agrees, and recommends that where positive and negative goodwill exist they can be netted off. If there is an excess of negative goodwill, this will be shown as a liability in the balance sheet. Should a standard be introduced, companies who have previously written off goodwill which would not be fully written off under the new rules will not be required to reinstate the undepreciated portion in the balance sheet; companies with goodwill as an unchanging asset will be required to depreciate it henceforth and the amount that would have been written off already had the standard been in effect should be deducted from reserves as a prior year adjustment.

10

Deferred Taxation

The basic approach to business taxation in the UK is that the tax charge should be computed with reference to the net profits shown in accounts, prepared according to generally accepted principles. However, the authorities have recognised the defects in conventional accounting and the flexibility available to accountants and directors due to the wide variety of accepted accounting policies for each type of transaction. In consequence there are certain rules used for converting accounting profit to taxable profit. Some of these rules simply disallow certain types of expenditure (such as the entertainment of domestic customers) and others specify particular accounting policies that must be followed in calculating profit for tax purposes, whether or not used for the accounts (for example, the Inland Revenue does not recognise LIFO methods of stock valuation). These adjustments are regarded as permanent differences between tax and accounting profits and, being non-recurring, they are part of the tax computation process in the year in which they occur.

There are, however, certain rules which switch items dealt with in one time period for accounting purposes into another for tax purposes. Thus, the application of these rules will produce the same total taxable profit as accounting profit over a period of years, but not year by year. Items which, for tax purposes, are dealt with in different periods from the accounting periods in which they are properly allocated, give rise to 'timing differences'. The purpose of accounting for deferred taxation is to restate the annual tax charge as though timing differences did not exist.

The principal timing differences are:

1. Depreciation of fixed assets—the tax assessment will normally allow depreciation in an earlier period than its allocation for accounting purposes (in particular with plant and machinery, where since 1972 100% depreciation may be claimed in the year of purchase for tax purposes).
2. Interest received or payable is accrued in accounts, but is only recognised for tax purposes when actually received or paid out.
3. Provisions for repairs and maintenance, for pension costs and for bad debts will be accrued in accounts but are only allowable as an expense for tax purposes when actually incurred.
4. Stock appreciation relief is a special allowance granted to businesses where the values of stocks have increased. There was uncertainty over how long the allowance would continue to be granted and it was thought that the relief might be withdrawn after a few years. However, stock relief is now an established tax allowance and after six years any relief claimed cannot be 'clawed-back' even if stocks fall in amount below the level six years earlier.

It is necessary to adjust the actual tax charge in respect of timing differences if the accruals concept is to be followed, because the tax rules are made for administrative convenience and do not claim to be acceptable methods of presenting accounting information. Furthermore, the figure of profit after tax has a special significance in that it is the amount of profit actually attributable to the owners of a business. It is undesirable that this should be distorted by tax charges which are based on recognising income or expenditure in different periods to those in which they are recognised for accounting purposes.

10.1 Accounting for timing differences

The essential feature of a timing difference is that it reverses itself over time. Thus, any adjustment to the tax charge for accounts purposes will also be reversed in due course. For example, if fixed assets are acquired, the whole of the cost may be available to offset against profits for tax purposes as capital allowances. Only the normal amount will be charged as depreciation in the accounts. The taxable profit will thus be lower than the accounting profit. In later periods the tax computation will bring in accounting profits before depreciation and the capital allowances will already have been fully utilised. The taxable profit will therefore exceed the accounting profit. The business has in effect delayed the tax payment from the earlier period to a later one.

If this distortion is to be removed from the accounts it will be necessary to set up a provision equal to the amount of tax saved by the use of capital allowances, and to charge the amount of the provision, together with the actual tax charge, as the total liability to business taxation. The provision will be credited in the accounts to a deferred taxation account and treated as a long-term liability. In later years transfers from the deferred tax account will be made back to the profit and loss account, offsetting the higher tax charges in those years.

Example

A limited company makes £1,000 profit a year before depreciation. During Year 1 new plant is bought costing £600, depreciated at $33\frac{1}{3}\%$ *p.a.* on cost, but 100% capital allowances will be claimed. A tax rate of 50% is assumed. The corporation tax in Years 1 to 3 is calculated thus:

Year 1

	£	£
Accounting profits	800	
add depreciation	200	
	1,000	
less capital allowances	600	
taxable profit	400	
Tax at 50%		200

Year 2

	£	£
Accounting profit	800	
add depreciation	200	
	1,000	
tax at 50%		500

Year 3

Accounting profit	800	
add: depreciation	200	
	1,000	
Tax		500
Total tax in period		1,200

If deferred taxation is ignored, the tax charged in the accounts will be shown as above. If deferred taxation is to be applied, the following will result:

Deferred taxation charge	£	*Balance*	*Profit and loss account*		£
Year 1					
Timing difference					
Capital allowance	600		Profit before tax		800
Depreciation	200				
	400		Tax	200	
Tax at 50%	200	200	Deferred tax	200	400
			Net profit		400
Year 2					
Capital allowance	—		Profit before tax		800
Depreciation	200				
	(200)		Tax	500	
			Deferred tax	(100)	400
Tax at 50%	(100)	100			
			Net profit		400
Year 3					
Capital allowance	—		Profit before tax		800
Depreciation	200				
	(200)		Tax	500	
			Deferred tax	(100)	400
Tax at 50%	(100)	—			
			Net profit		400

Thus the total tax charged is £1,200 at a rate of £400 *p.a.*

The deferred taxation account evens out the distortions created by the timing difference, and the correct trend of post-tax profits is shown. The balance of £200 on the deferred taxation account in Year 1 represents a provision against that amount of future tax which will be charged at a higher rate than the nominal rate (*i.e.* in Year 2 the rate of tax appears to be $\frac{£500}{£800} = 62\cdot5\%$ before the deferred taxation adjustment).

The transactions which result in a timing difference are called 'originating differences'. Thus the purchase of plant in the above example creates a timing difference and in Years 2 and 3 the surplus of depreciation charged over the capital allowances available represents the reversing differences. An originating difference is always cancelled out in the following accounting periods by a reversing difference or differences.

10.2 'Permanent' timing differences

The example in the previous section considers a single transaction which creates a timing difference. But for the majority of businesses such transactions are continuously incurred. In particular, the purchase of fixed assets may provide originating differences each year which outweigh reversals. Furthermore, in a period of inflation the value of such purchases is likely to increase and the total on the deferred tax account will rise. Indeed, during the period 1973–7, the combined effect of first year allowances on the purchase of fixed assets and stock relief (treated as a timing difference at the time) was to produce deferred tax accounts that were so large as to upset the ratios of shareholders' funds to debt in the case of many companies. For companies whose borrowing was controlled by trust deeds specifying the relationship between equity capital and other funds, the existence of large and growing deferred tax accounts proved a serious embarrassment.

Critics of the original accounting standard on deferred taxation, SSAP 11, argued that where net originating timing differences were likely to be incurred each year the balance on a deferred tax account was meaningless. The liability was theoretical in such a case. The argument was accepted in a new exposure draft, ED 19, and SSAP 11 was withdrawn. The position now is that timing differences need not be accounted for if there is a reasonable probability that future originating differences will outweigh the effect of reversals.

10.3 Deferral and liability methods

A complication is introduced if the rate of taxation changes. The deferred tax transfer is calculated by applying the current tax rate to the total of timing differences. But if the tax rate alters after an originating difference has been recognised in the deferred tax accounts, there is the problem of deciding which rate to apply to the reversing differences. Using the original rate will eventually bring the deferred tax account back to zero. This is known as the deferral method, and it assumes that the originating difference creates a sum of tax deferred in that year, and paid in later years, and that the purpose of the deferred tax account is to account exactly for this difference.

In contrast, the liability method looks to the actual amount of tax that will be paid in the future. Should the rate change after an originating difference, the amount of tax ultimately paid will not be the same as if the tax had all been paid in the first year. The method therefore acknowledges the ultimate liability by maintaining the deferred tax account at the rate at which payment of tax will be made, and this, since we cannot know future rates, is always taken to be the current rate.

When the tax rate changes, the balance brought forward on the deferred tax account is recalculated to show the new rate and the difference between the balance at the old and at the new rates is shown as a component of the deferred tax charge in the profit and loss account.

After a period in which both methods were in general use, the acceptance of the principles of current cost accounting rendered the deferred method unsuitable. CCA requires that liabilities be shown at their value to the business. The liability method computes the deferred tax liability in this way; the deferral method is historic.

10.4 Trading losses

If a business incurs a trading loss it will normally be able to offset the loss against future trading profits and thus will pay no tax until the losses are wholly extinguished. If a credit balance on deferred taxation exists at the time of a loss, and it is reasonably certain that future profits will be available to absorb present losses, the taxation represented by the deferred tax account will not be paid (*i.e.* reversing differences will reverse during a period in which tax is not payable). To the extent that the losses cover reversing differences, transfers may be made back to profit and loss account.

10.5 Revaluation of fixed assets

Inflation is not yet recognised for tax purposes. If an asset is sold for more than it was bought, capital gains tax is payable (subject to a variety of exemptions). If the asset is sold for more than its written down tax value, a balancing charge may be payable (or the proceeds will be offset against other capital allowances carried forward in a 'pool'). In each case the tax liability is incurred on disposal. However, as mentioned on page 101, it has become common for assets to be revalued when their market prices become seriously out of line with book values. The reserves will be increased at once by the amount of the revaluation but no tax liability will be incurred until the asset is disposed of. An originating timing difference is thereby set up and a transfer to deferred tax account should be made.

If, however, it is not intended to dispose of the asset in the foreseeable future, the originating difference can be ignored. The argument is the same as that discussed under 'Permanent' timing differences (p. 119) in that the deferred tax liability is not a real liability of the business and should not be shown as such until it becomes a real liability.

10.6 SSAP 15 Accounting for Deferred Taxation

SSAP 15 is the second attempt at a standard accounting practice for deferred tax. It is intended that deferred tax be accounted for on all originating timing differences of material amount, other than any tax reduction which can be demonstrated with reasonable probability to continue for the foreseeable future.

The first attempt, in SSAP 11, did not provide such flexibility. However, 'reasonable probability' should be demonstrated with reference to a programme of capital expenditure providing a stream of capital allowances, or to other such originating timing differences. Where an asset has been revalued it must be clear that the asset is to be retained within the business. In the case of stock relief, stock values should not be likely to fall in the foreseeable future.

SSAP 15 provides that the liability method be used for computing tax deferred; SSAP 11 permitted a choice of liability and deferral methods.

The transfer to or from deferred taxation account should be shown as a component of the tax charge in the profit and loss account, although deferred tax on extraordinary items should be shown as part of the total make-up of such items. On the balance sheet the deferred tax account should be shown as such, distinct from shareholders' funds and from current liabilities. A note to the accounts should indicate the nature and amount of the major elements comprising the net balance of the deferred tax account.

11

Foreign Currency Translation

Many businesses carry out trading transactions in foreign
countries and a growing number own subsidiaries abroad.
The accounts for such businesses will be maintained in the
local currency and this must be converted into sterling before
transactions can be included in the accounts of UK concerns.
Two types of problem arise:

1. Accounting for transactions where the exchange rate
   changes during the transaction (realised exchange differences);
2. Converting into sterling the accounts of businesses com-
   piled in a foreign currency.

11.1 Realised exchange differences

If a British company contracts with an American firm to buy
American wheat and is invoiced for \$20,000 when the
exchange rate is £1 = \$2.00, the \$20,000 invoice will be
recorded in the books as £10,000. If the pound then loses
value on world exchanges and at the time of payment is
worth only \$1.90, it will cost the British company £10,526
to buy \$20,000. The £526 represents a loss of exchange due
to circumstances beyond the control of the company (although it might have covered its position by buying dollars
on the forward exchange market). The correct way to treat
this loss in the accounts is the subject of debate between
those who would treat it as a normal trading item, and those
who would distinguish it as an extraordinary item and
perhaps not show it in the profit and loss account at all but

take it directly to reserve. The exposure draft which covers this point, ED 21, is dealt with below.

11.2 Conversion of amounts in foreign currency

The problem with completed trading transactions is at least confined to the correct presentation in accounts. But if amounts are shown in a foreign currency because the assets and liabilities concerned are held abroad, there is no settled theory on whether to use the exchange rate at the time the transaction took place—the historic rate—or that existing when the British accounts are made up—the closing rate. If a foreign subsidiary is owned by a British company who wish to prepare consolidated accounts, they will have access to the subsidiary's accounts only in the foreign currency. If the historic rate is used, each transaction making up the subsidiary's accounts must be converted into sterling at the rate at the time of the transaction. Trading transactions will usually be converted at average rates during the year; fixed assets and depreciation on the rates prevailing at the date of purchase; current assets, being realisable quickly, at the year end rate. The method will almost certainly produce a difference on the converted balance sheet between assets and liabilities, owing to the different conversion rates used. This difference remains 'hanging in the air', to be carried forward in the consolidated accounts as an adjustment of reserves.

The closing rate method will convert all items at the same rate—the rate ruling at the year end of the parent's accounts. The only exceptions will be for stocks purchased with sterling and remittances received in the year, which translate at the rates ruling at the time in accordance with the entries made in the books of the parent. Differences on exchange will therefore be small, but if the closing rate differs from that used the previous year then, even if the value of the subsidiary's net assets in the foreign currency is unchanged, they will nevertheless be given a different value in the UK accounts.

The theory of currency translations is so undeveloped that no definitive accounting practice has yet been recommended by the ASC. SSAP 6 referred to the difficulties of accounting for sudden sharp changes in exchange rates (*e.g.* devaluations from one fixed rate to another) but merely required the accounting policy adopted to be disclosed pending the issue of a new standard. Discussion of the position led to a further comment on this matter in ED 21 which supersedes SSAP 6 and ED 16. ED 21 *Accounting for foreign currency transactions* recommends that exchange differences should be dealt with in the profit and loss account and shown as extraordinary only if the item to which they relate is extraordinary.

If the closing rate method is used, the value of fixed assets held by a subsidiary will alter with the movement in the rate. ED 21 recommends that such differences should be dealt with directly in reserves, unless the amounts recover deficits previously charged to profit and loss or are deficits for which no cover exists in reserves.

Borrowings should always be converted at the current rate, as they may have to be repaid by the UK company out of domestic funds. However, where borrowing has financed assets held abroad, a loss on exchange on one will be balanced by a gain on the other and can be offset.

Although most UK companies used the closing rate method, the American standard (FAS 8) requires use of the temporal method. Multinational companies who published accounts both in the UK and US found that the use of the different methods produced markedly different profit figures on the same accounts. It is intolerable to have two different standards imposed on companies and efforts were being made in 1980 to produce a standard acceptable worldwide. This is likely to argue that companies with long-term investments abroad should use the closing rate method and take exchange differences to reserve, while companies carrying an exchange risk in respect of foreign operations should use either the temporal or the closing rate—whichever is most appropriate—but should take exchange differences to the profit and loss account. However, agreement hinges on the decision of the US Financial Accounting Standards Board and ED 21 will not become a standard until agreement is reached.

PART 3

Inflation Accounting

12

The Approach to Inflation Accounting

A fundamental assumption of accounts prepared under the historic cost convention is that the monetary unit in which values are expressed does not itself alter in value between one accounting period and the next. For many years this assumption has not been justified by experience. During the entire post-war period, inflation has been endemic in the Western world. The pace of inflation, as measured by the rate at which money loses its value to purchase goods and services, has varied—lower in years of world recession, higher in the years of greater economic growth—but the hopes of many that the problem would eventually go away have gradually come to look more and more unrealistic. It was these hopes that until recently prevented action to introduce a system of inflation accounting. In 1949 and 1952 the ICA discussed the problem in its recommendations on accounting *nos*. N12 and N15. These concluded that no suitable system of inflation accounting existed and that no change could be recommended to existing practice.

During the 1960s the rate of inflation worsened, particularly in the United Kingdom. Pressure from industry for recognition of the effects of inflation upon conventional accounts grew and the accountancy profession began to reconsider the question. The formation of the ASC marked a new phase, for it could hardly issue standards intended to promote a true and fair view, and not tackle the problem of inflation. Research in the first three years of the life of the ASC was directed towards adjusting accounts for changes in the purchasing power of money via a system called 'Current Purchasing Power' accounting ('CPP').

In 1973 ED 8, *Accounting for changes in the purchasing power of money*, was published. In that year the Government appointed a Committee of Enquiry, headed by Francis Sandilands, to consider 'Whether, and, if so, how company accounts should allow for changes (including relative changes) in costs and prices . . . and to make recommendations'. The Committee and the ASC were therefore working simultaneously but, as it happened, came to different conclusions.

In 1974 ED 8 became SSAP 7 with no material changes to the original proposals. The standard appeared representative of opinion in the US as well as the UK but was dubbed 'provisional' as the ASC recognised that the subject was too controversial to insist on uniformity of practice. There was a growing body of opinion which rejected CPP and considerable academic debate over alternative schemes.

In 1975 the Sandilands Committee reported.[1] To the surprise of many in the accountancy profession, they rejected the arguments used to support SSAP 7 and instead proposed that inflation accounting be based on the changes in prices experienced by each business entity. The system was called 'Current Cost Accounting' ('CCA'), the name deliberately chosen to contrast with historic cost accounting. CCA was more acceptable to industry than SSAP 7 and the Government announced its general acceptance of the Sandilands Report soon after publication. A steering group, chaired by Douglas Morpeth, was set up under the ASC to decide how to implement CCA in practice and to work out a new standard accounting practice.

In December 1976 the work of the steering group was published as ED 18 *Current Cost Accounting*. The exposure draft recommended the adoption of CCA along the lines of the Sandilands Report but added refinements to increase the flexibility of the system. The reception of ED 18 by the profession, industry and the Government was at first favourable, until widespread doubts began to be expressed over the complexity of the draft, the apparent freedom given to directors to choose their own figure of retained profits, and the proposal that CCA should

---

[1] Report of the inflation accounting committee, *op. cit.*

compulsorily replace historical cost accounting. These doubts led to an ICA vote against the compulsory introduction of CCA.

But there remained pressure from Government and industry for a standard. A fresh approach, still based on CCA, was made with ED 24 in 1979 and this became SSAP 16 in 1980 —Europe's first official break with historical cost accounting.

This chapter examines the theoretical concepts upon which CPP and CCA are constructed and reviews the defects of historical cost accounting and CPP accounting. The theory of CCA is introduced in the following chapter and SSAP 16 is outlined in Chapter 14.

12.1 Conventions of profit

There are three major concepts of profit used in accounting as well as many varieties of the basic themes. These three conventions are outlined below. An alternative approach, used in economics and based on discounting future cash flows, is outlined in an appendix to this chapter.

Convention 1—the historical cost convention.

> *Provided capital is maintained in monetary terms, all increases in the net assets are profits. Net assets are measured at original monetary cost to the business.*

This convention is the one most widely used in the Western world and is the starting point for teaching bookkeeping. All assets and liabilities are recorded in the books of the business as they arise, at the money cost to the business at that time. Subsequent changes in prices are, in general, ignored. So long as the business retains net assets which, when valued at cost (less any amounts deducted for depreciation, obsolescence *etc.*) equal the opening capital, all increases in the net assets may be treated as distributable profit.

Thus, if the business started the year with capital of £1,000 and stock which cost £1,000, and if during the year half the stock was sold for £700 the balance sheets would be:

	Start of year	End of year
	£	£
Stock	1,000	500
Cash	—	700
	1,000	1,200
Capital	1,000	1,000
Profit	—	200
	1,200	1,200

£200 in cash can be removed leaving the opening capital of £1,000 represented by stock of £500 and cash £500. £200 is therefore the profit. In the profit and loss account would appear

	£
Sales	700
less cost of goods sold	500
Profit	200

Convention 2—Current Purchasing Power

Provided capital is maintained at a constant purchasing power, all increases in net assets are profits. Net assets are revalued each year by the change in purchasing power of money.

CPP was developed to meet a criticism of historical cost accounting, which was that in a period of inflation the value of money is falling and preserve capital expressed as a sum of money is illusory, since each year the money will buy less than before.

Since capital is owned by whoever owns the business, it is important to measure the decline in the value of money in terms of the rate of price increases experienced by the owners. Thus, if prices generally are rising at 10% *p.a.* but the owner of the business consumes goods the price of which has risen by 20%, then that is the effective rate of inflation for the owner and the 10% rate experienced elsewhere is irrelevant.

However, businesses are owned by a great many people and it is impracticable to find out what rate of inflation each experiences. An average must be used and the average thought by the ASC to be most representative of the inflation perceived by the majority of people is that expressed in the retail price index.

Under CPP the balance sheets of the previous and the present accounting periods are converted into the same units —£'s of current purchasing power. The difference between the values of net assets thus derived is the profit. Conversion is effected by multiplying historical cost amounts by the change in the retail price index between the date of acquisition and the date to which the accounts are prepared. Net assets are no longer expressed in pounds but in pounds of current purchasing power and the distinction between capital and retained profits vanishes, leaving a single figure of equity interest.

Real assets such as fixed assets and stocks are deemed to maintain their purchasing power over time, while assets or liabilities whose value is fixed in money terms—cash, debtors, creditors and loans—lose value as prices rise. Such monetary items are deemed to be acquired at the year end date.

Thus, monetary items are expressed in the current balance sheet at par, while those of the previous year are revalued by the change in the RPI during the year. The non-monetary assets are expressed in terms of current purchasing power in both balance sheets. A business holding net monetary assets is shown to be worse off in a period of inflation, while a business with net monetary liabilities gains.

Continuing the example used for Convention 1, assume the RPI rose by 20% during the year. The net assets at the start of the year were £1,000 at cost. Assuming the stock had been purchased at the end of the preceding year, the net assets are restated in the CPP accounts at £1,200. The closing balance sheet contains £700 in cash, which is valued at par and half of the original stock. This will be restated at £600 (half of £1,200):

	Start of year	End of year
	£C	£C
Stocks	1,200	600
Cash	—	700
	1,200	1,300
Equity interest	1,200	1,300

Profit is the change in the net assets. Both balance sheets are stated in terms of the purchasing power of the pound at the year end. They are therefore directly comparable and the profit (also in terms of the year end value of the pound) is therefore £C100. The designation '£C' is required, since the pound will have a different purchasing power at each different accounting date.

The profit recorded under CPP differed from that shown by the historical cost convention, because the first £100 of the historic profit was required to maintain the purchasing power of the cash proceeds in terms of the stock consumed. The historical cost profit was calculated without any attempt to restore the purchasing power of the assets given up by the sale.

Convention 3—Current Cost Accounting

Provided the value of assets to the business is maintained, all increases above that value are profits. Net assets are measured in terms of their value to the business.

CCA does not regard capital as a sum of money due to the owners of the business but looks to the business itself. The monetary figures in the accounts represent real assets and under CCA no profit is recognised until sufficient has been charged against income to maintain the value of assets consumed in earning that income. This will normally require the valuing assets at their replacement cost and this will be determined irrespective of movements in the RPI.

Thus, if in the example the price of the stocks sold had risen by 10% in the year the profit and loss account would show

	£
Sales	700
less cost of stock sold	550
Profit	150

The difference between the historical cost of the stock sold and its replacement cost at the date of sale—£50—is treated as a holding gain. Such a gain, although a 'profit' in the conventional sense, must be retained so that the stock sold can be replaced. If the entire gain of £200 is distributed, the business will be unable to recover its position measured in terms of the value of its assets at the start of the year.

Similarly, at the end of the year the stock remaining is valued according to its value to the business, in order that the balance sheet will accurately reflect the value of net assets. The increase in the value of the stock over historic cost is a holding gain. Both holding gains are credited to a revaluation reserve which is treated as part of the long-term capital of the business.

The balance sheets will show:

	Start of year £	*End of year* £
Stock at value to business	1,000	550
Cash	—	700
	1,000	1,250
Capital	1,000	1,000
Profit	—	150
Stock revaluation reserve	—	100
	1,000	1,250

These three conventions, although presented here in a greatly simplified way, serve to illustrate difficulties in deciding how to measure profit. The historical cost convention ignores movements in prices and uses the money cost of assets. CPP and CCA attempt to measure profit and capital in terms of the real net assets employed in the business. However, while CPP values the business from the viewpoint of the owner, CCA values the business itself and does not look to the ownership. If all prices are rising at the same rate these methods produce identical results. Over a long period prices may well move closely together, but between one year and another it is not likely that the prices relevant to a business will have changed at the same rate as the RPI. The choice of accounting convention will therefore be crucial in determining the reported profit.

The debate over which convention should be used in financial reporting has not yet concluded, despite the widespread support for the proposals of the Sandilands Report. At the heart of the controversy is the question of which convention correctly accounts for the effects of inflation. It is probable that the matter will continue to be the source of debate for many years and that the search for more refined conventions will continue.

12.2 The needs of users of accounts

The Sandilands Report starts by discussing the meaning of inflation and how it can be measured, and then examines the theory of profits and values. It concludes that there are several concepts of profit that could be applied, depending on the requirements of the users of accounts. Since the appropriate concept, and the appropriate method of valuing assets, depends on the needs of users, the report then considers these needs. The recommendation for CCA is based upon the conclusions of the study and it is therefore necessary to discuss the needs that were regarded as central in the report.

The unit of measurement
The unit of measurement has traditionally been the currency of the country concerned. However, the CPP method adopts a new unit, the pound of current purchasing power. The meaning of this unit is discussed in detail below. The Sandilands Report (henceforth 'Sandilands') put forward five propositions which were not discussed but were simply stated as the chief requirements of all classes of users of published accounts. The propositions are that the unit of measurement

(a) Should be equally useful to all users;
(b) Should not change from year to year;
(c) Should be the same for all enterprises presenting financial statements;
(d) Should preferably be a physical object which could be exchanged by users of accounts;
(e) Should represent a constant value through time.

In Chapter 2 money measurement was stated as an essential axiom. The propositions of the Sandilands Report clarify the requirement. The report does not assume that all five points will be met in any particular unit of measurement. The presumption is that a unit should be able to satisfy as many of these criteria as possible.

The valuation of assets
The report considers the needs of the various 'user groups' who rely on accounts. The principal user group is said to be the shareholders of a corporate body, and they are thought to want accounts which:

(a) Prove that the management can account for all the funds entrusted to them;
(b) Provide the shareholders with an accurate assessment of the value of the funds invested in the business so that they can calculate the return on their investment and try to predict the future income the business is likely to earn.

The need for management to be accountable is met in any case by the legal requirement that all companies be audited, but the auditors do not comment on how the funds of the company have been used. The valuation of assets according to their cost allows the movements of funds to be traced, while any other form of valuation must remove the link of historic cost.

Criterion (b) requires that a value be placed upon assets, such valuation being made in the context of the present and expected future position of the business. There are two widely accepted ways of valuing assets to show their value to the business (replacement cost, net realisable value) of which replacement cost normally is the most relevant. (The methods are described in Chapter 13.)

The measurement of profit

Sandilands argues that shareholders and others will find that, of the three conventions mentioned above, CCA is the most relevant. This convention—based on charging against income the value to the business of assets consumed in order to earn that income—is expanded by Sandilands and SSAP 16 to include an analysis of all other monetary gains recorded in the books of the company. These are classified as 'operating gains' (profit as described in Convention 3), 'holding gains' (the difference between the actual cost and the replacement cost of assets) and 'extraordinary items'.

Operating gains show how efficiently the business is being run, while the total gains represent the change in financial state and thus the value of the shareholders' interest. Historical cost and CPP accounting do not present such information.

The Liquidity Position

One of the fears of anyone dealing with a business is that it may collapse and be unable to pay its debts in full. Creditors and other lenders of finance, such as debenture holders and banks, are thought to be far more concerned with the ability of the business to pay its debts than its future prospects (except in so far as its prospects will affect its ability to pay its debts). Shareholders too are concerned about the immediate stability of a company to which they have entrusted their money.

Accounts should therefore show the financial position of the company at the year end and also explain how that position changed during the past year. This latter point is now covered by SSAP 10 (see Chapter 23). Since the conventional balance sheet shows the assets classified into those easily turned into cash and others, and liabilities classified into those repayable in the near future (usually taken to mean within one year) and others, it was not thought that further changes were required.

Sandilands discussed the needs of users such as employees, the State, investment analysts *etc.*, as well as the better known users, such as shareholders and creditors, and decided that within the context of accounting for inflation these groups could all be regarded as satisfied, provided

shareholders' needs were satisfied. In other words, the needs
of shareholders include all the likely requirements of other
user groups. This conclusion does not hold for matters
beyond the scope of direct financial accounting—for
example, employees are often concerned about their own
prospects for employment and pay—but this was beyond
the brief of the Sandilands Committee. However, further
consideration was provided by 'The Corporate Report' (see
Chapter 24). Historical cost accounting, and the alternative
concepts can now be appraised in the light of user needs.

12.3 The criticisms of historical cost accounting

Before starting a revolution it is prudent to ensure that what
is to come is preferable to what is to be overturned. Thus,
conventional accounting—accounts prepared under the
historical cost convention—must be shown to be inadequate
against the systems proposed as alternatives. This section
will describe briefly the inadequacies of conventional
accounts in a period of inflation, as established by Sandilands and many other leading authorities.

The falling value of money
It was stated in Chapter 2 that profit measurement hinged
on how the capital of an enterprise was evaluated. The
historical cost convention assumes that a pound in one year
is worth a pound at any other time and that capital can be
suitably measured by the pounds that needed to be expended
to acquire the net assets. In a period of inflation this assumption cannot be tenable. Consumer prices in the UK doubled
between 1975 and 1980. An enterprise whose capital was
unchanged in historical cost terms over the period could be
roughly halved in size compared to other enterprises.
Clearly the owners of the capital will be less well off, despite
maintaining the money value of the capital. A method of
measuring which reflects 'well off' in *real* terms is needed.

CPP measures capital in terms of the general purchasing
power of money, while CCA adjusts for the specific price
changes of the assets employed in an enterprise. Despite
the differences between these methods (of which more
below) both attempt to restore the genuine measurement of

capital—a task which, due to inflation, historical cost accounting is unable to perform.

In addition, inflation has made it almost impossible to compare the results of different enterprises, because the assets employed in various businesses, at cost, will have different values depending on the date of purchase.

The undervaluation of assets

As the value of the pound falls, so real assets become more valuable than the amounts at which they are stated in conventional accounts. The response of conventional accounting, revaluations, has been mentioned in Chapter 8. This response does not adequately meet the needs of users for a comprehensive statement of the value of assets, because it is arbitrary and confined to certain types of assets. CCA explicitly values assets at their value to the business. CPP values them according to the purchasing power the sums invested in those assets can be said to represent.

The overstatement of profit

The understatement of asset values mentioned above leads to an overstatement of operating profits, since the cost of the assets used up in earning those profits is understated. CPP raises the cost of assets consumed to equal the purchasing power they had at the time of sale, while CCA values them at value to the business—usually at the replacement cost—at the time of sale. Both methods therefore seek to report operating profit as the increase in the 'real' capital of a business. The chief assets which are understated are stocks and fixed assets. Holding gains on stock are ignored completely by historical cost accounting as there is no mechanism for recording such gains, and the idea that holding gains exist is in any case contrary to the philosophy behind the convention. Fixed assets are valued at cost, and depreciation is also charged as an appropriation of the original cost. Therefore the charge does not match against income the full cost of the fixed assets consumed in earning the income.

The distorting effect holding gains on stock have on conventional profit figures in a time of rapid inflation was recognised in 1974, when a special relief for UK business taxation was announced. The relief, calculated by deducting the increase in the value of stocks over the year from an adjusted figure of taxable profits, was regarded as a temporary measure pending the introduction of inflation accounting. The very existence of such a relief made the work of the ASC and the Sandilands Committee all the more significant, because efforts to introduce inflation accounting in the past have always been seen as somewhat academic and irrelevant to the 'real world'. Now the real world had recognised the need to do away with a system of accounting that was no longer telling the truth, and the pressure was on the 'academics' to produce a superior system which was both theoretically sound and of practical use.

The solution proposed by the ASC in SSAP 7 was the CPP method. Despite strong and widespread criticism, CPP is still regarded by many accountants as the best available method of dealing with inflation accounting. The critique of the method advanced in the Sandilands Report, which helped swing opinion towards CCA, is now summarised.

12.4 Criticisms of CPP accounting

Most of the criticism of CPP lies not in theoretical faults but in the relevance and usefulness of the method. It appears to be giving the shareholder what accountants think he ought to know, rather than what management wishes him to know, or indeed what he himself might wish to know. Sandilands laid some stress on the difficulty of understanding CPP accounting compared to other systems of inflation accounting. The detailed points which led to the rejection of CPP as the best available method for accounting for inflation follow.

The unit of measurement

The criteria that a unit of measurement should meet were listed by Sandilands and have been discussed above. The CPP unit, a pound of constant purchasing power at a given date, is said to meet none of those criteria fully. It is not equally useful to all users of accounts, since each will find the RPI of different relevance to their own particular pattern of expenditure. It changes each year as previous years' accounts are updated, and is not constant. It will differ each year and indeed each month, making it impossible to compare accounts made up to different dates. It cannot be exchanged and can only be imagined as an abstract unit. The fifth criterion—constant value through time—is approached more closely by a CPP unit than any other proposed unit, but the limits of the RPI itself limit the usefulness of the CPP unit. The RPI does not measure all goods and services, and ceases to be directly comparable between periods if the pattern of consumers' expenditure changes, changing the weighting given to the different items making up the index.

The conclusion of the report is 'a unit of measurement with an absolute value through time is unattainable and the search for such a unit is illusory. We see no advantage in drawing up accounts in current purchasing power units rather than in units of money'.

The measurement of net assets

CPP accounts do not show the value of assets to the business, only the purchasing power of the sums of money invested in them. Because of this it is not possible to measure the efficiency of different businesses in terms of the rate of return on invested capital. Nor does CPP accounting provide a more reliable guide to the market value of assets than does historic accounting.

The concept of profit

The criterion advanced by Sandilands was that profit should be calculated by charging against income the cost of assets consumed, such cost being the value to the business at the time of sale. CPP accounting will only produce such a figure if the RPI has increased by precisely the same amount as the prices of the actual assets consumed by the business. Otherwise it is measuring the profit that *would* have been earned if all assets had increased in price at the same rate as the RPI—which may be interesting as a piece of additional information, but is not what the average investor wants to know.

The meaning of monetary gains

Monetary gains and losses are inevitable using a CPP system of measurement. But is a monetary 'gain' the same thing as a profit? Consider a simple case, a business financed by share capital of £100 and a loan of £100, holding an asset (say a piece of land) that was bought for £200 at the start of the

current year. There is no trading in the year or changes in
the net assets. However, during the year the RPI rises 20%.
Conventional accounting shows no profit or loss. CPP
shows the following:

	Last year £	This year £	
Asset (land)	240	240	(£200 cost × $\frac{120}{100}$)
Shareholders' interests	120	140	(The balancing item)
Loan	120	100	(Last year's value updated; no change this year)
	240	240	

In CPP terms the shareholders have gained £20 of current
purchasing power pounds from the lenders of the loan. The
problem is that the profit cannot be divorced from the assets,
but is simply bound up in the comparison of balance sheets.
Should the business try to distribute the profit, part of the
land would have to be sold and it would realise whatever
land was worth on the open market—its 'value to the
business'—which might or might not be the same as its CPP
value. The transfer of purchasing power to shareholders
from lenders is real enough, bearing in mind the reservation
that purchasing power varies from person to person. However, the way of measuring it is questionable.

In the CCA approach it is the value of the asset that rises,
and the shareholders' interests rise with it. If the price of
land had risen by, say, 25% the two years' balance sheets
would be thus:

	Last year £	This year £
Asset (land)	200	250
Shareholders' interests	100	150
Loan	100	100
	200	250

and it would be up to the individual shareholder to decide to what extent they were better off as a result of the appreciation in value of the land. The providers of the loan have enjoyed no benefit from the appreciation in value, and the business itself shows no profit, only a holding gain, indicating that its physical size has not altered.

Conclusion

When the Sandilands Committee applied the criteria derived from their study of the needs of users of accounts to the recommendations in SSAP 7, it was forced to conclude that CPP failed to meet users' needs.

There has since been some defence of CPP, in particular the argument that it alone tries to measure the effects of inflation (defined as the fall in the purchasing power of the pound) while other proposals, notably CCA, only measure changes in relative prices and not inflation as such. None the less the criticisms of CPP accounting were to prove decisive in swinging opinion away from CPP in general and SSAP 7 in particular. The concept of purchasing power was not so easily destroyed, despite the attack on it in the Sandilands Report, and survives in the continuing controversy about the treatment of monetary items in CC accounts, and in SSAP 16's suggestion that a note showing how shareholders' equity has changed after allowing for changes in the general price level should be published as additional information with CC accounts.

13

The Theory of Current Cost Accounting

13.1 The logic of CCA

Current cost accounting is based on the approach to profit theory outlined in Chapter 2. At the heart of CCA is the intention of measuring the capital of a business in such a way that the distorting effect of price changes during the accounting period is removed. Net assets are measured at their value to the business and a profit will not be recognised until assets consumed or liabilities incurred in earning income have been replaced or provided for respectively at the value to the business they had at the time the income was earned. The balance sheet discloses net assets at their value to the business allowing a more realistic appraisal to be made of the return on capital and of the market value of assets than is possible under historical cost accounting ('HCA').

CCA does not employ an index of general purchasing power, nor does it use the HC accounts except as the starting point in the preparation of CC accounts. The system of measurement throughout is value to the business. The unit of measurement is (in the UK) pounds, not pounds of a constant purchasing power. It follows that CCA does not attempt to value a business according to the funds invested in it by the owners. It restates the net operating assets— normally fixed assets, stocks and monetary working capital —at current cost and leaves it to the owners to decide if the value of their investment has kept pace with inflation and economic growth.

The Sandilands Report (and ED 18) provided a detailed and highly theoretical approach to CCA. SSAP 16, which had made it a compulsory form of financial reporting for large enterprises in the UK, is not as radical as ED 18 and attempts to graft CCA onto existing HC accounts. There are, therefore, certain differences between the theory and SSAP 16's practice. The emphasis in this book is on the practical aspects of financial accounting and the following discussion is intended as a broad guide to the thinking behind SSAP 16.

13.2 Profits and gains

Under the HC convention operating profit is identical to the monetary gain on trading transactions. The gain is calculated by deducting from money proceeds of sale the money cost of the assets consumed or sold. Under CCA a third factor is introduced—the current cost of the assets consumed or sold at the time of disposal. There are therefore two types of gain which together comprise the total 'profit'. The operating gain is the difference between the sale proceeds and the current cost of the asset at the time of sale, while the holding gain is the difference between current cost and historical cost.

It is the holding gain which measures the effects of inflation (or more precisely, measures the impact of changes in the input prices affecting the business). Such a gain is not regarded as distributable profit under CCA. The distributable gain is the operating gain which, by being calculated after making full provision to replace the assets sold or used, genuinely measures the extent to which the transaction has increased the net assets (and therefore the capital) of the business.

The expressions 'operating' and 'holding' gain were introduced by Sandilands to clarify the confusing terminology used previously. However, SSAP 16 does not speak of gains but 'adjustments' which have to be made to the HC accounts These adjustments take two forms:

(a) Adjustments to the profit and loss account which, by eliminating holding gains, present as profit only the operating gains.
(b) Adjustments to the balance sheet so as to present the net operating assets at current cost. These adjustments, which do not affect the profit and loss account because they are restricted to the net assets held at the end of the

accounting period, are called 'revaluation surpluses or deficits' in SSAP 16.

In addition it should be noted that extraordinary items are also subject to current cost adjustments and the amount of any extraordinary profit or loss will be after deducting the appropriate holding gain or loss on the asset concerned.

The distinction between these types of gains is brought out in the following examples:

(a) A business sells a unit of stock for £20 which cost £10. At the time of sale the stock had a current cost of £16. Under CCA theory there is a £4 operating gain and a £6 holding gain. (Under SSAP 16 a £6 adjustment to the historical cost gain of £10 would result in a CC profit of £4.)

(b) The same sale is made but the proceeds are £14. The holding gain is the same but there is an operating loss of £2. (A £6 adjustment to the HC profit of £4.)

(c) The stock is held to the end of the accounting period when its current cost is £17. It is shown in the balance sheet at that value and a £7 revaluation surplus is credited to owners' equity (and treated as undistributable because the gain is unrealised).

(d) The business operates a machine which cost £2,000 and has a life of five years. After a year the machine would cost £2,600 to replace new. The CC depreciation charge is 2,600/5 = £520 as this is the current cost of the asset consumed in the year. (A depreciation adjustment of £120 is added to the HC charge of £400. This is a form of holding loss because the value that the business is losing through depreciation is increased as the replacement cost of the asset increases.)

(e) A business sells a factory which cost £20,000 for £50,000. The factory has a total estimated life of thirty years and is twenty-one years old. The current cost at the time of sale was £40,000. Assuming the sale was not a normal transaction, a revaluation surplus of £34,000 (40,000 − (9/30 × 20,000)) and an extraordinary profit of £10,000 will be recorded.

(f) The factory is not sold but held at the end of the year when its value to the business is £45,000. The revaluation surplus is £39,000. (If CCA accounts are prepared for the first time the whole surplus will be recorded at once; normally the surplus will have built up each year as the current cost is compared to the historical cost.)

The CCA approach, at first sight greatly different to HC accounting, is not in fact so drastic a change as it may seem. The treatment of revaluations and extraordinary items is very close to that discussed in Chapter 5 where it was argued that all unrealised profits had to be regarded as undistributable and that realised capital gains and extraordinary items should be classified as distributable only if the funds were not required to be retained in the business. The purpose of the calculation of value to the business (or current cost) is to compute accurately what under historical cost is expressed so vaguely, namely the amount which must be deducted from sale proceeds to maintain the business at a given operating capacity.

It must be remembered that the measurement of net operating assets at current cost is an accounting representation of operating capacity and not a technical or physical measure. It is arguable that the managers of a business will have a clearer idea of the true capacity than can be shown by any accounting convention. But CCA is intended to provide a more effective way to account for business transactions than has been used before, and a more relevant method of measuring operating profit, free from some of the major distortions which the user of accounts is unable to measure and which have rendered HC accounts unsuitable explanations of business transactions.

13.3 The valuation of assets

In the discussion above, the concept of 'value to the business' has been used interchangeably with 'current cost'. To be more precise, the purpose of current cost accounts is to measure assets at their value to the business and there are in SSAP 16 two bases applicable—'net current replacement cost' and 'recoverable amount'. Assets are to be measured at the lower of these two values.

The notion of value to the business is different in kind both from historical cost and from sale values. The argument, advanced originally by Professor J. C. Bonbright, is that the best measure of the value of an asset is its deprival value—how much worse off a business becomes if it is deprived of an asset it previously owned. The justification for this approach is that the alternative is to value the asset by how much better off the business is owning it and this creates awkward problems.

Suppose, an item of trading stock cost £100, would cost £150 to replace but could be sold for £200. Valuation on the basis of how much better off the business is owning the asset would require a value of £200—before it had actually made the sale, thus anticipating realisation and recognising profit earlier than is acceptable both in current practice and in accounting theory. However, the deprival value is £150 because the business can replace the stock at that price. Valuation by deprival does not anticipate realisation and does not involve a guess of the eventual market price but is based on the objective price of replacement.

The normal measure of value to the business is therefore replacement. Replacement cost will tend to be identical to historical cost except in the case of stocks and fixed assets. Allowance must be made for depreciation and technical change in physical assets but the general principle is that replacement cost is the current market price the business would pay to acquire the assets it currently owns in the same state and age.

There are times when assets are not replaceable in the market or when a business would not wish to replace them at all. In these cases the appropriate value is the recoverable amount, *i.e.* the net amount the business could obtain on disposal in the normal course of business. This is identical to the HC concept of net realisable value and the rule of the lower of replacement cost and recoverable amount is applied in the same way as the HC rule of the lower of cost and NRV (see p. 76).

Sandilands suggested a third measure might also be valid in special cases—economic value. This is the net present value of the future earnings of an asset and is relevant in those cases where an asset is capable of earning income but has no realistic recoverable amount (perhaps because it is specific to the one business). The practical relevance of economic value is so limited that it is likely to be ignored. The measure of value to the business under SSAP 16 is therefore the lower of the net current replacement cost and recoverable amount. An illustration of the calculation of replacement cost for fixed assets is in Chapter 14.

13.4 Monetary items

Monetary items comprise trade debtors and creditors, accruals and prepayments, bank balances and overdrafts, long-term finance, taxation and deferred taxation and in fact every item neither part of owners' equity nor a physical asset. These items are characterised in having a fixed money value which having been determined by some past transaction is not subsequently altered whatever may happen to prices. The replacement value is therefore equivalent to the money (or historical) value and the balance sheet valuation of monetary items under CCA is identical to the treatment under HCA.

There is however some controversy over the effect of monetary items on the measurement of current cost profit. It is necessary to distinguish between working capital (trade debtors and creditors accruals and prepayments) and other monetary items.

A business may have a positive or negative working capital (positive meaning debtors exceed creditors). During a period of inflation the value of working capital is likely to rise even though the volume of transactions giving rise to debtors and creditors is steady or even declining. A business with a positive working capital must continually increase its financial investment while a negative working capital position means a continual inflow of cash. Because these financial burdens or benefits are permanent, given the assumption of a going concern with no significant changes in debtor or creditor relationships expected, a CCA gain or loss can be recognised. Since the purpose of CCA is to remove the impact of price changes, the working capital gain or loss is calculated as the difference between the money increase in working capital, less the increase that would have been recorded had prices stayed constant. There is further consideration of the calculation in Chapter 14.

Working capital varies directly with trading and the gain or loss associated with it can be regarded as part of the CC operating profit. But other monetary items do not vary in the same way. Taxation is fixed annually according to the tax laws in force at the time; hire purchase finance or a mortgage will be related to a particular asset and the repayments will be fixed over the period of the loan; long-term finance such as medium-term bank loans or loan stock may be raised to support general business development and will have no direct bearing on day-to-day trading (or changes in prices). Hence any adjustment for long-term monetary items would have to be treated separately from the other current cost adjustments which are all linked to trading.

Normally a business has an excess of long-term monetary liabilities over long-term monetary assets and it is this case which is considered in detail. The converse, a business holding net monetary assets, cannot easily be dealt with under CCA since such assets can produce nothing of themselves but can only be lent to others. SSAP 16 states there is no settled treatment for this case.

Sandilands argued that no credit should be taken for holding net long-term monetary liabilities because as inflation raised the value of the assets financed by the liabilities, so owners' equity is increased and no further adjustment is needed (see p. 143). Furthermore it would be misleading to report any gain because it would only be receivable when the business was wound up and this would be inconsistent with the going concern concept.

The argument of SSAP 16 is that a business is continually realising its assets through normal business transactions, *e.g.* fixed assets are depreciated over their lives, such depreciation being a realisation of part of the asset. The business applying CCA will charge the full replacement cost of all assets used up or sold against profit. But if part of the finance for assets has come from long-term debt, which is fixed in money terms, then that part of the replacement adjustment relating to long-term finance is not needed. (Consider the employment of a machine wholly financed by a loan. Whatever happens to the replacement cost of the machine, provided the business charges depreciation on the historical cost basis, then sufficient funds will be retained to pay off the loan when the machine is fully depreciated and scrapped.)

SSAP 16 recognises the devaluing of long-term finance by inflation through a requirement that a 'gearing adjustment' be applied to the other current cost adjustments, reducing the total of the adjustments in the ratio that long-term finance bore to the total capital employed during the accounting period. The gearing adjustment is therefore retrospective, looking back to the assets used during the past year and the finance available at the time. It does not imply anything about necessary finance in the future. This crucial point is considered further in section 14.6

14

SSAP 16 Current Cost Accounting

SSAP 16 'Current Cost Accounting' was published in April 1980. Unlike previous official pronouncements on inflation accounting it does not seek to persuade or argue a case. The standard requires that all UK enterprises over a certain size produce current cost accounts for accounting periods starting on or after 1 January 1980.

The theory of CCA outlined in Chapter 13 is the foundation on which the standard builds. This chapter is concerned with how it is to be implemented in the case of a normal trading/industrial company. There are many special cases and certain problems, which are beyond the scope of this book (and which indeed are still the subject of experimentation). Furthermore it has been made clear by the ASC that SSAP 16 may itself be replaced in a few years as experience of CCA is amassed. It is therefore stressed that the appearance of a standard does not close the debate which has now gone on for more than a decade.

SSAP 16 applies to all companies listed on the Stock Exchange plus any other company with two out of the three following criteria:

(a) More than 250 employees;
(b) Turnover over £5m;
(c) Balance sheet total (fixed assets, investments, current assets) over £2·5m.

But there are exemptions for insurance companies, investment trusts and property investment companies, and for all non profit-making organisations.

The standard in fact applies to any entity which fulfils the size criteria and wishes its accounts to show a true and fair view. But as there are very few such entities aside from companies, they are not dealt with in this book.

One of the crucial features of SSAP 16 is that it gives companies a choice as to how to present CCA information. Indeed, CC accounts may be presented as the only accounts (provided the Companies Acts are complied with insofar as they refer to HC information). Few companies are likely to go so far in the next few years. Most will choose to provide CC accounts as supplemental to the main HC accounts but the reverse is also allowed—HC accounts being supplemental to CC accounts.

Whichever route is chosen, CC accounts will consist of a profit and loss account, balance sheet, notes explaining the bases and methods used, and, if the CC accounts are the main accounts, a CC Source and Applications of Funds statement.

14.1 The profit and loss account

SSAP 16 envisages that CC accounts will normally be prepared starting with the HC accounts and making certain adjustments. The format of the profit and loss account specifically recognises this. Although companies have flexibility in how it may be set out, the normal layout will be as below.

The profit and loss account starts with the HC profit before interest and tax and applies the current cost operating adjustments to derive current cost operating profit. This profit figure represents the surplus the business has generated over and above all amounts needed to maintain its operating assets and is the closest accounting measure of the theoretical profit described in Chapter 2.

To this profit is then applied the cost of long-term finance which is the interest payable, less the gearing adjustment. Taxation will be as in the HC accounts and the profit derived is the current cost profit attributable to shareholders —*i.e.* the change in the equity interest having made allowance both for changes in input prices and the benefits and costs of outside finance. It is essential that the CC profit and loss account shows both the operating profit and the profit attributable to shareholders since the first relates to the

EXAMPLE OF PRESENTATION OF CURRENT COST ACCOUNTS

Y Limited and Subsidiaries

Group current cost profit and loss account for the year ended 31st December 1980

1979 £000		1980 £000
18,000	Turnover	20,00
2,420	Profit before interest and taxation on the historical cost basis	2,900
1,320	Less: Current cost operating adjustments (note 2)	1,510
1,100	*Current cost operating profit* . . .	1,390
(170)	Gearing adjustment . . . . . (166)	
180	Interest payable less receivable . . . 200	
10		34
1.090	Current cost profit before taxation . .	1,356
610	Taxation	730
480	*Current cost profit attributable to shareholders*	626
400	Dividends	430
80	Retained current cost profit of the year	196
16·0p	Current cost earnings per share . . .	20·9p
5·2%	Operating profit return on the average of the net operating assets	6·0%

£000	**Statement of retained profits/reserves**	£000
80	Retained current cost profit of the year	196
1,850	Movements on current cost reserve (Note 4)	2,054
NIL	Movements on other reserves . . .	NIL
1,930		2,250
14,150	Retained profits/reserves at the beginning of the year	16,080
16,080	Retained profits/reserves at the end of the year	18,330

business as a whole and the second to the owners. HC accounts have of course reflected the same split in showing profit before and after interest.

The current cost operating adjustments comprise cost of sales, depreciation and monetary working capital. These are now described.

14.2 The cost of sales adjustment ('COSA')

The principles of CCA require that each sale is matched with the cost of sale calculated at current cost. Some businesses may be able to compute the current cost of their sales directly, *e.g.* an aircraft manufacturer turning out two aircraft a month can calculate the current cost of each. But in the main businesses will have to use shortcut methods. The most common is the averaging method, which uses suitable indices of prices in order to approximate the average volume increase in stock during the year. The difference between the volume increase and the total increase is attributable to price changes, and it is this sum which must be deducted from HC profit as the cost of sales adjustment.

The averaging method presupposes that replacement cost is the appropriate base for measuring current cost—it will be so in the vast majority of cases because where a business is forced to value its stock at net realisable value, the business is unlikely to be a going concern and current cost accounts will be irrelevant.

Price indices can be obtained from Government publications (a set of tables entitled 'Price indices for current cost accounting' have been specially published to assist in the preparation of CC accounts) or constructed by companies using suppliers' price lists and their own experience of price trends. Where standard costing is employed, the price variances compared to purchases will show the rate of inflation applicable.

The averaging method assumes fairly even stock *volumes*. If stocks alter in volume during a trading cycle, the cost of sales adjustment should be calculated for shorter periods than the year (or accounting period). However as HC stock valuations are required and as most businesses do not value stocks more frequently than once a month, the monthly calculation of the cost of sales adjustment will often be the most accurate measure that can be obtained.

The cost of sales adjustment applies to all categories of stocks and work in progress. The various cost elements making up work in progress must be treated separately, *e.g.* labour costs adjusted by changes in wages rates, overhead costs according to the average movements in salaries, rents *etc.*

Example 1—Cost of sales adjustment for raw materials
A business dealing in gubbins has the following information in its trading account for 1977, prepared under the historical cost convention. The stocks are valued using FIFO, and represent three months' purchases. The average cost at which they are stated is therefore that of mid-November before each year end.

	£ 000
Opening stock	250
Purchases	1,600
	1,850
Less closing stock	300
Historic cost of sales	1,550

Detailed records of cost movements have not been kept but an index of the price of gubbins is available, calculated to the *middle* of the month:

November	1980	100
December	1980	100
January	1981	102
November	1981	110
December	1981	112
January	1982	112

It is necessary to calculate the average price of the gubbins, which in this case is 106.5, as an arithmetic average of the opening and closing figures, $\left(\dfrac{100 + 102}{2} + \dfrac{112 + 112}{2} /2 \right)$.
If the index is known not to have risen smoothly during the year, it is necessary to calculate the average as the average of

the twelve monthly index numbers. The cost of sales adjustment is calculated thus:

Adjusted opening stock
£250,000 × 106.5/100 = £266,250
Adjusted closing stock
£300,000 × 106.5/110 = £290,454
The current cost of sales is therefore:

Opening stock	£266,250
Purchases	£1,600,000
	£1,886,250
Less closing stock	£290,454
Current cost of sales	£1,575,796

The increase in the cost of sales—the cost of sales adjustment—is £1,575,796 — £1,550,000 = £25,796.

The cost of sales adjustment is unaffected by the volume of purchases in the period. It relates solely to the average stocks held because the need for the adjustment only arises on stocks which are bought in one period and sold in another at which time the replacement cost has changed. A business that sold its stocks on the day of purchase would have no need for a COSA, nor would one which experienced no change in the replacement cost despite the general rate of inflation outside. In the (unlikely) example of a business with no stocks on hand at any year end but some trading during each year, the COSA would be calculated for the periods during which stocks were actually held.

Normally the COSA will be a deduction from HC profit, reflecting increases in prices. It is however possible for certain stocks to have falling replacement costs—consider the electronics industries and the massive falls in the prices of computers, calculators and similar equipment during the last twenty years. Commodities tend to be very price-volatile and long periods of falling prices are often experienced, especially in times of economic down turn. So a COSA which leads to an addition to HC profit can be experienced, indicating that the business can replace its stock as it sells it with a decreasing investment. It should be noted that falling prices in a time of general inflation can be a signal for disaster and some critics of SSAP 16 argue that it could be highly misleading at such a time to produce accounts which report an increase over the HC profit.

14.3 The monetary working capital adjustment ('MWCA')

Just as rising input prices impose a cost on a company attempting to maintain its stock volumes, so will a company which maintains normal debtor/creditor relationships find that rising input prices impose a burden (if MWC is positive) or provide a benefit (if negative) rather than the MWC adjustment. SSAP 16 requires that the MWC adjustment be computed in the same way as the COSA and for the same periods, acknowledging the intimate relationship between the volume of stocks, debtors and creditors which must exist in virtually all companies. For example, as stocks are sold so debtors rise; if stocks are built up creditors also increase. The MWC adjustment therefore applies (with the COSA) the principles of CCA to working capital as a whole. Indeed, there are special cases where a COSA cannot be applied, *e.g.* where stocks are held in order to realise capital gains as in certain commodity deals. In those cases SSAP 16 requires that a MWC adjustment be applied to the working capital which will include such stocks.

MWC comprises items used in the day-to-day running of the business—trade debtors, prepayments, trade creditors, accrued expenses, trade bills and turnover tax payable or receivable will all be included in the net figure; but debtors or creditors relating to the purchase of fixed assets would be excluded. The chief difficulty lies with the treatment of bank overdrafts. For some companies an overdraft is a short-term measure to tide the business through a cash-tight period and in such a case the overdraft replaces trade credit and is therefore part of MWC. But many companies have permanent overdrafts, regularly 'rolled-over' by the banks. In such a case it is arguable that the overdraft is basically long-term finance, does not alter with the day-to-day trading and therefore comes into the gearing calculation rather than the MWC adjustment. The question is more than academic because the MWCA comes 'above the line' in determining operating profit while the gearing adjustment comes 'below'.

SSAP 16 attempts to be flexible, suggesting that any portion of an overdraft which fluctuates with other elements of MWC can be included with it; the rest must be deemed long term.

It is easier to make this suggestion than to decide in practice how to divide an overdraft and there is a strong presumption in the Guidance notes published with the standard that it would have to be shown that the overdraft fluctuated directly with the cyclical nature of trading before any part of it could be deemed MWC. (SSAP 16's fore-runner ED 24 was firm that all overdrafts were part of long-term debt.)

Cash balances would normally be ignored, unless a cash float had to be held as part of the business (*e.g.* in shops). Cash is not an operating asset in the CCA sense because it can produce nothing directly.

When calculating the MWCA, the same indices should be applied as are used for COSA. Creditors will move very closely with stock prices since the bulk of the trade creditors of the average company are for stocks. Debtors may not move unless the business is careful to maintain precise profit margins. Thus if there is likely to be a material impact on the MWC an index of selling prices should be used instead. If different indices are used then the price-increase in debtors will have to be calculated separately from that of creditors and the one deducted from the other.

There may be cases where the MWC is not only negative but exceeds the amount of stocks. This will probably arise with businesses with fast turnover, buying on credit but selling for cash such as supermarkets. In this case the excess of negative MWC is not funding the stocks but is a form of long-term finance and is therefore excluded from the MWCA and added to the gearing adjustment calculation.

14.4 The depreciation adjustment

The current cost of fixed assets consumed during a period will not be measured by HC depreciation for this is linked to the acquisition cost, not the current cost, of the assets concerned. The depreciation adjustment is the amount needed to raise the HC depreciation charge to the current cost charge. There is some debate as to whether the charge should be based on average or year-end values but it is unlikely the difference will be material. Because fixed assets have to be revalued at current cost at the year end in any case (to prepare the CC balance sheet) the depreciation adjustment may more conveniently be based on those values, providing due allowance is made for acquisitions and disposals during the period.

A calculation of current cost depreciation is given in section 14.11 It will be seen that backlog depreciation (as described in Chapter 8) is not charged against current cost profit but is transferred to reserves. This is because current cost accounts measure the cost of earning income in the current period, not the effect of current price changes on *past* consumption of fixed assets.

The depreciation adjustment should always be a charge against CC profit. For it to be a credit, the replacement cost of the assets concerned would have to have fallen and in such cases the historical cost convention requires that the assets be written down in the books to the lower value. Since HC depreciation is charged, following SSAP 15, on the revalued amount, the HC accounts would automatically be adjusted to reflect changed values and no further CC adjustment would arise. In such a case the amount of writeoff would not be added to the normal depreciation charge but would be charged against profits as an exceptional or extraordinary item.

When fixed assets are disposed of, the resulting gain or loss on book value should be adjusted to reflect the current cost value of the asset. Normally this will equal the sales value since by definition the recoverable amount is the net realisable value and this in turn, being the market value of the asset is effectively net current replacement cost. Hence the sale proceeds will equate to current cost and there will be no current cost operating profit or loss on the disposal (*i.e.* the HC profit or loss on disposal will be charged or credited as a current cost adjustment).

CCA looks at the full cost of earning income. Assets which have been fully written off under (prudent) HC rules may still be in use. Such as asset should be brought into the accounts at the appropriate net current replacement cost, assigned a life and depreciated as if newly acquired. This is important because many businesses have assigned very short lives to fixed assets as a way of increasing depreciation charges in recognition of inflation. Under CCA there is no point in this practice and no justification for its continuance.

14.5 The CC balance sheet

The purpose of the balance sheet under CCA is to show the operating assets employed in the business at their value to the business, and to show how they were financed. Where assets are valued differently to the HC accounts, the differences are assigned to a 'current cost reserve'. The current cost adjustments are also transferred to this reserve, which forms part of the owner's equity and which in general is not distributable if it is intended to maintain the physical capacity of the business. This is discussed further below.

Unlike Sandilands, SSAP 16 is unwilling to break the link with the HC accounts. Assets not accounted for in the HC balance sheet will not appear in the CC balance sheet derived from it. (Sandilands allowed all assets to be appropriately valued, including goodwill.) Hence the CC balance sheet will not attempt to value the business as a whole but restates the HC accounts. Where an HC balance sheet is given, the CC balance sheet need not be as detailed provided it clearly shows the totals of net operating assets and net borrowing (although these may be given as a note). These totals are important because they form respectively the basis on which the return on capital can be measured and the basis for calculating the gearing adjustment.

The valuation of property
Property—freehold or leasehold land and buildings— presents a special problem under CCA because there is no obvious replacement cost for land, and in some cases buildings. The guidance notes identify specialised and non-specialised buildings. Specialised buildings are those not frequently dealt with on the open market and the current cost must be based on the cost of construction. Non-

specialised buildings, probably the majority of industrial and commercial property, comprising ordinary shops, offices, factories and warehouses, can be valued at open market value with reference to similar properties in the same area. The land under specialised buildings should also be valued this way as land prices tend to vary with area rather than the use to which the land is put. SSAP 16 does not refer to the need for frequent independent valuations of property but the guidance notes do suggest that valuations by properly qualified valuers take place at least every five years.

As with HC accounts, land is not depreciated in CC accounts and where land and buildings are valued as a single unit, a split has to be made to derive the amount on which depreciation of the buildings can be charged.

The valuation of plan

Plant—used in this context to denote all kinds of machinery, fixtures and equipment used within a business—will be valued at the lower of net current replacement cost and the recoverable amount. These two amounts will normally be fairly similar so that the difference should not be material. (It will only be the manufacturer or distributor of a particular item of plant who finds a major difference between the two measures.) Recoverable amount is basically the price on the secondhand market but the concept of net current replacement cost is a little more complicated. A longstanding criticism of the concept has been that as technical changes take place so existing plant ceases to be comparable to newer models. However, the current cost may still be determined via the concept of gross current replacement cost. The cost of the 'modern equivalent asset' can be taken as a starting point, adjusted to reflect the changes in technology to derive the gross current replacement cost of the asset in service, and this is then reduced to net by taking account of the proportion of the life of the asset remaining compared to its total life.

Example 2

A company uses a standard Gubbins extractor in the manufacture of gubbins. The machine was purchased four years ago at a cost of £12,000. The company estimates that its future life will be six years, producing about 14,000 gubbins a year. The machine is still available from the manufacturers at a price of £20,000 but a new Super extractor is also available at a cost of £25,000; this has a life of eight years but an annual output of 28,000 gubbins for running costs equivalent to that of the standard model. The price of the Super has not changed during the year. The company wishes to prepare CCA accounts for the first time and must value the extractor at replacement cost.

Solution

Gross current replacement cost must first be estimated. The cost of an identical model to that in use is £20,000. The cost of a modern equivalent asset, the Super, is £25,000 for double the output over eight years in comparison to the Standard's ten years of useful life. The adjusted cost is therefore:

$$£25,000 \times \frac{14,000}{28,000} \times \frac{10}{8} = £15,625$$

Gross current replacement cost is the lower of the cost of an identical model or a modern equivalent, and it is therefore £15,625.

In order to value at net current replacement cost, the gross figure is adjusted by the life remaining on the existing asset. The net current replacement cost is therefore £15,625 $\times \frac{6}{10}$ = £9,375. In the accounts, the gross current replacement cost of £15,625 and the depreciation of £6,250 (£15,625 − £9,375) will be shown under fixed assets. The revaluation surplus is £3,625 (£15,625 − £12,000). The calculation of backlog depreciation is as follows:

	£	£
Total depreciation to be disclosed		6,250
Depreciation charged in first three years, on historic cost at $\frac{£12,000}{10}$ per annum	3,600	
Depreciation charged in fourth year on current cost at $\frac{£15,625}{10}$	1,562	

	£	£
Total depreciation charged to profit and loss		5,162
Backlog set off against revaluation surplus		1,088

Note: The depreciation charge in the fourth year is based on the average value of the machine, in this case equal to the year end value.

When there is a large quantity of plant to be revalued it may be quite impractical to attempt to value each, just as it can be impossible to value each item of stock. Suitable indices should be used either for individual assets or groups of similar assets.

Management may object to revaluing a particular asset on the grounds that it is not intended to replace it at all. However, this criticism is invalid. CCA measures the current costs incurred during the past period; it does not look to the future when a different set of assets might be used. It is concerned with things as they are.

Stock valuation

During the year the cost of stocks sold is adjusted to current cost via the COSA. At the end of the year the stocks on hand are also revalued to current cost in a separate exercise. When it is found necessary to write stocks down to net realisable value in the HC accounts the same valuation will apply to the CC accounts.

Contracts may present problems if the work is specialised to the business and estimates would have to be made of how much the work done would have cost had it all been done at the year end date. However, the revaluation surpluses or deficits on stocks should not in general be so large as to make the choice of valuation base critical.

14.6 Net borrowing and the gearing adjustment

The final adjustment to the HC profit and loss account required by SSAP 16 is the gearing adjustment. This is the proportion of the current cost operating adjustments attributable to finance provided as external debt rather than as owners' equity. The formula for calculating the gearing adjustment is

$$G = \frac{L}{L + S} \times A$$

where G is the amount of the gearing adjustment
          L is the average net borrowing in the period
          S is the average owners' equity in the period (measured at current cost)
          A is the current cost operating adjustments.

The gearing adjustment will always reduce the total of the current cost operating adjustments (if these are a deduction from HC profit, the gearing adjustment will be an addition to it and vice versa).

Net borrowing is the excess of monetary liabilities over monetary assets. All such items are included, other than those used in the monetary working capital adjustment. In particular cash balances and short-term deposits will be reckoned in with monetary assets, while such deferred liabilities as deferred taxation and provisions will be included with loan stock, debentures, mortgages and bank loans as monetary liabilities. Usually businesses have an excess of monetary liabilities over monetary assets. Should the reverse hold no gearing adjustment is made because the business then has no *real* outside debt—there may be some debt but if it is counterbalanced by monetary assets which could be applied in paying the debt off, then the business is not in reality a net borrower.

In the special case of nationalised industries whose ownership is vested in the Government and whose debt is also principally supplied by the Government, SSAP 16 provides that no gearing adjustment should be made. However, to be consistent, nationalised industries must show interest *after* tax and extraordinary items.

For all other businesses making a gearing adjustment, SSAP 16 suggests that interest be shown netted off against the gearing adjustment in the profit and loss account (see example, p. 155). The reason is that the interest charge fulfils two functions—it should maintain the value of the borrowed funds compared to general inflation and in addition should provide a real return. The business financing part of its operations from long-term fixed debt will gain as inflation reduces the real value of the debt, but will incur interest charges fixed at rates which the lenders will hope will compensate for the loss caused through inflation. It is therefore reasonable to regard the interest charge as an offset to the gearing adjustment and to treat the net of these two items as the 'real' interest charge borne by the business.

In fact this will be true only in certain special circumstances but it provides a useful approximation when examining accounts.

In calculating the gearing adjustment a number of points must be borne in mind:

(*a*) The shareholders equity must be after revaluing assets to current cost. (It makes no difference if current cost adjustments are charged since they are only then credited to the current cost reserve—itself part of shareholders' funds.)

(*b*) The gearing adjustment is applied to the current cost operating adjustments. Some businesses have under the HC convention revalued assets and accordingly charged higher depreciation in the normal HC accounts. This extra charge is not subject to the gearing abatement. Consequently businesses with identical assets but different policies on revaluation will have different gearing adjustments. To avoid this difficulty SSAP 16 allows the gearing adjustment to be at the level it would be if no revaluations were incorporated into the HC accounts. In practice any distortions are unlikely to be material.

(*c*) Where a company chooses to make CC accounts its main accounts the figure of operating profit will already have all the current cost adjustments included. There will therefore be no basis on which a gearing adjustment could be calculated. It is not clear what the ASC recommends in this situation but presumably the company could estimate what the operating adjustments would have been and produce a gearing adjustment accordingly. This point is of course an extension of (*b*) taken to the ultimate.

Example 3
Consider a business set up on 1 January with £60 of equity
and £40 of debt bearing interest at 5% per annum. During
the year £100 of stock is bought and then sold for £140 at a
time when the replacement cost to the business was £115.

Calculation of gearing adjustment
Assuming the sale took place in the middle of the year, the
average equity interest is then the mean of the opening
and closing figures. In this example the HC equity will equal
the CC equity (since any current cost adjustment will merely
be transferred from revenue to current cost reserves). The
HC profit is £38 (sales 140 — cost of sales 100 and interest
2). The closing equity interest is therefore £98 and the
average in the year

$$\frac{60 + 98}{2} = £79.$$

The debt is constant at £40 and the gearing proportion is

$$\frac{40}{79 + 40} = 34\%$$

The current cost profit and loss account is

	£
Profit as in HC accounts	40
Less: COSA	(15)
	25
Gearing adjustment (34% of 15)	5
Interest payable	(2)
Current cost attributable profit	28

The closing balance sheet is

	£	
Cash	138	
Equity—capital	60	
—Revenue reserve	28	
—current cost reserve	10	(COSA less gearing)
Total equity	98	
Fixed debt	40	
	138	

This example illustrates the fundamental problem with the gearing adjustment. How much profit can be distributed? If the CC attributable profit is distributed, the equity interest becomes £70. In real terms it is greater than at the start of the year (input prices have risen 15%: the opening equity would need to be 69 to maintain its value). The gearing calculation therefore appears to be on the prudent side.

But if a dividend of £28 is paid out, the business as a whole shrinks in real terms. The opening capital employed of £100 would need to be £115 to be maintained in real terms After distribution of £28 it would actually be £110. (The real value of the debt has fallen by 15% of £40 = £6, while £1 is retained through the overprudent gearing calculation.)

The decision must be made; is the business to be maintained in real terms or is it just the equity interest which should be maintained? If the former then either the distribution of profit should be restricted to the CC operating profit (and the gearing adjustment regarded as irrelevant) or the debt must be maintained in real terms which means it must be increased by new borrowing. Many businesses do attempt to maintain the real value of debt so as to preserve the operating capacity of the whole enterprise (not just that part financed by equity capital), but in times of rapid and increasing inflation this can mean continually borrowing more and capital markets are not well structured to cope. Should Government policy be to curb monetary growth as an anti-inflation weapon, this may make it impossible for many businesses to borrow adequately. Profit distribution is then restricted to the CC operating profit (after interest and tax) so that the substance of the business is maintained by steadily boosting the equity to balance the falling real debt, or, if profit distribution is maintained at higher levels then the business shrinks. HC accounting will contribute to the latter likelihood by reporting higher profits than under CCA.

The gearing adjustment does not, of course, alter the reality of business; what it does is to measure the falling value of fixed borrowings in a time of inflation and force management to decide how to finance future operations.

14.7 The current cost reserve

All current cost adjustments to the HC accounts are transferred to the current cost reserve, which is itself regarded as
part of shareholders' funds. The movement on reserve in
any year will normally comprise:

(a) The cost of sales adjustment.
(b) The Monetary working capital adjustment.
(c) The depreciation adjustment.
(d) Profit or losses on the disposal of fixed assets which are
    eliminated when the assets are revalued at current cost.
(e) The net increase in the value of fixed assets held at the
    balance sheet date over the cumulative increase in the
    previous year.
(f) The net increase in the valuation of stocks over the
    cumulative increase in the previous year.
(g) The gearing adjustment (with opposite arithmetic sign
    to the net operating adjustments (a–d)).

SSAP 16 requires that the movements be shown as a note
to the current cost accounts. It is also suggested that the
balance on the reserve be shown divided between realised
and unrealised elements. Realised current cost reserves are
those adjustments passed through the profit and loss
account—*i.e.* the COSA, MWCA, gearing and asset disposal
adjustments. The total amount realised represents the total
charged against the HC profits by way of CC operating
adjustments since CC accounts were started. Since the HC
reserves include profits before that time which were not
subject to the CC adjustments, it would be unwise to draw
any conclusions from the relative size of the CC reserve and
the remaining (HC) reserves in the balance sheet, or indeed
the relative size of the realised and unrealised parts.

14.8 Special matters

Group accounts
Group accounts should be produced on the same basis as
the accounts of subsidiaries. There may be problems where
some subsidiaries fall under the criteria of SSAP 16 and
others in the group do not, or where CCA information is

lacking, as in the case of most foreign subsidiaries. It will be up to the directors of the parent company to produce the most relevant group accounts given the information available and to note deficiencies.

Where the subsidiaries of a group have material inter-company accounts, and where external debt is handled on a group basis it is necessary to be consistent when calculating the MWC and gearing adjustments. It is recommended that each subsidiary calculates its own MWCA, including inter-group debt, providing all companies in the group treat such debt the same way. The gearing adjustment however should be calculated on a group basis rather than be the sum of the subsidiaries gearing adjustments.

Goodwill

As stated on page 110, goodwill which consists largely of undervalued assets should be eliminated on the adoption of CCA. Where goodwill already exists in HC accounts, the transactions which created goodwill should be reviewed and that part of the goodwill which related to undervalued assets should be set off against the revaluation surpluses arising. Thus goodwill in CCA accounts will be genuine goodwill relating to the cost of acquiring the business over and above the cost of the net assets.

Foreign currency translation

The CCA requirement that net assets be stated at value to the business means that overseas assets and liabilities should be translated at the exchange rates ruling on the balance sheet date (the 'closing' method). Differences on consolidation of foreign subsidiaries will then be price differences caused by the movement of exchange rates and should be transferred to reserves.

14.9 CCA and profit distribution

To most accountants and businessmen the chief merit of any form of inflation accounting is in providing better measurements of profit than are obtainable under HC accounts.

There is therefore great interest in whether CCA provides

a good guide as to how much profit is available each year for distribution. This topic has already been discussed with reference to the HC convention (see p. 65) and the general principles apply with equal force to CCA profits. But there are a number of points to consider. SSAP 16 specifically states 'the current cost profit attributable to shareholders should not be assumed to measure the amount that can prudently be distributed'. This is a somewhat disappointing statement bearing in mind the long debate over CCA and the claims for its usefulness. However, undoubtedly the CCA operating adjustments do attempt to measure profit after replacing the assets sold or consumed in the process of earning income, and to that extent the current cost operating profit (after deducting interest and tax) is a reasonable measure of the amount of money that the business could distribute without reducing its capacity. SSAP 16 points out that the decision to distribute any amount must look to the availability of cash, the future needs of the business and the ability to borrow. Indeed unless a business is steadily raising its borrowing to match the erosion of the external debt measured by the gearing adjustment, it should regard the funds covered by the adjustment as non-distri- butable, leaving the current cost operating profit as the measure of what can be released. But if borrowing can be maintained without jeopardising the credit standing of the business and without increasing the interest burden unduly, the current cost profit attributable to shareholders could be taken as the distributable amount.

In law, companies can still distribute the full amount of the HC profit, even if they prepare CC accounts showing a lower current cost profit. The 1980 Companies Act forbids the distribution of unrealised profits but does not refer to current cost accounts. SSAP 16 has no binding authority on this matter although it will strongly influence what is regarded as 'best practice'. It could be argued that a business distributing profits in excess of its attributable current cost profit is deliberately reducing its capital and it may be legitimate to ask how it can do this and remain a going concern. As CCA becomes better understood it is likely that the current cost accounts will be seen as a better guide to performance and the amounts that can fairly be distributed than the HC accounts and that the latter will cease to be widely used for this purpose.

14.10 Criticisms of SSAP 16

In Chapter 12 HC and CPP accounting were criticised from the standpoint of CCA. It is now necessary to review CCA, as introduced by SSAP 16, and to consider its shortcomings and the developments to be expected in the next few years. It should be remembered that there is still a substantial body of opinion which holds that inflation accounts are misleading and irrelevant to management, as well as being complicated and hard to understand. Such criticism was the downfall of ED 18.

Does SSAP 16 account for inflation? SSAP 16 states '. . . it is not a system of accounting for general inflation'. If the input prices affecting a business stay the same during the year while in the economy generally prices rise, say, at 50%, the CCA accounts will produce the same result as HC accounts, even though the substance of the business will be worth some 66% of the previous value. However, it is possible to measure shareholders' equity in each year under CCA and deflate the figures by the changes in general purchasing power, thus indicating how the equity has performed against average prices in the economy. Indeed the guidance notes suggest such a note be supplied with the accounts.

The usefulness of CCA is that in any given year the accounts of different businesses will be much more comparable than has been the case under HC accounting and in particular ratios of operating profit to operating assets will give a fair indication both of the absolute performance of management and of the relative profitability of different businesses and industries.

The gearing adjustment has aroused considerable controversy and its theoretical foundations are still to be fully resolved. The technicalities of the arguments, which relate in part to still fiercely debated economic theories of capital and value, are beyond the scope of this book. Briefly, the problem is that while the gearing adjustment is based on the ratio of debt to equity in the period just ended, the concept only makes sense if it is assumed future finance will be available to replace assets used and that in turn requires assumptions about the similarity of the future to the past. The concept also forces the question, what are the accounts saying? Are they measuring the entire business however financed, or that part which is financed by equity capital?

The doubts about the gearing adjustment probably mean that the figure of current cost operating profit will be more widely used than that of profit attributable to shareholders.

The link with original costs, central to HC accounting, is broken by CCA (though not CPP accounting which applied the same index figure to all HC amounts). While the current cost operating adjustments are widely accepted, the current cost balance sheet puts values on the physical assets which are not directly substantiated in arms-length transactions. SSAP 16 emphasises that the CC balance sheet is not a valuation of the business; however, there are fears that it may be so interpreted. Furthermore while HC accounting is objective, an element of subjectivity must creep into CC figures and SSAP 16 is the first accounting standard to require a system less objective than the one it replaces.

Despite criticism the case for CCA remains that it provides a more useful and relevant system of measuring business performance than HC accounts and in particular for providing a profit figure based explicitly on the concept of profit and capital advanced (in Chapter 2) as the foundation of modern accounting. HC accounting, which developed rather as a refinement of book-keeping techniques than as a scientific approach to measuring business transactions, has failed to provide satisfactory results in periods of inflation. As inflation seems to be built in to the world economic system, it is unreasonable to argue, as some accountants have done, that it is better to divert effort into stopping inflation than to accounting for it. We cannot wait for what seems a very far off change in the basic structure of the economic climate and some form of CCA is essential if accounting is to have anything to contribute.

14.11 Example of current cost accounts

This example demonstrates the application of SSAP 16 to

conventional financial accounts. It is necessarily simplified, and has been based on the more detailed workings shown as an appendix to the Guidance Notes on SSAP 16 issued by the ASC. The reader is strongly recommended to read the Guidance Notes and to obtain copies of the published accounts of companies producing current cost accounts.

In this example the current cost accounts of Z Ltd are shown first, followed by the workings based on the historical cost accounts.

Z Limited

1. Current cost profit and loss account for the year to 31 December 1981

		£000
Turnover		64,000
Historical cost profit before interest		5,200
Less: Current cost operating adjustments		3,120
Current cost operating profit		2,080
Gearing adjustment	(910)	
Interest payable (net)	1,000	
		90
Current cost profit before taxation		1,990
Taxation		700
Current cost profit attributable to shareholders		1,290
Dividends		300
Retained current cost profit of the year		990

Statement of retained profits	
Retained current cost profit of the year	990
Movements on current cost reserve	1,998
	2,988
Reserves at 1 January 1981	12,540
Reserves at 31 December 1981	15,528
Earnings per share	18·4p

Current cost balance sheet at 31 December 1981

		£000
Assets employed		
Fixed assets		18,808
Net current assets		
Stock	8,220	
Monetary working capital	4,500	
Total working capital	12,720	
Dividends	(300)	
Other current liabilities (net)	(700)	
		11,720
		30,528
Financed by		
Shareholders' funds		
Share capital		8,000
Current cost reserve	9,036	
Other reserves	6,492	
		15,528
		23,528
Loan stock		6,000
Deferred tax		1,000
		30,528

Notes to current cost accounts
A. A general explanation of the purpose of current cost accounts can be used to introduce the remaining notes

B. Fixed assets and depreciation
The gross current cost of fixed assets has been derived as follows.

Plant and specialised buildings have been restated using appropriate Government indices applied to the historical costs.

The current cost of land has been estimated by the directors.

Asset lives have been reviewed on the introduction of current cost accounting and the existing asset lives were found to be adequate.

Total depreciation charged in the CC profit and loss account represents the average current cost of the proportion of fixed assets consumed in the period. The depreciation adjustment of £850,000 is the difference between the depreciation charge in the HC and CC accounts.

The adjustment of £900,000 on the disposal of fixed assets represents the difference between the historical and current cost net values of the assets in question at the date of disposal.

C. Working capital
This includes stocks and trade debtors less trade creditors.

In order to allow for the impact of price changes on working capital two adjustments are made to the operating costs calculated on the historical cost basis, one on stock and the other on monetary working capital. The adjustments are based on movements in appropriate Government indices.

D. The gearing adjustment
A proportion, called the gearing proportion, of the net operating assets of the business is financed by borrowing. As the obligation to repay borrowing is fixed in monetary amount, irrespective of price changes on the proportion of assets so financed, it is unnecessary to provide for the impact of price changes on these assets when determining the current cost profit attributable to shareholders. Thus, the gearing adjustment has been applied which abates the current cost operating adjustments by the average gearing proportion in the year.

2. Current cost operating adjustments

	£000	£000
Cost of sales	810	
Monetary working capital	560	
	———	1,370
Depreciation	850	
Fixed asset disposals	900	
	———	1,750
Total		3,120

3. Financing of the net operating assets

	£000
Fixed assets	18,808
Working capital	12,720
	31,528
Share capital and reserves	23,528
Dividends	300
Total shareholders' interests	23,828
Loan stock	6,000
Deferred tax	1,000
Other current liabilities	700
Net borrowing	7,700
	31,528

4. Fixed assets

	Gross CRC £000	Depreciation £000	Net CRC £000
Land	4,610	–	4,610
Plant and Machinery	26,910	12,712	14,198
	31,520	12,712	18,808

5. Current cost reserve

Balance at 1 January 1981		7,038
Revaluation surpluses		
Land	300	
Plant and machinery	1,118	
Stocks	930	
		2,348
Monetary working capital	560	
Gearing	(910)	
		(350)
Balance at 31 December 1981		9,036
Of which realised		2,210
unrealised		6,826

The realised element represents the net cumulative total of the current cost adjustments which have been passed through the profit and loss account.

Workings to the current cost accounts

The historical cost accounts on which the current cost accounts are based are given below.

Historical cost profit and loss account for the year ending 31 December 1981

	£000
Turnover	64,000

	£000
Trading profit (including 1,000 on disposal of fixed asset)	5,200
Interest payable	1,000
Profit before taxation	4,200
Taxation	700
Profit attributable to shareholders	3,500
Dividends	300
Retained profit for the year	3,200

Statement of retained profits	
Retained profit of the year	3,200
Revenue reserves at 1 January 1981	5,502
Revenue reserves at 31 December 1981	8,702

Historical cost balance sheet at 31 December

	1981	*1980*
	£000	£000
Fixed assets	12,202	11,502
Current assets		
Stock	8,000	6,000
Debtors	10,500	9,000
Cash	3,000	2,000
	21,500	17,000

	1981	1980
Current liabilities		
Trade creditors	6,000	5,000
HP creditors	700	1,000
Overdraft	2,300	3,000
Taxation	700	750
Dividends	300	250
	10,000	10,000
Net current assets	11,500	7,000
	23,702	18,502
Share capital	8,000	6,000
Reserves	8,702	5,502
Shareholders' funds	16,702	11,502
Loan stock	6,000	6,000
Deferred tax	1,000	1,000
	23,702	18,502

Workings to produce current cost accounts

A. Calculation of fixed assets at current cost.

The movements of fixed assets in the historical cost accounts are:

	Land cost	Plant and Machinery cost	dep'n	net	Total
1 January 1981	1,800	14,200	(4,498)	9,702	11,502
Disposals	—	(1,600)	600	(1,000)	(1,000)
Additions	1,000	1,700	—	1,700	2,700
Depreciation			(1,000)		(1,000)
31 December 1981	2,800	14,300	(4,898)	9,402	12,202

Depreciation in the historical cost accounts on plant and machinery is on the straight line basis with an average plant life of fourteen years. The HC charge in 1981 is thus approximately 14,300/14 = 1,000.

There are three stages in the CC calculations—to revalue plant to 1 January 1981 values, to determine average and year end values and thence to calculate the depreciation charge. (The opening values at CC will normally be taken from the previous years CC balance sheet but in this example it is assumed CC accounts have not previously been prepared.)

The plant is sufficiently homogeneous for a single index to be valid to obtain current costs. All the plant used at 1.1.81 was obtained in 1973 and 1977 as follows:

Year of purchase	Index (mid year)	Historical Cost	Current Gross Cost	Depreciation on C.G.C.
1973	59·3	5,200	12,500	7,140
1977	93·8	9,000	13,680	3,910
Assets in use at 1.1.81		14,200	26,180	11,050

Index at	31.12.80	142·5
	30.6.81	149·2
	30.12.81	154·6

The depreciation charge for the year, based on average current cost is as follows:

Assets at gross current replacement cost 1.1.81	26,180
Less: disposals in year (at G.C.R.C)*	3,000
	23,180
Adjusted to the average value (mid year) for 1981 $(23,180 \times 149\cdot2/142\cdot5) =$	24,270
Additions in year (assumed to be at average GCRC)	1,700
	25,970
The depreciation charge is 1/14 = (say)	1,850
The HC charge is	1,000
Depreciation adjustment	850

* Assumed that the CRC of disposals is 3,000 and depreciation 1,100.

The revaluation surplus and the transfers to current cost reserve are:

Assets in use at year end which were held at the start of the year: (£000)

	Current cost	*Depreciation*
Balance 1.1.81	26,180	11,050
Less: disposals	3,000	1,100
	23,180	9,950

The revaluation surplus is measured by the change in the index over the year. This is $(154 \cdot 6 - 142 \cdot 5)/142 \cdot 5 = 8 \cdot 5\%$

The revaluation amounts are therefore 1,968 (cost) and 845 (depreciation).

For assets acquired during the year and for the depreciation charge made in the year, the appropriate surplus is the average increase in the index, which is the year end figure divided by the average for the year. This is $(154 \cdot 6 - 149 \cdot 2)/149 \cdot 2 = 3 \cdot 6\%$.

The revaluation amounts are 62 (cost) and 67 (depreciation) on the acquisitions at current cost of 1,700 and depreciation charge of 1,850 respectively. The total transfer to current cost reserve for revaluations on plant is $(1,968 + 62) - (845 + 67) = 1,118$.

Land is valued by the directors at say 4,610 following a valuation of 3,310 in 1980. As 1,000 was added in 1981 the revaluation surplus is 300.

Fixed asset disposals. The proceeds were £2000. The net current replacement cost was $(3,000 - 1,100) = £1900$ at the time of sale. Thus the current cost profit on disposal was 100 and the difference between that and the HC profit of £1000 is charged as a current cost adjustment.

B. The cost of sales and monetary working capital adjustments

The relevant price index is as follows:

October 1980	173·3	October 1981	197·9
November	175·4	November	200·1
December	177·4	December	202·4
January 1981	179·6	January 1982	204·4
September	195·6		

The index is calculated to the middle of each month. The following month end index numbers are calculated as midpoints between the mid-month numbers.

30 November 1980	176·4	20 November	1981	201·3
31 December 1980	178·5	31 December	1981	203·4

Monthly average for 1981—190·7.

Cost of sales adjustment
In the example stock is assumed valued first in first out and to have risen steadily in volume over the year. The opening stock was three months purchases and the closing stock five months.

The adjusted opening stock is therefore

$$6,000,000 \times 190\cdot7/175\cdot4 = 6,523,375$$

and the adjusted closing stock

$$8,000,000 \times 190\cdot7/197\cdot9 = 7,708,943$$

The adjusted increase in stock is 1,185,568, (say) 1,190,000.

The original stock increase is 2,000,000, therefore the COSA is 2,000,000 — 1,190,000 = £810,000.

Stock revaluation
The closing stock must be valued at current cost in the balance sheet. The appropriate index number is that for the end of December.

For 1980 the revaluation was $6,000,000 \times 178\cdot5/175\cdot4 =$ (say) 6,100,000.

For 1981 the revaluation is $8,000,000 \times 203\cdot4/197\cdot9 =$ (say) 8,220,000.

Since the current cost reserve already holds 100,000 relating to 1980, it is the increase in the stock revaluation, 120,000 that is added to the reserve in 1981.

Monetary working capital adjustment
In this example trade debtors and trade creditors are deemed to comprise monetary working capital and all other debtors and creditors are reflected in the gearing adjustment.

Assuming that it is fair to use the same index as for the COSA and that the average age of debtors and creditors is one month, the calculation of the MWCA is (in £000):

Opening MWC (9,000–5,000) = 4,000.
Closing MWC (10,500–6,000) = 4,500.
Adjusting opening MWC 4,000 × 190·7/176·4 = 4,324.
Adjusting closing MWC 4,500 × 190·7/201·3 = 4,263.
Adjusted decrease in MWC = (say) 60.
The unadjusted increase in MWC is 500, thus the MWCA is 500 − (−60) = 560.

C. The gearing adjustment

Net borrowing is as follows:

	Opening £000	Closing £000
Loan stock	6,000	6,000
Deferred tax	1,000	1,000
HP creditors	1,000	700
Bank overdraft	3,000	2,300
Taxation	750	700
Cash	(2,000)	(3,000)
Total net borrowing	9,750	7,700
Shareholders' funds (at current cost)	18,540	23,528
Dividends	250	300
Total shareholders' funds	18,790	23,828
Total capital employed	28,540	31,528

The gearing proportion is the average of net borrowing to capital employed and is therefore:

$$\frac{\left(\dfrac{9,750}{28,540} + \dfrac{7,700}{31,528}\right)}{2} = 29\cdot3\%$$

The gearing adjustment is 29·3% of the current cost operating adjustments. As worked out above these are:

	£000
Depreciation	850
Fixed asset disposals	900
COSA	810
MWC	560
	3,120 × 29·3% = 914·2 (say) 910

D. Current cost reserve

£000	Unrealised surpluses				Realised	Total
	Land	Plant	Stocks	Total		
1 January 1981	1,510	5,428	100	7,038		7,038
Revaluations	300	1,118	120	1,538		1,538
Transfer to Profit and loss		(850)		(850)		(850)
		(900)		(900)		(900)
Current cost operating adjustments					3,120	3,120
Gearing adjustment					(910)	(910)
Total	1,810	4,796	200	6,826	2,210	9,036

PART 4

Group Accounts

15

The Legal and Accounting Framework

Group accounts are prepared both because there is a legal requirement to do so and because accounts that omitted the results of subsidiaries would be unacceptable to users, and would not be thought to show a true and fair view of the business concerned. In this chapter the reasons for this position are amplified and a summary of the legal requirements for group accounts is given. The remaining chapters of Part 4 discuss the accounting practices that are generally accepted in the United Kingdom as being the right procedures to use in the preparation of group accounts.

15.1 Definition of terms (*section references are to the Companies Act 1948*)

Subsidiary: a company is a subsidiary of another if either

(a) That other is a member of it and controls the composition of its board of directors; or
(b) The other holds more than half in nominal value of its equity share capital; or
(c) The first-mentioned company is a subsidiary of any company which is that other's subsidiary. (S 154)

Holding company: a company is deemed to be another's holding company if, but only if, that other is its subsidiary. (S 154)

Group accounts: The group accounts laid before a holding company shall be consolidated accounts comprising

(a) A consolidated balance sheet dealing with the state of affairs of the company and all the subsidiaries to be dealt with in group accounts;

(b) A consolidated profit and loss account dealing with the profit and loss of the company and its subsidiaries. (S 151)

15.2 The need for group accounts

When a company acquires shares in another, the purchase or acquisition is normally treated as an investment. Following the historic cost convention, the investment would be valued at cost in the accounts of the owning company. Should the investment be in a profitable company which does not distribute all its profits each year, the 'true' value of the investment—equal to the proportion of the equity share capital held multiplied by the net assets of the company —will rise each year. The shareholders of the investing company would be ignorant of this position as long as the investment was stated at cost. (They would learn about losses as they were incurred by the owned company, since provision for reductions in value are made under the historic cost convention and, under the prudence concept, as soon as they are known to have taken place.)

It can be argued that when the shareholding in the 'owned' company is small, the value of the net assets which that shareholding represents is irrelevant. The investment can only produce dividends, since the shareholding is not large enough to influence the policy of the directors of the 'owned' company. However, when the shareholding is large, such influence is acquired. Clearly, at the extreme of 100% ownership the investing company has control over whatever the owned company does. Even if the shareholding is not large enough to give control, but in some other way the directors obey the directors of the investing company, the investment is more than a share certificate with the right to receive dividends. If a dividend is paid, it will be with the consent of the investing company. It thus ceases to represent a genuine return on funds invested but becomes a deliberate transfer of funds from one company to another. What matters to the investing company is the actual profits of the controlled company, because it can use its power to have all or none paid as dividend. Moreover, control of the directors brings control of trading activities, and the controlled company can if it be wished, be run as a division or branch of its governing body. The only limits on the control are legal safeguards for minority shareholders (*i.e.* other shareholders in the controlled company for whom the shares are only an investment) and when a holding reaches 90% there is virtually no power left to the minority shareholders except for appeal to the Department of Trade or to the Court against blatant fraud.

Thus, when there is control of one company by another it is fallacious to treat the relationship as no more than that of investor and investee. Instead the position is that of holding company and subsidiary, and the key to the relationship lies in the economic reality screened behind the legal facade. The effect of control through voting power, or influence over directors, effectively turns the subsidiary into a division of the holding company. It follows that if the accounts of the holding company are to present a true and fair view of its position, they must incorporate the accounts of the subsidiary in a suitable form. The form regarded as possessing the greatest utility to shareholders and other users of the holding company's accounts is that of consolidated accounts. The purpose of consolidated accounts is to present the result of all companies within a group as if they were a single company, making necessary allowances for shares in subsidiaries owned by persons outside the group. An alternative is to present the accounts of subsidiaries separately but to publish them in the same document as the accounts of the holding company itself. Occasionally this method is used in practice, but it forces the user of the accounts to make the consolidation adjustments for himself in order to derive the relevant information, and for this reason is undesirable in the vast majority of cases.

The importance of control as the rationale for group accounts has been stressed by some accountants, who believe that it is misleading to make a 50% shareholding the normal criterion of the existence of a group. It is argued that if a company is controlled by another, the shares held by the controlling company in the subsidiary are of no consequence; conversely, if a majority holding (over 50%) of the voting shares does not provide control, then the holding does not effectively render the investee as a subsidiary—despite the apparent legal relationship. However, the definition given by S 154 above is in general use, and will be applied henceforth.

The development of group accounts in the UK was stimulated by certain practical considerations as well as by the theoretical case argued above. During the pre-war years, holding companies were used by some boards of directors as a way of keeping commercial activities secret. There was no requirement to publish group accounts and so shareholders in a public company that owned private companies (even substantial companies) would receive the profit and loss account and balance sheet relating to the holding company alone. The profit and loss account might contain only details of dividends paid by subsidiaries (but not their profits), and the balance sheet might state the cost of the shares in the subsidiaries (but not the net assets). Thus, the shareholders of the public company would be effectively denied the most relevant information and it would be difficult for most of them to inquire at Companies House and to look up the accounts of the subsidiaries for themselves.

Many leading public companies did go beyond the legal minimum and prepared group accounts, leading the field in improvements to financial reporting then in the same way as they do today. As a result, accounting theory and expertise was accumulated until it became possible for the Companies Act 1948 to make it mandatory for all holding companies to publish group accounts. It should be emphasised that the Act specifies only that group accounts should be prepared, and goes on to give details as to the manner of presentation and exceptions to the rule; it does not give the accounting rules which must be applied to carry out consolidations, leaving it to the accountancy profession who, applying the criterion of the true and fair view, must ensure that group accounts are satisfactory.

15.3 Basic legal requirements

The preparation of group accounts
The definition of group accounts given in S 151 makes it clear that group accounts are to be similar in presentation to ordinary company accounts. They are to be presented

together with the accounts of the holding company (S 150). However, if the consolidated profit and loss account deals with all of the subsidiaries, complies with the Companies Acts and shows how much of the consolidated profit or loss is dealt with in the accounts of the holding company, then a separate profit and loss account for the holding company need not be presented (S 149).

In addition, the accounting years of holding company and subsidiaries must coincide, unless the directors feel there are good reasons against it (S 153). If they do so feel, the group accounts must incorporate the results of the latest financial year of the subsidiaries concerned (S 152).

In practice this is often encountered when there are foreign subsidiaries; it is expedient for their financial years to end before that of the holding company, so that there is sufficient time for accounts to be prepared which can be incorporated in the group accounts, without holding up publication of the latter due to delays in the transmission of information, the preparation of currency conversion *etc.*

Disclosure of subsidiaries
The Companies Act 1967 requires that a holding company must state in its accounts in respect of each subsidiary:[1]

(*a*) Its name;
(*b*) Its country of incorporation, if different to that of the holding company;
(*c*) The identity and proportion of issued shares of the subsidiary held, out of each class of share (but only those shareholdings relevant for the purposes of S 154 of the Companies Act 1948). (Section 3.)

In the case of a subsidiary incorporated outside the UK, or trading outside the UK, the directors may conceal that it is owned by the holding company if they feel disclosure would be harmful and if the Department of Trade agrees.

In addition, any company owning more than 5% of the nominal value of the issued equity share capital of another, which is not a subsidiary, must state in its accounts:

(*a*) The name of the company in which shares are held;

---

[1] Large groups need only list principal subsidiaries.

(*b*) Its country of incorporation if different to that of the investing company;

(*c*) The class and proportion of shares held;

(*d*) Particulars of any other shares held (whether equity or not).

The same exemptions apply as to subsidiaries.

If shares in another company are valued at more than 10% of the total assets of the investing company, details corresponding to (*a*), (*b*) and (*c*) above are required. This provision is a good example of the law being used to prevent economic realities being concealed behind formal accounting conventions.

Exemptions to the preparation of group accounts

A holding company which is itself a wholly-owned subsidiary of a company incorporated in Great Britain is exempt from producing group accounts (S 150). This is because all the relevant information can be found in the group accounts of its holding company. A wholly-owned subsidiary has all its share capital owned either directly or via other subsidiaries, by its holding company.

A company liable to produce group accounts can leave out some or all of its subsidiaries from the consolidated accounts if the directors believe that:

(*a*) Inclusion is impracticable, or of no real value particularly in relation to the cost of carrying out the consolidation; or

(*b*) Inclusion would be misleading or harmful to the business; or

(*c*) The businesses of holding company and subsidiary are so different that it would be unreasonable to present them as part of a single undertaking.

The directors are at liberty to use option (*a*), but (*b*) and (*c*) require the approval of the Department of Trade.

When a subsidiary is not included in group accounts, the reason for this and details of the company's share in its profits must be produced instead.

An alternative to full consolidation is the production of two or more sets of consolidated accounts, one of which includes the holding company. This procedure is used, for example, by the Hawker Siddeley Group Ltd, which presents separate accounts for its subsidiary Hawker Siddeley Canada Ltd, on the grounds that Canadian law restricts the Group's freedom to deal with its subsidiary in certain ways.

Certain information required for a single company does not need to be altered in the case of a holding company. The items involved are:

1. Particulars of directors' emoluments, pensions and compensation for loss of office;
2. Particulars of loans to directors;
3. Particulars of investments in other companies (subject to the disclosure of holdings in excess of 5% mentioned above);
4. Particulars of emoluments of employees earning over £10,000 *p.a.* With regard to directors' emoluments, the amounts shown in the accounts of the holding company must contain emoluments received via subsidiaries, whether or not group accounts are prepared (S 196).

SSAP 14 Group accounts

SSAP 14 was issued as the UK counterpart to IAS3 *Consolidated financial statements*, which preceded it. SSAP 14 is based on the UK Companies Acts, and it repeats the requirements of the Acts in almost all respects. Its definitions include:

(*a*) *Financial statements* Balance sheets, profit and loss accounts, statement of source and application of funds, notes and other statements which collectively are intended to give a true and fair view of financial position and profit or loss.
(*b*) *Group accounts* Financial statements of a group.
(*c*) *Consolidated financial statements* One form of group accounts which presents the information contained in the separate financial statements of a holding company and its subsidiaries as if they were the financial statements of a single entity

SSAP 14 gives a different set of exemptions from the

requirement to prepare group accounts in consolidated form than do the Companies Acts. A subsidiary may be excluded from consolidation if:

(a) Its activities are so dissimilar from those of other Group companies that it would be misleading to present consolidated financial statements; or

(b) Although the holding company owns directly or indirectly more than half the equity share capital it does not own more than half the voting capital or it is restricted in its ability to appoint the majority of the directors; or

(c) The subsidiary operates under restrictions which significantly impair control by the holding company over the subsidiary's assets and operations for the foreseeable future; or

(d) Control is intended to be temporary.

The directors must state in the Group accounts the reason why any subsidiary is excluded. SSAP 14 requires the following accounting treatment in such a case;

1. If there are dissimilar activities, separate financial statements should be provided, combined if appropriate with the statements of other non-consolidated subsidiaries with similar activities. The separate statements should provide:

(a) A note of the holding company's interest;
(b) Particulars of intra-group balances and transactions;
(c) A reconciliation with the amount included in the consolidated financial statements for the group investment in the excluded subsidiary, which should be stated under the equity method of accounting (see Chapter 18).

2. If the holding company does not have real control the subsidiary should be treated either under the equity method or as an investment at cost (or valuation), less any provision.

3. If control is impaired by restrictions, the subsidiary should be treated as an investment, valued at cost plus the group's share of profits or losses since the date of acquisition to the date the restrictions took effect. No further

profits should be recognised (but losses must be provided for). The group accounts should disclose the subsidiary's net assets, profits or losses for the period, dividends paid to the holding company and any provisions made to write down the value of the investment.
4. If control is temporary, the subsidiary should be treated as an investment and stated as a current asset at the lower of cost and net realisable value.

Changes in the group

The group will include its share of a subsidiary's profit or loss, and net assets, from the date of acquisition, and up to the date of disposal. On acquisition the net assets of the subsidiary are to be accounted for at 'fair value', either in the subsidiary's own accounts or as a consolidation adjustment. The difference between the revalued net assets and the purchase consideration will be the premium or discount on acquisition (otherwise known as goodwill—see section 9.5). The effective date for accounting for acquisitions and disposals is the earlier of:

(*a*) the date on which consideration passes; or
(*b*) the date on which an offer becomes unconditional.

15.5 Approaches to consolidation

The Companies Acts require consolidated balance sheets and profit and loss accounts to be prepared, but do not detail the methods to be used. As mentioned at the start of this chapter, reliance is placed upon the accountancy profession and the overall rule of a true and fair view. The method thought to give the 'truest and fairest' view has been the 'acquisition method; the alternative is the 'merger', or 'pooling of interests', method. In the UK the acquisition method, which assumes that a holding company always takes over its subsidiary, had unquestioned dominance both in theory and practice until, in 1971, ED 3 opened a new controversy. This exposure draft allowed the use of the merger method—where a partnership rather than a purchase is assumed to have taken place—in certain carefully specified cases. The merger method had been growing in popularity in the US, and the UK profession has always been careful to heed transatlantic trends. However, the merger method has come under attack from accountants both here and in the US, and there are legal doubts about its applicability to Britain.

ED 3 never became an SSAP and is now officially out of print. For this reason, and because UK companies still use the acquisition method almost unanimously, the merger method is not discussed in the main chapters on consolidation. As a guide, the essential differences between the methods are that under the acquisition method the profits of a subsidiary up to the date of takeover are 'frozen', in the sense that they cannot be regarded as profits of the holding company which it can legally distribute to its own shareholders. The merger method, only thought applicable when the merged companies are of a reasonably similar size, and where merger is effected by the exchange of shares rather than by the payment of cash for shares, assumes that the interests of the companies are pooled and that all profits are now group profits since there is no outright purchaser. The shareholders of the new group are deemed to be the same as the shareholders of the previously independent companies.

In the following three chapters, the acquisition method is employed to explain the mechanics of carrying out consolidations, and the generally accepted solutions to particular problems are indicated. In order to appreciate the differences between consolidated and unconsolidated accounts, the balance sheets of The Delta Metal Company Limited, given on p. 200, should be examined. Delta is one of a minority of companies which state their own and the group's balance sheet on one page. This practice is ideal for bringing out the effects of consolidation upon the balance sheet of a company which owns subsidiaries.

The reader will note that the consolidation process makes four kinds of alterations to the balance sheet of The Delta Metal Company Limited itself.

1. All totals of assets, current liabilities and long-term borrowings are altered. This is because the assets and liabilities of the subsidiaries are added to those of the parent company.

2. The asset 'Subsidiary companies' vanishes from the consolidated balance sheet. It is replaced by the real assets and liabilities of 1. above.

3. Outside shareholders' interests appear in the consolidated balance sheet. These are the other shareholders of those subsidiaries which the parent does not wholly own. The total net assets of the subsidiaries are consolidated, but since less than 100% of the shares are owned in some cases, allowance must be made for the assets attributable to the outside shareholders.

4. The reserves attributable to the shareholders of The Delta Metal Company Limited are higher in the consolidated balance sheet. The profits of subsidiaries, ignored in the parent company's own balance sheet, are brought into the consolidation showing shareholders the true value of their holdings.

The Delta Metal Company Limited
Balance sheets at 30 December 1978

	Notes	Group 1978 £m	Group 1977 £m	Holding company 1978 £m	Holding company 1977 £m
Source of Capital					
Preference capital	12	**2·81**	2·81	**2·81**	2·81
Ordinary capital	12	**35·68**	35·67	**35·68**	35·67
Reserves	13	**121·52**	104·22	**57·10**	47·20
		160·01	142·70	**95·59**	85·68
Outside shareholders' interests		**4·39**	4·45	**—**	—
Long-term borrowings	14	**43·14**	35·96	**41·08**	34·73
Short-term borrowings	14	**35·19**	38·29	**28·92**	27·84
Deferred taxation	15	**1·27**	1·84	**(1·66)**	(1·32)
		£224·00	£223·24	**£163·93**	£146·93
Employment of capital					
Fixed assets	22	**118·39**	108·10	**—**	—
Subsidiary companies	21	**—**	—	**195·92**	177·88
Associated companies and trade investments	23	**28·16**	24·12	**3·25**	0·61
Current assets					
Stocks and work-in-progress	17	**121·10**	106·02	**—**	—
Debtors		**87·87**	81·70	**1·41**	0·95
Cash		**3·89**	3·89	**0·03**	0·01
		212·86	191·61	**1·44**	0·96
Deduct: Current liabilities					
Creditors	18	**100·81**	87·59	**24·67**	21·61
Current taxation	19	**6·55**	5·79	**3·96**	3·70
Dividends		**8·05**	7·21	**8·05**	7·21
		115·41	100·59	**36·68**	32·52
Net current assets		**97·45**	91·02	**(35·24)**	(31·56)
		£244·00	£233·24	**£163·93**	£146·93

16

The Consolidated Balance Sheet

16.1 Introduction

In practice, consolidations are carried out as a 'memorandum' exercise; the workings are not part of the normal double-entry bookkeeping system. The companies in the group retain their separate books throughout. The accountants will normally prepare a set of working papers which start with the final accounts of the companies in the group and build up to the consolidated accounts. In the examples used here we shall approximate such working papers by using a 'worksheet' approach, and this is in practice how the job is tackled for simple consolidations.

In the working papers a fundamental distinction is made between real assets and liabilities (*i.e.* those having an existence beyond the group) and inter-company items (*e.g.* loan to subsidiary). The latter arise because of the nature of group structure and would disappear if all the companies in the group were to be amalgamated. Such items must therefore be cancelled out as part of the consolidation process. The consolidated accounts therefore present the group as it really is, which is, of course, the purpose of the exercise.

In this chapter the simplest form of consolidation is introduced first, followed by successively more complex points until all of the important features met in consolidations have been discussed. The typical form of accounts of a small industrial company has been used but the principles apply to all consolidations.

16.2 The simple group:

The basic approach—100% subsidiary

Example 1

On 1 January 1977 Lord Ltd acquired Serf Ltd, by causing Serf Ltd to be incorporated and subscribing for all the shares. At the year end, Lord prepares its annual accounts and Serf will prepare accounts for the first time. Lord then consolidates Serf's figures with its own to form the group accounts. The balance sheets on 31 December are:

Assets employed	Lord			Serf		
	£	£		£	£	
Fixed assets	Cost	Dep'n	Net	Cost	Dep'n	Net
Land freehold	50,000	10,000	40,000	—	—	—
Leasehold	7,000	2,000	5,000	4,000	500	3,500
Plant	28,000	21,000	7,000	9,000	1,000	8,000
Motor vehicles	12,000	7,500	4,500	2,400	600	1,800
	97,000	40,500	56,500	15,400	2,100	13,300

Investment in subsidiary:			
shares at cost		1,000	
Long-term loan		10,500	
Current Assets			
Stocks		12,000	2,500
Debtors		8,000	3,000
Cash		500	150
		20,500	5,650
Current liabilities			
Creditors		6,000	4,500
Taxation		2,800	600
Dividend		1,000	—
		9,800	5,100
Net current assets		10,700	550
		£78,700	£13,850
Financed by			
Share capital			
£1 ordinary shares		50,000	1,000
Reserves			
Capital		10,000	
Retained profits		13,700	2,350
		73,700	3,350
Deferred tax		5,000	
Long-term loan		—	10,500
		£78,700	£13,850

The first step in consolidation is to add together all real assets and liabilities and then to eliminate the inter-company items. It is convenient to rewrite the balance sheets as a list of items, so that every item may be traced through to the final consolidated accounts. The list is reproduced below; experienced students will not need to write out the accounts in full for every consolidation, but will put the majority of items straight into the consolidated accounts. The worksheet for Lord and Serf is as follows:

	Lord £	Serf £	Consolidation £
Freehold land —*cost*	50,000	—	50,000
—*deprec.*	10,000	—	10,000
Leasehold land—*cost*	7,000	4,000	11,000
—*deprec.*	2,000	500	2,500
Plant —*cost*	28,000	9,000	37,000
—*deprec.*	21,000	1,000	22,000
Motor vehicles—*cost*	12,000	2,400	14,400
—*deprec.*	7,500	600	8,100
Shares in subsidiary	1,000	—	*Note 1*
Loan to subsidiary	10,500	—	*Note 2*
Stock	12,000	2,500	14,500
Debtors	8,000	3,000	11,000
Cash	500	150	650
Creditors	6,000	4,500	10,500
Taxation	2,800	600	3,400
Dividend	1,000	—	1,000
Share capital	50,000	1,000	*Note 1*
Capital reserve	10,000	—	10,000
Retained profits	13,700	2,350	*Note 3*
Deferred tax	5,000	—	5,000
Loan from parent	—	10,500	*Note 2*

The notes refer to items which need special attention on consolidation. All other items have been added together and the totals will appear in the consolidated accounts.

Note 1: Shares in subsidiary: to the parent company, Lord, the shares are an asset acquired when Serf was formed. But in the group accounts what matters is the net assets those shares represent. The shareholders of Lord want to know what net assets are held in Serf rather than the cost of the shares in it, thus 'piercing the legal veil of incorporation'.

Hence, in the consolidated accounts, the shares of Lord will be shown as the shares of the group and those of Serf are eliminated. Similarly, the investment in Serf's shares shown in Lord's own accounts is eliminated; it is replaced by the net assets that it represents. The working papers could show these eliminations in terms of double-entry as the debit in Lord's accounts balances the credit in Serf's accounts. But such double-entry is not the equivalent of normal bookkeeping, merely part of the workings; in later examples the double-entry approach to working papers will be used to deal with more complicated cases.

Note 2: Loan to/subsidiary/from parent: again, in the consolidation a debit in the accounts of one company is cancelled out by a credit in the accounts of the other. Such a loan is purely an inter-company transaction which does not alter the reality of the group's financial position at all. In the same way as a man who puts money from one pocket into another is no richer than if it had been left undisturbed, so the distribution of assets or liabilities between companies in a group is irrelevant when measuring the total net assets of the group in order to account to shareholders.

Note 3: The treatment of the *reserves of a subsidiary* poses a special problem in consolidations. In this case all the reserves of Serf were earned after it was formed. The profits are therefore genuine profits of the group and could be distributed by Lord to its shareholders (following a dividend paid by Serf to Lord). Thus, in this case a simple consolidation of the reserves is appropriate—later examples will deal with cases where the reserves of a subsidiary are not necessarily reserves of its parent.

When reserves are consolidated they are often known as 'consolidated reserves', the name implying that some of the reserves are held in subsidiaries and cannot be distributed by the parent until a dividend is received by it from those subsidiaries.

The inter-company items having been dealt with, the group balance sheet can be prepared. The layout follows that of the parent company as closely as possible. The reader should trace each item through from the worksheet, to confirm that the consolidated balance sheet represents the true state of the group as far as the shareholders of Lord are concerned.

Example 1: Solution

Lord Ltd and Subsidiary
Consolidated Balance Sheet at 31 December 1977

	£	£	£
Assets employed			
Fixed assets	*Cost*	*Dep'n*	*Net*
Freehold property	50,000	10,000	40,000
Leasehold property	11,000	2,500	8,500
Plant	37,000	22,000	15,000
Motor vehicles	14,400	8,100	6,300
	112,400	42,600	69,800

	£	
Current assets		
Stock	14,500	
Debtors	11,000	
Cash	650	
	26,150	
Current liabilities		
Creditors	10,500	
Taxation	3,400	
Dividend	1,000	
	14,900	
Net current assets		11,250
		£81,050
Financed by		
Shareholders' funds		
Share capital—£1 ordinary shares		50,000
Capital reserve		10,000
Retained profits		16,050
		76,050
Deferred taxation		5,000
		£81,050

In this example all assets and liabilities have been listed in the worksheet and shown in detail in the answer. Henceforth, for the sake of simplicity, only the 'skeleton' figures of fixed assets and net current assets will be shown in the examples under the heading 'Assets employed'. This will allow concentration on the remaining figures, which are the important ones in consolidations. All items normally included as 'Assets employed' in consolidated accounts are derived by simple addition of the figures in the accounts of the various companies making up a group. (The sole exception, goodwill, is dealt with in the next example.)

Pre-acquisition reserves and goodwill; Example 2

Now assume that Lord acquired Serf when Serf was an established independent company. The acquisition date is 1 January 1977 and Lord paid £3,000 for the whole of the share capital. At the time, the reserves of Serf consisted of £1,000 (all retained profits).

At the year end (31 December 1977), consolidated accounts are prepared for the first time. The balance sheets of the two companies before consolidation are as follows:

	Lord £	Serf £
Fixed assets	56,500	13,800
Investment in subsidiary shares	3,000	
Loan	10,500	
Net current assets	8,700	1,050
	£78,700	£14,850

	Lord £	Serf £
Share capital	50,000	1,000
Capital reserve	10,000	—
Retained profits	13,700	3,350
Shareholders' funds	73,700	4,350
Deferred tax	5,000	
Loan		10,500
	£78,700	£14,850

Lord's net current assets are £2,000 less than in Example 1—
the difference is the extra cash used to pay for Serf. The
procedure for consolidation is the same as before, but there
are two new points:

(*a*) Lord paid £3,000 for Serf and for this acquired net
assets of £2,000 (represented by £1,000 share capital and
£1,000 reserves as at the date of purchase). Why did Lord
pay the extra £1,000? The company presumably believed that
future profits of Serf would repay the investment and therefore the true value of the company was £3,000. The extra
£1,000 is therefore goodwill (this is discussed in theory in
Chapter 9). However, goodwill in this case is recorded only
when consolidation is carried out, because only then is the
cost of the investment (in Lord's accounts) eliminated and
the actual assets acquired substituted. If consolidation had
been carried out at the time of purchase, £2,000 of net assets
would have replaced £3,000 of cash paid for them, and a
difference would appear in the accounts. The extra payment
of £1,000 is an asset, even though it is not included in the
accounts of Serf. It represents part of the value acquired by
Lord. If the group accounts are to show a true and fair view,
the goodwill must be recognised in the consolidation.

Such goodwill is called 'goodwill on consolidation'. Some
accountants prefer to write it off against the reserves of the
holding company in the year of acquisition, rather than
carry it forward indefinitely as an intangible asset. Others
write it off over a period of years, or not at all. In the
examples that follow goodwill is shown as an asset, but the
reader is reminded that opinions differ in regard to the treatment of goodwill and that an SSAP is expected which should
reduce the range of accounting policies used to deal with it.
(*b*) Lord acquired Serf when the latter had already earned
profits. These profits cannot be regarded as profits of the
holding company. They comprised part of the purchase
consideration for cash paid by Lord. If Lord were to treat
Serf's pre-acquisition reserves as its own profits, it would in
effect be treating capital as profits. The matter may be
clarified with reference to profit theory, in which only an
increase in net assets over a period of time can be considered
profit. When Lord exchanged its cash for Serf's shares, its

net assets remained the same (if goodwill is considered as an asset). Thus only Serf's profits earned after the date of acquisition can be considered by Lord as profits made on its investment and thus distributable to its shareholders.

The reserves of Serf at the date of consolidation must therefore be divided into those earned before the date of acquisition and those earned after. The latter are added to the reserves of Lord; the former cancelled out against the cost of the investment in Serf. Both workings are shown below.

Worksheet for Example 2

	Lord £	Serf £	Consolidated £
Fixed assets	56,500	13,800	70,300
Investment in subsidiary—			
shares	3,000	—	*Note 1*
loan	10,500	—	*Note 2*
Net current assets	8,700	1,050	9,750
Shares	50,000	1,000	*Note 1*
Capital reserve	10,000	—	10,000
Retained profit	13,700	3,350	*Note 3*
Deferred tax	5,000	—	5,000
Loan from parent	—	10,500	*Note 2*

Note 1: The treatment of the cost of shares and share capital and reserves thereby acquired provides the calculation of the 'cost of control'. The cost of the acquisition of Serf is compared to the net assets effectively acquired, as represented by the shareholders' funds at the date of acquisition. It is often helpful to use double-entry format to ensure that the figures are easy to trace from original balance sheets to the final accounts.

Cost of Control

	£		£
Cost of shares in Serf	3,000	Share capital of Serf	1,000
		Pre-acquisition reserves	1,000
		Goodwill (balancing item)	1,000
	£3,000		£3,000

Note 2: The two loan items cancel each other out.
Note 3: The reserves of the group consist of Lord's reserves plus the post-acquisition reserves of Serf. At the year end

Serf's reserves are £3,350; the reserves at the date of acquisition were £1,000. Therefore the post-acquisition reserves are £(3,350 − 1,000) = £2,350 and the total reserves of the group—the consolidated reserves—are £13,700 plus £2350 = £16,050.

Example 2: Solution

Lord Ltd and Subsidiary
Consolidated balance sheet at 31 December 1977

Assets employed

	£
Fixed assets	70,300
Goodwill on consolidation	1,000
Net current assets	9,750
	£81,050

Financed by
Shareholders' funds

	£
Share capital	50,000
Capital reserve	10,000
Consolidated revenue reserves	16,050
	76,050
Deferred taxation	5,000
	£81,050

Inter-company accounts

As with the loan in Example 1, intercompany current accounts are offset against each other. A frequent problem, though perhaps encountered more in examinations than in practice, is the inter-company accounts which do not agree. The solution is always to make any necessary adjustment to the parent company's accounts.

Example 3

On 31 December Lord's accounts show a balance due from Serf of £250. Serf's accounts show a debt to Lord of £200. On 29 December Serf had sent £50 to Lord, but the money was not received by the year end.

In this case Lord's account with Serf must be adjusted as

if the cash had actually been received by 31 December. The adjustment is not recorded in Lord's books but only in the working papers. The £50 is designated as cash in transit and will appear as such in the Group accounts if material—if not, it will be added to the ordinary cash figure. After the adjustment, the current accounts cancel each other out.

Proposed dividends by subsidiary

If a dividend is paid by a wholly-owned subsidiary, there is no effect on the shareholders of the holding company. The group accounts already include the profits earned by the subsidiary. A dividend merely transfers cash from one bank account to another, and the retained reserves of the subsidiary fall while those of the holding company rise. If, however, a dividend is proposed but has not been paid by the year end, the holding company may not have made any entry in its own accounts for the dividend; in the subsidiary's accounts, however, it will be shown either as a current liability or be credited to the inter-company current account and will have been deducted from reserves. The usual procedure is to add back the proposed dividend to the subsidiary's reserves and to remove it from current liabilities or from the inter-company current account. Furthermore, even where the holding company has brought the proposed dividend into its accounts and debited the current account with the subsidiary, these entries are also reversed. The aim is to reproduce, in the working papers, the position before the dividend was declared. Remember that no change is made to the accounts of the individual companies, only to the accounts used as the raw material for the consolidation workings.

Dividend paid out of pre-acquisition profits

Pre-acquisition profits are regarded as part of the investment made in the subsidiary and thus as part of the capital of the holding company. A dividend paid out of such profits to the holding company is therefore a return of capital. The effect is to reduce the cost of the purchase of the shares, just as, if a car is bought for £2,000 and then a 10% cash refund is given, the cost is £1,800. The refund of £200 is not regarded as income.

Thus, if a dividend is paid out of pre-acquisition profits,

the appropriate treatment by the holding company is to credit the 'cost of shares in subsidiary' account, reducing the balance of the account. This transaction should be recorded in the accounts of the holding company before the consolidation workings are begun. It is a permanent adjustment to the holding company's own accounts.

Acquisition during the year

If a company is acquired during its accounting period, then the purchase consideration is assumed to be for the company as at the date of purchase, including all profits earned up to that date. If accounts are not produced up to the date of the purchase but only at the end of the normal accounting period, the profits earned during that period must be split between those earned before and those earned after the purchase. Sometimes internal accounts are available; if not, profits may have to be arbitrarily divided on a time basis.

Example 4

A company is acquired on 31 May. The company prepares accounts once a year at 31 December. The reserves on 1 January were £1,000 and on 31 December £2,200. The pre-acquisition profit is therefore £1,000 plus $\frac{5}{12}$ of £(2200 − 1000) = £1500. The remaining £700 ($\frac{7}{12}$ of £1200) is profit applicable to the holding company. Time apportionment is not the best way of dividing profits. It is far better to make up accounts to the nearest day possible to the take-over, since most businesses experience fluctuations in activity during a year and profits do not accrue evenly each month. However, the preparation of accounts is time-consuming and may be thought too expensive in relation to the amounts involved. Time apportionment is the easiest solution and in the absence of further information it should be used, both in examinations and in practice.

Capital reserves on consolidation

In the cost of control computation, it has hitherto been assumed that the cost of shares was equal to or exceeded the net assets acquired. It is possible for shares to be acquired at less than their apparent worth as measured by net assets, and thus for 'negative goodwill' to be created. Thus if Oyster

Ltd acquires Pearl Ltd for £1,500 when Pearl has a share capital of £1,000 and retained profits of £800, Oyster will have made an apparent profit of £300 on the deal. The problem is how to treat this negative goodwill (also known as 'capital reserve on consolidation'). The first edition of this book presented the conventional case for treating a capital reserve on consolidation as a permanent and undistributable part of shareholders' funds. The reserve was not to be netted off against any positive goodwill nor credited as a profit to the profit and loss account.

The ASC discussion paper 'Accounting for goodwill' (see Chapter 9) argues that there is no difference in kind between positive and negative goodwill and that the treatment should be the same, namely that goodwill should be treated as a fixed asset (or liability) subject to depreciation over a suitable period related to the future earnings of the business acquired. This view is likely to replace the previous view on dealing with negative goodwill.

When preparing a consolidation, it is essential to calculate the goodwill for each subsidiary separately as different depreciation rates may apply. The student should show positive and negative goodwill separately in the balance sheet and make no assumption about depreciation unless instructed to do so.

Revaluation of assets

It should be plain that the historic cost convention has been retained when valuing subsidiaries, in that the purchase consideration is taken as the nominal value of shares plus reserves to date. In the absence of inflation-adjusted accounts, the holding company must estimate the current value of a potential subsidiary, and will not look at book amounts except as a guide to such values. In an inflationary economy, current values will normally exceed historic values, and goodwill therefore will normally be created upon the acquisition of subsidiaries whose accounts are prepared under the historical cost convention.

Such goodwill, as pointed out in Chapter 9, reflects the undervaluation of the assets of the subsidiary, rather than the genuine ability of the company to earn 'super profits' through its reputation, established trade or products *etc.* A good example is the £169 million of goodwill in the balance sheet of the GEC group.[1] Created as a result of the take-over of English Electric in 1968, it shows the undervaluation of English Electric's assets rather than its potential for future profits.

A way of eliminating goodwill created through under-valuation of assets is by revaluing the assets themselves. This should be carried out on acquisition, and the pre-acquisition reserves of the subsidiary should be written up at the same time. The net effect is to reduce goodwill and raise the value of fixed assets in the consolidated balance sheet. The theory of revaluations has been described in Chapter 5, but a much more significant development will be the adoption of current cost accounting. Under CCA the fixed assets will be stated at current values in the accounts, regardless of prospective take-overs. The purchaser of a company will therefore know the current value of the business, and any surplus paid for the shares over their net asset value will be much closer to genuine goodwill than under historic cost accounting.

Revaluation after acquisition is a much more difficult matter. The increase in values should be apportioned into the pre- and post-acquisition periods so that the reserves can be adjusted appropriately. Deciding exactly when changes in value arose is tricky, since it depends upon a reconstruction of the state of the subsidiary at the time of take-over and must be a subjective assessment. This is why revaluation at the time of take-over is highly desirable.

16.3 Minority interests

We now assume that the holding company owns less than 100% of the subsidiary's share capital.

Example 6

On 1 January 1977 Atom Ltd bought 80% of the shares of Electron Ltd for £4,000, when Electron had a share capital of £1,000 and £2,000 of reserves. The balance sheets at 31 December 1977 are:

---

[1] See the Annual Accounts of General Electric Company Limited, from 1969 onward.

	Atom £	**Electron** £
Fixed assets	20,000	3,000
Shares in subsidiary	4,000	—
Net current assets	32,000	4,000
	£56,000	£7,000
Share capital	40,000	1,000
Reserves	16,000	6,000
	£56,000	£7,000

The problem in this case is that the shareholders of the Atom group own only 80% of the shares of Electron, which means that they are entitled to 80% of the profits and, upon a winding up, to 80% of the net assets. This could be dealt with in two ways. The group accounts could include 80% of the assets, liabilities and reserves of Electron, and thus ignore the existence of minority shareholders in that company. This method is never used in practice, partly because of the legal interpretation of the wording of the Companies Acts, but mainly because the effective control of Atom (or any holding company) is over the whole of the subsidiary. The minority can only be passive receivers of the dividends. The majority shareholding means that the holding company appoints the directors and can alter the constitution of the subsidiary (except in rare circumstances). Actions taken by those directors will affect all the assets and liabilities of the subsidiary. Thus, to show a true and fair view of the relationship between holding company and subsidiary, all the assets, liabilities and reserves of the subsidiary are consolidated with those of the holding company and if there are minority interests, those interests are calculated and shown as a separate liability in the group accounts. This method should always be used both by the student and in practice.

The calculation of minority interests is made in the working papers by ascribing to them the nominal value of their shares, plus their proportion of the reserves of the subsidiary. The distinction between pre- and post-acquisition has no relevance for this calculation. The minority shareholders are entitled to their share of the reserves at the date of the accounts. The group accounts are prepared in order to show the position from the point of view of the members of the holding company. Thus, the interest of the minority, as far as group shareholders are concerned, is a liability. Many companies include minority interests as a sub-heading within the category 'shareholders' funds'. Such treatment is reasonable, in the sense that the sums due to the minorities are not true liabilities, *i.e.* future repayment does not have to be made. On the contrary, the sums represent the extent of the investment made in the subsidiary by the minority shareholders. However, it must be remembered that the minority interest is a liability, in the sense that it is a sum due to persons other than the group shareholders. The presentation of the group accounts should make this clear.

Example 6; Workings
The assets are added together as before. The following are the calculations that must be made to the remaining items on the balance sheets:

Division of Electron's Share Capital

	£		£
Atom—80% (to cost of control A/c)	800	Share capital	1,000
Minority interest—20%	200		
	£1,000		£1,000

Division of Electron's Reserves

	£		£
Minority interest—20% (to minority interests account)	1,200	Reserves	6,000
Pre-acquisition reserves—80% of £2,000 (to cost of control A/c)	1,600		
Post-acquisition reserves—80% of £(6,000–2,000)	3,200		
	£6,000		£6,000

Cost of Control Account

	£		£
Cost of shares in Electron	4,000	Shares in Electron	800
		Pre-acquisition reserves	1,600
		Goodwill	1,600
	£4,000		£4,000

Group Reserves

Reserves of Atom	16,000
Reserves of Electron	3,200
	£19,200

Minority Interests

	£
Shares in Electron	200
Share of reserves in Electron	1,200
	£1,400

Example 5: Solution

Atom Ltd and Subsidiary
Consolidated Balance Sheet at 31 December 1977

Assets employed	£
Fixed assets	23,000
Goodwill on consolidation	1,600
Net current assets	46,000
	£70,600

Financed by Shareholders' Funds	
Share capital	50,000
Reserves	19,200
	69,200
Minority interests	1,400
	£70,600

Note that the minority interest is simply 20% of the share-holders' funds of Electron Ltd at the end of the year. Had there been negative reserves, then a negative reserve figure would have been offset against the share capital allocated to the minority. If the shareholders' funds was itself a negative item, as is sometimes experienced when businesses are started, the minority interest would be shown as a deferred asset in the group accounts.

In such a situation, the directors would probably prefer not to consolidate the subsidiary's results. If there was to be a proposed dividend outstanding at the end of the year, it would be added back to the reserves of the subsidiary as before. Minority interests will not be altered because the minority have a share in the dividend, and if this is added back to reserves, their share of the reserves is increased by the identical amount.

Minority interests—some special points
1. Goodwill: In the example of Atom and Electron above, goodwill has been valued from the point of view of the holding company only. Yet had the holding company acquired a 100% interest in Electron, it is reasonable to assume that the payment would have been raised by 25% $\left(\dfrac{100 - 80}{80}\right)$ and therefore that goodwill would also be one quarter higher. Strictly speaking, therefore, goodwill should be valued at £2,000 and the minority interest raised by £400, thus making full allowance for the 'true' figure of goodwill that attaches to the subsidiary as a whole. Yet such an adjustment is never carried out in practice, probably because of the difficulties in relating the theoretical concept of goodwill in this case—the £400 is unrealised—to the historic cost convention. In addition, it relates purely to the minority interests and is only of technical interest to the members of the holding company.

2. Inter-company sales: A similar problem is met if sales take place between companies in a group and if a profit element is included in the sales price (*i.e.* if Electron sold to Atom goods costing £500 for £600). From the group viewpoint, the profit is not realised until the goods are sold outside the group. If Atom has resold the goods by the year end there is no difficulty. If, however, they are still in stock, there is a problem of valuation. Valuations should be at

cost, meaning cost to the group, (or, under CCA, value to the group), if unrealised profit is not to be recognised. Thus, it is necessary to write down stocks acquired from another group company, to the cost to the group of the acquisition of the stocks. The group would therefore value the goods at £500 and the profit taken by Electron will be deducted from the group profit. (But the goods continue to be valued at £600 in Atom's own accounts.)

However, when there is a minority interest, as with Electron, it can be argued that the sale of the stocks is a legitimate sale from Electron to Atom, and that, as far as Electron is concerned, the profit has been realised. The minority are not affected if there is to be a write-down for group purposes, but they may not want a write-down of profits in which they have a share.

Possible solutions to the problem are to:

(a) Eliminate all unrealised profits in the group accounts and reduce the interest of both group shareholders and the minority shareholders in due proportion. The minority interest in the group accounts will then be understated, but is shown correctly in the accounts of the subsidiary; the minority receive only those accounts.

(b) Eliminate the entire profit from the group reserves, thus reducing them by more than the rightful share but showing minority interest correctly in the group accounts.

(c) Eliminate only that part of profit applicable to group shareholders. Both group and minority interests are then shown correctly but stocks are still overstated in the group accounts.

Solution (a) is probably the soundest of the three but practice varies. It is therefore important that the policy chosen to deal with unrealised profits on inter-company transactions be stated, if the amount is material. In practice this is rarely the case and no mention is made in most group accounts of the accounting policy chosen. Where it is mentioned solution (a) is favoured. This solution must be used when there are no minority interests.

Solution (a) will be used in later examples in this book.

16.4 Piecemeal acquisitions

Suppose that on 30 January 1977 Lock Ltd buys 25% of the ordinary shares of Jaw Ltd, another 10% on 1 July, another 35% on 1 December and the remaining 30% on 31 December 1977. How do we consolidate Jaw with Lock on 31 December?

The problem is to pinpoint the date Jaw joined the Lock group as a subsidiary. In law that is determined when more than half of the equity share capital has been acquired. Thus the purchase on 1 December turned Jaw, previously an associate (see Chapter 18) into a subsidiary. However, if it was always Lock's intention to acquire Jaw, then the earlier purchases are more significant than mere additions to a trade investment; they mark the start of Jaw's absorption into the Lock group. There are two ways of dealing with Jaw's consolidation:

(a) If control was premeditated, each purchase should be treated separately. The reserves attaching to each block of shares purchased should be calculated at the date the block was acquired and credited to the cost of control account in the working papers.

(b) If control is retained, as it were, by accident—the 1 December purchase being undertaken as a distinct exercise separate from the previous purchases—it is inappropriate to treat profits made between 30 January and 1 December, or between 1 July and 1 December (pertaining to the 25% and 10% blocks respectively) as profits available for distribution. Instead the 70% holding achieved on 1 December is treated as though it was a single purchase made on that date.

These treatments cannot affect the real assets and liabilities of either company. What they alter is the value put on the purchase and hence both the goodwill and the reserves available for distribution.

Example 6
Facts as above. Reserves of Jaw were £50,000 on 1 January and profits are made at a rate of £2,000 a month during the year. Using treatment (a) reserves are split as follows:

Purchase date	Equity acquired	Total reserves (cumulative) £	Pre-acquisition reserves £
	%		
30 Jan.	25	52,000	13,000
1 Jul.	10	62,000	6,200
1 Dec.	35	72,000	26,200
31 Dec.	30	74,000	22,200
Total	100		£67,600

Treatment (b)

1 Dec.	70	72,000	50,400
31 Dec.	30	74,000	22,200
Total	100		£72,600

The difference between these two methods, is that £5,000 will be distributable as profit under treatment (a) and not under treatment (b). Goodwill will be £5,000 higher under (a) than under (b). Method (a) is therefore less conservative, valuing the holding more highly. The choice in practice depends on the intent of the directors of the holding company at the time when the initial purchases are made; but application of the prudence convention will obviously come down in favour of method (b).

16.5 The sale of shares in subsidiary

In all examples so far, the holding company has bought and retained shares in the subsidiary. We now assume that some of the shares are sold. The key point is to distinguish between the profit or loss on the sale of the shares, and the treatment of the reserves attaching to the shares, which henceforth belong to the minority shareholders who buy the shares.

Example 7
Tap Ltd bought the whole of the share capital of Root Ltd on 1 January 1976 when Root's reserves were £40,000. On 31 July 1977 Tap sold 20% of its holding for £20,000. Immediately prior to the sale the balance sheets were as follows:

	Tap	Root
	£	£
Net current assets	36,000	64,000
Shares in subsidiary	60,000	—
	£96,000	£64,000
Share capital	30,000	12,000
Reserves	66,000	52,000
	£96,000	£64,000

The sale should be recorded separately first. The profit on the sale of shares will be computed by setting off the appropriate cost of purchase with the proceeds thus:

	£
Sale proceeds	20,000
Cost of shares sold:	
20% of 60,000	12,000
Profit	8,000

The profit figure of £8,000 should be treated as an extraordinary item, unless Tap habitually buys and sells the shares of its subsidiaries. It is also the basis for a capital gains tax assessment.

The effect of the sale on the consolidated accounts is as follows: the sale of shares effectively involves the disposal not only of the reserves attaching to those shares, but of any goodwill originally created on consolidation. Under the historic cost convention such goodwill may exist indefinitely, once created, but attaches to the shares. Because part of it now belongs to the minority it is necessary to recalculate the cost of control account.

Cost of Control (after sale)

	£		£
Cost of shares retained	48,000	Share capital retained	9,600
		Pre-acquisition reserves retained:	
		80% of £40,000	32,000
		Goodwill	6,400
	£48,000		£48,000

Minority interest now appears thus:

	£
Share capital	2,400
Reserves:	
20% of £52,000	10,400
	£12,800

Example 8: Solution

Tap and Subsidiary
Consolidated Balance Sheet at 31 July 1977

	£
Net current assets	120,000
Goodwill on consolidation	6,400
	£126,400
Share capital	30,000
Reserves	83,600
Minority interest	12,800
	£126,400

The net current assets comprise the £100,000 of original group assets plus the £20,000 proceeds of the sale of the shares in Root. The group reserves comprise:

	£
Original reserves of Tap	66,000
Post-acquisition reserves of Root:	
80% of £12,000	9,600
Profit on sales of shares	8,000
	£83,600

16.6 Complex groups

We now consider groups with two or more subsidiary companies. There is no particular problem where two or more subsidiaries are each directly owned by the holding company. The working papers are prepared as before for each subsidiary and final totals are added together. It is common, however, for subsidiaries themselves to have subsidiaries and occasionally for a holding company and a subsidiary jointly to own another subsidiary. The first type is known as a vertical group and the second as a mixed group. These are dealt with in turn.

16.7 Vertical groups

In dealing with complex groups it is essential to understand the nature of the relationship between the companies. The key points are:

1. The interest that the holding company has either directly or indirectly in each subsidiary;
2. The timing of acquisitions.

Example 8
Cell Ltd owns 80% of Molecule Ltd, who own 60% of Atom Ltd. Atom seems only indirectly linked to Cell, but Cell has control of Molecule and Molecule controls Atom, so that Atom is effectively controlled by Cell and is a sub-subsidiary of that company (refer to S 154 (*b*) of Companies Act 1948, page 171).

What is Cell's interest in Atom? Molecule is entitled to 60% of Atom's profits and of that 60%, Cell is entitled to 80%. The interest of Cell in Atom is therefore 80% of 60% = 48%. Although this is less than half, the effective control through Molecule is the binding factor which determines that Atom is a subsidiary in the Cell group.

If Cell's interest in Atom is only 48%, are there really any 'minority' shareholders? It transpires that there are two sets of minority shareholders in Atom. There is a set directly owning 40% of Atom. There is also a set owning the minority holding (20%) in Molecule, through which it has an interest in Atom. Its holding amounts to 20% of Molecule's 60% in Atom and thus this set has an effective interest of 12% in Atom. As a proof, the sum of the minorities interests, plus the interest of Cell, adds to 100% (40% + 12% + 48%).

Continuing the example two possibilities arise:

(*a*) That Molecule acquired Atom before Cell acquired Molecule;

(*b*) That Atom was acquired after Cell took over Molecule.

In addition a minor complication—negative reserves on acquisition and a loss incurred during the year—is introduced. This should present no difficulties, as treatment is the same as for positive reserves and profits.

The balance sheets at 31 December 1977 are:

	Cell £	Molecule £	Atom £
Fixed assets	65,000	8,000	4,000
Shares in subsidiary	49,000	8,000	—
Net current assets	93,000	21,000	6,000
	£207,000	£37,000	£10,000
Share capital	100,000	50,000	5,000
Revenue reserves	107,000	(13,000)	5,000
	£207,000	£37,000	£10,000

(*a*) *Holding Company acquires subsidiary after subsidiary acquires sub-subsidiary*

Assume that Molecule acquired its 60% interest in Atom in 1975 when Atom's reserves were £2,000. Cell acquired its 80% interest in Molecule on 30 June 1977, when Atom's reserves were £3,000 but accounts for Molecule were not available. On 1 January 1977 Molecule's reserves were £1,000.

Procedure: calculate the consolidation adjustment for each subsidiary separately, but cut out the intermediate step of consolidating Atom with Molecule. The following memorandum double-entry workings are needed.

Atom: Allocation of Share Capital

	£		£
Minority interests (52%)	2,600	Share capital	5,000
Cost of control	2,400		
	£5,000		£5,000

Atom: Allocation of Reserves

	£		£
Minority interests (52%)	2,600	Reserves	5,000
Pre-acquisition reserves:			
48% of £3,000	1,440		
(cost of control)			
Post-acquisition reserves			
48% of (£5,000 − 3,000)	960		
	£5,000		£5,000

Note: acquisition of Atom by the Group is deemed to be on 30 June 1977, not the date when Molecule acquired Atom's shares.

Atom: Cost of Control

	£		£
Cost of shares		Shares	2,400
(80% of £8,000)	6,400		
		Pre-acquisition	
		reserves	1,440
		Goodwill	2,560
	£6,400		£6,400

Note: it is Cell's share of Atom that is to be computed; thus, we compare the effective cost to Cell of the shares in Atom with the 80% share of Atom's shares and reserves acquired by Cell.

Molecule: Allocation of Cost of Shares

	£		£
Cost of shares in Atom	8,000	Cell (to cost of control of Atom); 80%	6,400
		Minority Interests 20%	1,600
	£8,000		£8,000

Note: the cost of the Atom shares in Molecule's accounts is to be eliminated from the group accounts and is replaced by the Group's share of Atom's net assets. Similarly, the minority interest is to be expressed as the minority's share of the net assets of Atom and so the cost attributable to the minority is debited to the minority interests' account.

Molecule: Allocation of Share Capital

	£		£
Cost of control: 80%	40,000	Share capital	50,000
Minority: 20%	10,000		
	£50,000		£50,000

Molecule: Allocation of Reserves

	£		£
Reserves	13,000	Minority interest:	
		20%	2,600
		Pre-acquisition:	
		80% of £6000	4,800
		Post-acquisition:	
		80% of £7000	5,600
	£13,000		£13,000

Note: Molecule had £1,000 of profits brought forward on 1 January 1977. By 31 December this had become a cumulative loss of £13,000. The loss during the year was therefore £14,000 (+ £1,000 − £14,000 = − £13,000). In the absence of further information it is assumed that the loss accrued evenly. On 30 June 1977 the balance on reserves must therefore have been £1,000 + (−£14,000/2) = −£6,000. Using the double-entry format, the negative reserves are shown as a debit entry in the working papers as above, and the allocations of the reserves will also be debits to their respective workings:

Molecule: Cost of Control

	£		£
Cost of shares	49,000	Share capital	40,000
Pre-acquisition loss	4,800	Goodwill on	
		consolidation	13,800
	£53,800		£53,800

Group: Minority Interests

	£		£
Atom: cost of shares	1,600	Atom: share capital	2,600
Molecule: reserves	2,600	Atom: Reserves	2,600
Balance	11,000	Molecule: share	
		capital	10,000
	£15,200		£15,200

Group: Revenue Reserves

Molecule	5,600	Cell	107,000
Balance	102,360	Atom	960
	£107,960		£107,960

Example 8: Solution to possibility (a)

Cell Ltd and Subsidiaries
Consolidated Balance Sheet at 31 December 1977

Assets employed

	£
Fixed assets	77,000
Goodwill on consolidation	16,360
Net current assets	120,000
	£213,360

Financed by
Shareholders' funds

Share capital	100,000
Reserves	102,360
	£202,360
Minority interests	11,000
	£213,360

Note: Goodwill comprises the goodwill on consolidation of both subsidiaries (Atom £2,560 and Molecule £13,800).

(b) Holding company acquires subsidiary before latter acquires sub-subsidiary

The same figures as in possibility (a) are used, but now Molecule is acquired on 1 January 1977 and acquires Atom on 30 June 1977.

Procedure: Atom joins the Cell group on 30 June 1977, when Molecule acquires its shares. In possibility (a), it joined the Cell group on the same date. The procedure for consolidation of Atom into the Cell Group is therefore as before and produces the same figures as in possibility (a). In this case it is only the different date of acquisition of Molecule by Cell which produces a change in the consolidated accounts. Molecule's share capital is allocated as before, but new working is required for the reserves.

Molecule: Allocation of Reserves

	£		£
Balance	13,000	Minority interests	
		(as before)	2,600
Pre-acquisition reserve:		Post-acquisition loss:	
80% of £1000	800	80% of £14,000	11,200
	£13,800		£13,800

Molecule: Cost of Control

	£		£
Cost of shares	49,000	Share capital	40,000
		Reserves	800
		Goodwill	8,200
	£49,000		£49,000

Example 8: Solution to possibility (b)

Cell Ltd and Subsidiaries
Consolidated Balance Sheet at 31 December 1977

Assets employed

	£
Fixed assets	77,000
Goodwill on consolidation	10,760
Net current assets	120,000
	£207,760

Financed by

	£
Shareholders' funds	
Share capital	100,000
Reserves	96,760
	196,760
Minority interests	11,000
	£207,760

Workings: Group Reserves

	£
Cell	107,000
Atom	960
Molecule	(11,200)
	£ 96,760

Goodwill

	£
Atom	2,560
Molecule	8,200
	£10,760

16.8 Mixed groups
The Cell group (Cell, Molecule and Atom) can be shown diagrammatically, thus:

DIAGRAM 1

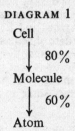

Here, Cell has direct control over Molecule; Molecule has direct control over Atom; Cell has indirect control over Atom. This is a 'vertical group'. Contrast this with the situation shown in Diagram 2—a 'mixed group'.

DIAGRAM 2

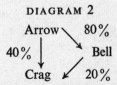

In Diagram 2 Arrow has direct control of Bell—but

neither Arrow nor Bell control Crag outright. However, Arrow's direct holding in Crag, plus its indirect ownership (through Bell) of another block of shares, gives it overall control. As with the example of the vertical group in Diagram 1, the financial interest of Arrow in Crag differs from its control of the share capital. In this case its financial interest is 56% (40% + 80% of 20%) but it has control of shares equal to 60%. Remember that it is the latter fact which makes Crag a subsidiary of Arrow under S 154 of the Companies Act 1948. If Bell's holding in Crag were 11%, the financial interest of Arrow would be 48.8%; but because Arrow had control of 51% of Crag's shares, Crag would still qualify as a subsidiary.

When one or more of the companies in a group is only in the group because all or part of its capital is held directly *and* indirectly by the holding company, as in Diagram 2, the group is described as 'mixed'. However, the consolidation procedure is the same as for vertical groups. The date of acquisition by the *group* is the key point. Bell joins the group the day the control of its shares passes to Arrow; Crag is not controlled until both Arrow and Bell have acquired their holdings in it. Thus, the date of acquisition is always the date of the latter of these two events. The only new factor compared with the vertical group is that there are three calculations of the cost of control—for Arrow's direct stake in Crag, for Arrow's indirect stake in Crag via Bell and for Arrow's stake in Bell.

17

The Consolidated Profit and Loss Account

The approach to the consolidated profit and loss account is similar to that of the balance sheet, except that it is important to produce the right presentation if S 149 of the Companies Act 1948 is to be complied with. That section gives exemption from publishing the profit and loss account of the holding company provided a certain format is used for the group presentation. In 1974/5, out of 295 leading UK groups, all published only a profit and loss account for the group which complied with S 149, and none published a separate profit and loss account for the holding company.[1] This form of consolidated profit and loss account is thus of great relevance and in this chapter it is assumed that S 149 is to be followed, and that the published group accounts do not contain a profit and loss account for the holding company.

17.1 The basic case: 100% owned subsidiary

As in Chapter 16, a simple case is used to begin with and the complications usually met in practice are gradually introduced.

Example 1

Gale Ltd has owned Fir Ltd for many years. Their accounts, made up to 31 December 1977, show the following:

---

[1] *Survey of Published Accounts, 1975, op. cit.*

	Gale £	Fir £
Turnover	150,000	45,000
Cost of sales	85,000	27,000
Depreciation	10,000	3,000
Trading profit	55,000	15,000
Dividend received	5,000	—
Interest payable	8,000	4,000
Profit before tax	52,000	11,000
UK taxation	20,000	4,000
Profit after tax	32,000	7,000
Dividend proposed	10,000	—
Dividend paid	—	5,000
Profit retained	22,000	2,000
Retained profit b/f	45,000	8,000
Retained profit c/f	67,000	10,000

The process of consolidation, as before, consists of adding together the separate figures but eliminating inter-company transactions and presenting the information in suitable form.

Worksheet

	Gale £	Fir £	Adjustment (Note 2) £	Consolidated £
Turnover	150,000	45,000		195,000
Depreciation	10,000	3,000		13,000
Trading profit	55,000	15,000		70,000
Dividend received	5,000	—	(5,000)	
Interest payable	8,000	4,000	—	12,000
Profit before tax	52,000	11,000	(5,000)	58,000
UK Tax	20,000	4,000		24,000
Profit after tax	32,000	7,000	(5,000)	34,000
Dividend proposed	10,000	—		10,000
Dividend paid	—	5,000	(5,000)	—

Note 1: as these are limited company accounts, only those items normally dealt with in published accounts will be consolidated. The cost of sales is not required by UK law or by professional standard (although it is required in the USA). It has therefore been ignored.

Note 2: the inter-company dividend comes from profit earned not by Gale but by Fir. To include it in Gale's profit would be double counting. It is therefore treated as though it had never been paid and is eliminated both from Gale's and Fir's figures.

Example 1: Solution

Gale Ltd and Subsidiary
Consolidated Profit and Loss Account
for the year ended 31 December 1977

	Notes	£	£
Turnover			195,000
Operating profit	1		70,000
Interest payable			12,000
Profit before taxation			58,000
Taxation			24,000
Profit after taxation	2		34,000
Proposed dividend			10,000
Retained profit for the year:			
Gale Ltd		22,000	
Subsidiary		2,000	
			£24,000

Statement of retained profit:

	£
Balance at 31 December 1976	53,000
Retained profit for the year	24,000
Balance at 31 December 1977	£77,000

Notes to the accounts
1. Operating profit is stated after charging £13,000 depreciation.
2. £32,000 of the profit available for appropriation in the year was dealt with in the accounts of Gale Ltd.

Explanatory notes
The layout shown above is typical of that used in practice, although there are various ways in which the same information can be disclosed. The solution complies with S 149 of the Companies Act 1948 by including *Note 2*. The division of retained profit for the year between holding company and subsidiary is given as an example of current 'best practice'; the information is not required by law. Similarly, the statement of retained profit, which many companies are now publishing, is regarded as best practice but is not a legal requirement. In the past, retained profits brought forward

were usually included as part of the profit and loss statement, but movements on reserves have become so important in recent years, in relation to the amounts disclosed in the profit and loss account, that the separation of the statement of current profits and the reconciliation of past reserves and reserves carried forward is useful in clarifying the results of the year's operations. In addition, the introduction of current cost accounting, as recommended by ED 18, will necessitate an appropriation account which will link the profit and loss account and the balance sheet.

The treatment of retained profits for the year *is* required in the form used in this example when the results of associated companies are to be consolidated. The requirement—part of SSAP 1 *Accounting for the results of Associated Companies*—is discussed in Chapter 18.

The use of a note to disclose depreciation may seem unnecessary in this example. The Companies Acts require a number of items of income and expenditure to be specifically disclosed in the accounts, but it is a matter of preference whether they are shown in a 'box' on the face of the accounts or shown by note. Modern practice inclines towards 'clean' accounts, simple and clear statements with all detail attached in notes. For this reason a note was shown as part of the solution.

17.2 An acquisition during the accounting period

Example 2
The facts are the same as in Example 1, except that Gale acquired Fir on 30 September 1977 and Fir's dividend was paid on 1 October in respect of the year to 30 June 1977.

An acquisition during the year presents the same problem as the consolidation of balance sheets. The profit shown in the accounts of the subsidiary cannot be regarded wholly as profit of the group. The consolidated accounts can treat as group profit only profits earned subsequent to the acquisition of the subsidiary. To achieve comparability, it is customary to start with the profits for the whole year for all group companies and then to deduct, in the profit and loss account, pre-acquisition profits arising from subsidiaries acquired during the year.

In Example 2 Gale has received part of Fir's pre-acquisition profits in the form of a dividend. In Gale's own accounts this will be deducted from the cost of shares in Fir. It does not affect the consolidation at all. As stated previously, all inter-company dividends are ignored, and the consolidation proceeds as if they had never been paid or proposed.

The acquisition took place during the year. There can be no disclosure in the profit and loss account of retained profits brought forward by the subsidiary. Instead they are offset in the consolidation workings against the cost of the shares in the subsidiary, as part of the cost of control calculation. Only the reserves of Gale can be brought forward in this case.

Example 2: Solution

Gale Ltd and Subsidiary
Consolidated Profit and Loss Account
for the year ended 31 December 1977

	Notes	£
Turnover		195,000
Operating profit	1	70,000
Interest payable		12,000
Profit before taxation		58,000
Taxation		24,000
Profit after taxation		34,000
Pre-acquisition profits of subsidiary		5,250
Profit after tax attributable to the members of Gale Ltd	2	28,750
Proposed dividend		10,000

		£
Retained profit for the year:		
Gale Ltd.	17,000	
Subsidiary	1,750	
		£18,750

Statement of retained profit:

	£
Balance at 31 December 1976	45,000
Retained profit for the year	18,750
Balance at 31 December 1977	£63,750

Notes to the accounts
1. Operating profit is stated after charging £13,000 depreciation;
2. £27,000 of the profit available for appropriation in the year was dealt with in the accounts of the company.

Explanatory notes: calculation of pre-acquisition profit:

Fir: Net profit after tax for year	7,000
Acquisition on 30 September	$= \frac{9}{12} \times £7,000$
Thus pre-acquisition profit	$= £5,250$

Accounts Note 2: Gale's own profit after tax, ignoring the inter-company dividend.

17.3 Minority interests

Minority interests are treated in the same manner as in the balance sheet: the total profits for group companies are added together and the share of minority shareholders in those profits is then deducted.

Example 3
Rolling Ltd has a 60% holding in the equity of Stones Ltd., which it has held for many years. The trading results for the year to 30 June 1978 are as follows:

	Rolling £	*Stones* £
Trading profit	30,000	18,000
Dividend received	6,000	—
	36,000	18,000
Taxation	16,000	6,000
Net profit	20,000	12,000
Dividend paid	10,000	10,000
Profit retained	10,000	2,000

Reserves at 30 June 1977 were Rolling—£120,000, Stones—£40,000.

Example 3: Solution

Rolling Ltd and Subsidiary
*Consolidated Profit and Loss Account
for the year ended 30 June 1977*

	Note	£
Operating profit		48,000
Taxation		22,000
Profit after taxation		26,000
Minority interests		4,800
Profit after taxation attributable to Rolling Ltd	1	21,200
Dividend		10,000
Retained profit for the year:		
by Rolling Ltd	10,000	
by Subsidiary	1,200	£11,200
Statement of retained profits:		
Balance at 30 June 1977		144,000
Retained profit for the year		11,200
Balance at 30 June 1978		£155,200

Note 1: £20,000 of the profit available for appropriation in the year has been dealt with in the accounts of Rolling Ltd.

Explanatory note; minority interests are 40% of Stone's profits for the year (40% of £12,000 = £4,800). Retained profits are £10,000 in Rolling's accounts, plus 60% of the retained profits in Stone's accounts (60% of £2,000 = £1,200). Retained profits brought forward—Rolling's reserve plus 60% of Stone's reserves.

Example 4
The facts are as in Example 3, but here Stone was acquired on 1 January 1978, and paid its dividend on 30 June 1978.

Procedure: in this example, Stone's profits must be divided into three components: minority interests, pre-acquisition and post-acquisition profits. Thus:

	£
Stone's profits in year	12,000
Minority interests (40%)	4,800
Pre-acquisition profits ($\frac{6}{12} \times 60\% = £12,000$)	3,600
Post-acquisition profits ($\frac{6}{12} \times 60\% = £12,000$)	3,600
	12,000

The treatment of the dividend presents a problem, since it is not known whether it relates to the period before or after acquisition. If, as is most likely, it is the dividend for the whole year to 30 June 1977, it must be apportioned with $\frac{6}{12}$ taken as a reduction of the cost of the shares in Stone and $\frac{6}{12}$ included as part of the retained profits in the accounts of Rolling.

Example 4: Solution

Rolling Ltd and Subsidiary
*Consolidated Profit and Loss Account
for the year ending 30 June 1978*

	Note	£	£
Operating profit			48,000
Taxation			22,000
Profit after tax			26,000
Minority interests		4,800	
Pre-acquisition profits of subsidiary		3,600	8,400
Profit attributable to Rolling Ltd	1		17,600
Dividend			10,000
Profit retained for the year:			
Rolling Ltd	7,000		
Subsidiary	600		£7,600

Statement of retained profits:

Balance 30 June 1977	120,000
Retained profit for the year	7,600
Balance 30 June 1978	£127,600

Note to accounts

1. £17,000 of the profit available for appropriation in the year was dealt with in the accounts of Rolling Ltd.

Explanatory note: working to Note 1. Net profit in Rollings books in Example 3—£20,000. As dividend of £6,000 has to be halved, £3,000 must be deducted giving £17,000 dealt with in Rolling's accounts.

17.4 Preference shares

The dividends received on a holding of preference shares in a subsidiary are treated in the same way as dividends on equity shares. In the year of acquisition of the preference shares, the dividend may have to be apportioned between the amount to be offset against the cost of the shares and the amount retained in the profits of the holding company. The date of the acquisition of the ordinary shares is normally irrelevant to this calculation. If preference shares are acquired before ordinary shares, no consolidation is necessary (unless the voting rights of the preference shares carry control of the company) until sufficient ordinary shares are acquired to give control.

18

Associated Companies

18.1 Accounting for associated companies

The Companies Acts require the consolidation of the accounts of subsidiaries with their holding companies. Nothing is said about holdings of up to 50% or the treatment of consortium companies set up by a number of separate companies where each member of the consortium has a say in its management. However, there is no reason why the interests of one company in another should not be consolidated in the accounts of the first company. The limits to such a procedure are dictated by common sense: plainly the interest of a company in another, when its shareholding is 5% of the total equity interest, will be limited to the receipt of dividends. To consolidate the accounts will produce a misleading financial report since the 'holding' company will be claiming a control it does not have and the minority interest deduction in the consolidated profit and loss account will be 95% of the profits of the 'subsidiary'.

On the other hand, it is arguable that a substantial minority stake—say 40%—is influential and may provide control in practice (the other shareholders may each have small holdings and be unable or unwilling to combine their voting strength). Furthermore, in the case of a 40% holding, traditional accounting only recognises the dividends declared and not the profits accruing to that holding; yet these may be much greater than the dividend and may be material in comparison to the profits of the investing company.

By the late 1960s, leading public companies had begun

to account for significant—but under 50%—holdings in other companies, to provide more information for users of their accounts. Indeed, the idea that traditional accounting was inadequate to deal with significant minority holdings had become so prevalent that the first publication of the ASC was an exposure draft called *Accounting for the results of Associated Companies*. In 1971 came ED 25, with the same title. ED 25, issued in 1980, revises SSAP 1 and is the basis for the following discussion. ED 25 defines a company as an associate if it is not a subsidiary and if:

(*a*) the investing group or company's interest is effectively that of a partner in a joint venture or consortium, and the investing group or company is in a position to exercise a significant influence over the associated company; or

(*b*) the investing group or company's interest is for the long term and is substantial, and, having regard to the disposition of the other shareholdings, the investing group or company is in a position to exercise a significant influence over the associated company.

In both cases it is essential that the investing group or company participates (usually through representation on the board) in commercial and financial policy decisions of the associated company, including the distribution of profits. A 20% holding is the usual indicator of an associated company; it would be unusual for a company owning 20% of another to exercise no influence over that company. However, the definition in ED 25 makes it clear that 20% holding is not by itself a sufficient condition. A company holding up to 50% of the equity of another may regard its holding as being a trade investment and may have no desire to wield any influence over the policies of the 'investee'. In such a case it is exempt from the requirements of SSAP 1.

18.2 Accounting treatment

A subsidiary is consolidated in full with its holding company: each asset and liability is added to those of the parent to produce the group accounts and minority interests are then expressed as a liability of the group. An associate is a company in which the investing company has only a minority holding, and in order to express this important difference in the consolidated accounts, the profits accruing to the holding company are disclosed as a separate figure in the profit and loss account, and the total value of the shares in the associate (the due proportion of net assets) is shown as a single figure in the balance sheet. The mechanics of consolidation are brought out in the examples later in this chapter.

18.3 Consolidation of associated companies in an investing group

'Investing group' denotes a group already preparing consolidated accounts (*i.e.* a holding company which has one or more subsidiaries). The following procedure is to be used.

Profit and loss account
1. Profits before tax: the group's share of profits or losses in associates before tax should be shown separately from its own profit or loss before tax.
2. Taxation: the tax attributable to the group's share of profits in associates should be shown separately.
3. Extraordinary items: the group's share of extraordinary items of associates would normally be included with group extraordinary items, but would be shown separately if material.
4. Profit retained for the year: the group's share of retained profit in the accounts of associates should be shown separately.
5. Other items: the consolidation procedure is not a full consolidation and items such as depreciation or income from property need not be disclosed unless significant in the context of the group accounts.

Example 1

Mammoth Holdings Ltd own 75% of the equity shares of Tusk Ltd and 25% of the equity in Elephant Ltd, which it regards as an associate. Consolidated accounts have been

prepared for Mammoth and Tusk. It is now required that
the latest available accounts of Elephant be consolidated
with those of the Mammoth group. The profit and loss
accounts are as follows:

	Mammoth & Tusk *Year ending* *31 December 1977* £	Elephant *Year ending* *30 September 1977* £
Turnover	550,000	140,000
Operating profit	175,000	52,000
Investment income	5,000	8,000
Profit before taxation	180,000	60,000
Taxation	80,000	20,000
Profit after taxation	100,000	40,000
Minority interests	10,000	—
Profit attributable to Mammoth Ltd.	90,000	
Dividends paid	—	10,000
Dividends proposed	30,000	10,000

Profit retained for the
year:
  by Mammoth 52,000
  by Subsidiary 8,000

	60,000	20,000

The shares in Elephant were acquired on 1 January 1977.
The dividend paid by Elephant was declared on 30 August
and paid 29 September.

Example 1: Solution

Mammoth Holdings Ltd and Subsidiary
Consolidated Profit and Loss Account
for the year ending 31 December 1977

	Note	£	£
Turnover			550,000
Operating profit			175,000
Share of profits of Associated company			11,250
Profit before taxation			186,250
Taxation—Company and Subsidiary		80,000	
—Associated company		3,750	
			83,750
Profit after taxation			102,500
Minority interests			10,000
Profit attributable to Mammoth Holdings Ltd			92,500
Dividends			30,000
Profit retained for the year:			
by Mammoth Holdings Ltd		52,000	
by Subsidiary		8,000	
by Associated company		2,500	
			62,500

Note to the accounts
1. £82,000 of the profit available for appropriation was dealt with in the accounts of Mammoth Holdings Ltd.

Workings to Solution to Example 1
(a) Choice of accounts: it is not essential that the accounting dates of holding company and associate coincide. See section 18.5 on miscellaneous points.
(b) Turnover: only the holding company's and subsidiary's turnover are consolidated.
(c) Operating profit is the profit of holding company and subsidiary. The group's share of the associate's profits or losses is then added to obtain the total group profit before taxation.
(d) Investment income, in so far as it consists of dividends

from the associate, must be eliminated from the overall consolidation. In this case we know that the income is wholly derived from the associate, because it is 25% of the total dividends declared by Elephant.

(e) Group's share is 25% of the post-acquisition profits of Elephant. Acquisition was on 1 January, 9 months before Elephant's year end. Thus the group's share of profits is: 25% of £60,000 $\times \frac{9}{12}$ = £11,250.

(f) Group's share of tax is taken as the proportion of the group's share of profit to total profit. Thus it is: 11,250/60,000 $\times$ £20,000 = £3,750.

(g) Profit retained in the associate is:

	£
Pre-tax profit	11,250
less tax	(3,750)
less dividend	(5,000)
	2,500

(h) Treatment of the dividend from Elephant: it has been assumed that the two dividends were declared out of post-acquisition profits. If either or both had been declared out of profit for the whole year to 30 September 1977, they would then be apportioned: a quarter to be offset against the cost of the shares in Elephant and three-quarters as investment income. However, as with dividends paid by a subsidiary, the consolidated accounts are only affected to the extent that the greater the dividend paid, the lower the amount of profit attributable to the group retained in the accounts of the associate.

Balance sheet

The investing group's interest in an associated company should be shown as:

(a) The group's share of the net assets other than goodwill of the associated companies; and

(b) The group's share of the goodwill of the associated companies together with

(c) The premium paid on the acquisition of the interests in the associated companies after attributing fair values to the net assets acquired.

This requirement treats associates in the same way as subsidiaries are treated by SSAP 14.

Example 2

The facts are as in Example 1. The reserves of the Mammoth group were £110,000 on 31 December 1977 before consolidation of Elephant's results. The cost of the shares in Elephant was £80,000.

At that time the fair value of Elephant's net assets was £300,000, thus goodwill on acquisition is £80,000 − (300,000/4) = £5,000.

Example 2: Solution

Mammouth Holdings

Consolidated Balance Sheet at 31 December 1977 (Extracts)

	£	£
Interest in Associated company		
Group's share of net assets (other than goodwill)	77,500	
Goodwill on acquisition of associate	5,000	
		82,500

	£	£
Revenue reserves		
Group companies: retained profits	110,000	
Associated company: retained profits	2,500	
		112,500

18.4 The consolidation of associated companies in the accounts of an investing company

When group accounts are not prepared, there is no adjustment to be made to the balance sheet in respect of associates. The investment in associates will continue to be shown at cost, less any amounts written off. A note of the company's share of the retained profits or losses of the associate is all that ED 25 requires.

However, the profit and loss account should be presented in consolidated form, bringing in the share of the associate's profits or losses as for an investing group. Thus, the layout used in Example 1 should be used in this case, although there will be no reference to subsidiaries or minority interests. A statement of how the profits retained for the year are divided between investing company and associate is vital; otherwise the balance sheet figure of reserves (which will not include reserves retained by the associate) will appear to be unreconciled with the profit and loss account.

18.5 Miscellaneous matters

(*a*) *Accounting dates*. In practice there is no reason why the financial years of an investing company and associate should coincide, nor is there any legal obligation on directors of the investing company to achieve similar year ends. ED 25 therefore allows the use of the accounts of associates made up to a date not earlier than 6 months before the date of the investing company's accounts, or very shortly after that date. (If the associate is listed on the stock exchange, only published financial information may be used.)

When there is a time-lag between the date of the associate's accounts and those of the investing company, as in Example 1, care should be taken to ensure that later information does not materially affect the view given by the earlier accounts.

When dates of accounts differ, the date to which the associate's accounts are made up should be disclosed, and if unaudited accounts are being used, that fact should also be disclosed.

(*b*) *Accounting adjustments*. If material, the same adjustments to remove the effects of inter-company transactions should be made as for a subsidiary. In the case of inter-company sales, the figures for turnover in the investing company's accounts need not be changed, since the sale to an associate is both legally and commercially a sale to an entity outside the group. However, unrealised profits on stock sold to or bought from an associate should be extracted from the accounts.

(*c*) *Exemption.* Associates can be omitted from the group accounts for the same reasons that apply to subsidiaries (see section 15.3).

(*d*) *Companies Acts provisions.* ED 25 does not override the Companies Act 1967 in respect of investments in other companies. (See Chapter 19.)

PART 5

Published Financial Accounts

19

The Accounting Requirements of the Companies Acts

United Kingdom governments have always respected the competence of the accountancy profession when framing company legislation. The Companies Acts are mainly concerned with defining the rights and duties of directors and shareholders. Comparatively little attention is given to accounts, apart from provisions that audited accounts be prepared each year, and certain amounts disclosed in the accounts. Beyond this the law has yet to go. The EEC is working towards standardisation of company accounts, but agreement between the member states has not yet been reached.

This chapter summarises the UK legal requirements, which are not only valid for this country but are used in many others where the influence of the UK profession has spread. The reader should bear in mind that the UK legislation requires the auditor to ensure that the accounts show a true and fair view. If an auditor is not sure whether an accounting practice is true and fair he must look in the first instance to accounting standards, and thereafter to generally accepted practices.

Note
The following summary deals only with the important provisions of the Acts. The reader requiring more detailed information is referred to the Acts themselves. All section references in this chapter are to the Companies Act 1948 unless otherwise stated.

19.1 The Preparation, Publication and Audit of Accounts

Every company is required to keep proper books of account in respect of money received and expended, sales and purchases, and assets and liabilities. Such books must give a true and fair view of the state of the company's affairs and explain its transactions (S 147). A profit and loss account and balance sheet must be laid before the company in general meeting once every calendar year, made up to a date not later than 9 months before the date of the meeting (S 148). The profit and loss account and the balance sheet must give a true and fair view of the profit or loss for the year and of the state of affairs at the end of the year, and must comply with Schedule 2 of the Companies Act 1967 (S 9, 1967 Act). Schedule 2 comprises the list of items to be disclosed and is summarised below.

At each Annual General Meeting, every company must appoint an auditor to hold office until the next AGM (S 159). His duty is to report on all accounts laid before the company and to say whether, in his opinion, they comply with S 9 of the 1967 Act (S 14, 1967 Act).

19.2 Disclosure of the profit and loss account

When internal accounts are prepared, a detailed profit and loss account is drawn up showing sources of income and each category of expenditure or charge against income. The Companies Act 1967 requires that certain items be disclosed, but there is no need for the complete profit and loss account to be published. Whether items are presented on the face of the accounts or as a note is left to the discretion of the directors, subject to the need to show a true and fair view. *The following items must be disclosed:*

1. Turnover
   Exemptions:
   (*a*) banking and discount companies;
   (*b*) any company which is neither a holding company nor a subsidiary of any body corporate and whose turnover is less than £1 million.

2. Depreciation

The amount charged by way of provision for depreciation, renewals or diminution in the value of fixed assets and separately, if any amount is charged by way of provision for renewals. If depreciation or replacement of fixed assets is provided by some method other than a depreciation charge or provision for renewals or is not provided, the method used or not used must be stated.

3. Hire of plant and machinery

4. Interest payable

Interest on loans, divided into:
(*a*) bank loans and overdrafts;
(*b*) loans repayable within five years from balance sheet date;
(*c*) other loans.

5. Auditors' remuneration (*including expenses*)

6. Directors' emoluments

(*a*) Aggregate amount of directors' emoluments (meaning all forms of remuneration);
(*b*) Aggregate amount of directors' or past directors' pensions;
(*c*) Aggregate amount of any compensation for loss of office. Each total is to be analysed into amounts paid:

(*i*) in respect of service as a director of the company or of its subsidiary while a director of the company;
(*ii*) in respect of other services.

In this context (*i*) is interpreted to mean fees and (*ii*) salaries. Further analysis must show the source of emoluments of each of classes (*a*) to (*c*) above divided between (*i*) the company, (*ii*) the company's subsidiaries, and (*iii*) any other source.

In addition the totals are to be analysed into:
(1) Chairman's emoluments, while chairman;
(2) Emoluments of the highest-paid director;
(3) The number of directors receiving emoluments in the brackets £0–£5,000, £5,000–£10,000 *etc.*;
(4) The number of directors waiving emoluments and the amount so waived.

Exemptions from (1)–(4) above apply to:
(*a*) Directors whose work is performed outside the UK;
(*b*) A company neither a holding company nor subsidiary and where total emoluments are less than £40,000.

7. *Employees earning over £20,000*

The number of employees in brackets of £5,000 as for directors.

8. *Income from (a) quoted and (b) unquoted investments*

9. *Net rental income from land*

10. *Taxation*
The charge to UK corporation tax, foreign tax and the amount of double tax relief; the basis on which the UK charge is computed and any special circumstances affecting taxation.

11. *Extraordinary items*

12. *Prior year adjustments*

13. *Dividends*
The aggregate amount paid and proposed to be paid for the year.

14. *Transfers to reserves and provisions*
(*a*) Amounts provided to redeem share capital or loans;
(*b*) The amount set aside for provisions other than depreciation of fixed assets, or amounts withdrawn from provisions and not applied for the purposes thereof.
(*c*) The amount, if material, set aside for transfer to or from reserves. This includes the transfer of retained profits to the Revenue Reserves (normally the final figure in the profit and loss account).

15. *Comparative figures*
The corresponding amounts for the preceding financial year.

19.3 Disclosure of the balance sheet

The requirements cover all items found in a balance sheet but most specify no more than that it should be disclosed.

Against some items, however, are detailed requirements. In modern practice these are invariably dealt with in notes, leaving the balance sheet an uncluttered set of key figures.

1. General layout

Authorised and issued share capital, reserves, provisions and other liabilities, fixed current and other assets should all be classified under headings appropriate to the business, with such particulars as are necessary to disclose their general nature.

2. Fixed assets

(*a*) The method used to arrive at the value of each class of assets must be disclosed (usually by showing the cost or valuation of the assets and the aggregate amount written off for depreciation);

(*b*) For revalued assets (apart from unquoted investments), there must be shown the years when so valued, the amount of valuation and, if valued during the current year, either the names or the qualifications of the valuers and the bases of valuation used.

(*c*) For all fixed assets other than investments shall be stated the aggregate amount of assets in each class acquired during the current year, and the aggregate amount of assets included in the previous year's balance sheet disposed of or scrapped in the current year.

(*d*) Land should be analysed into the following categories:

(1) Freehold;

(2) Long leasehold (unexpired lease at year end for more than 50 years);

(3) Short leasehold (unexpired lease less than 50 years).

3. Goodwill, *patents and trademarks*

The amount of goodwill, patents and trademarks shall be shown net of any amounts written off, and the method used to arrive at the amount shall be stated.

4. Investments

The aggregate amounts of quoted and unquoted investments shall be shown separately.

(*a*) Quoted investments are to be divided into those quoted on a recognised stock exchange (the UK stock exchange) and others. If the market value differs from the amount in the accounts, it shall be stated; the stock exchange value should also be stated, if lower than the market value.

(b) Unquoted investments in the equity share capital of another body corporate shall be shown at the value of the directors; alternatively, details of the income and reserves attributable to the investment should be given.

5. Current assets
There are no blanket provisions, except:

(a) The way in which stocks and work in progress have been computed (if material);

(b) If any current asset does not have a value on realisation at least equal to the stated amount, that fact is to be disclosed by the directors.

6. Loans
Two special types of loan are distinguished.

(a) Loans for the purpose of acquiring shares in the company, unless made in the ordinary course of business, must be disclosed if they are either for trustees for employees, or for employees themselves.

(b) Loans to officers of the company must be disclosed, showing;

(1) Amounts lent during the financial year to existing officers and to persons who became officers after receiving the loan;
(2) The amount of any such loans made before the financial year end and outstanding at the end.

Loans made in the ordinary course of business, and loans to employees for less than £2,000 are exempt from such disclosure.

7. Expenses not written off
Such 'quasi-assets' as preliminary expenses or the expenses of an issue of shares, must be disclosed under separate heads.

8. Current liabilities
As with current assets, only some of the items likely to be classified under this heading are specified for separate disclosure. These are:

(*a*) The aggregate amounts of bank loans and overdrafts;
(*b*) The aggregate amount of dividends payable.

9. Share capital

The classes of share capital are to be shown separately, and the authorised and issued capital in each class disclosed. In addition there must be noted:

(*a*) The amount of any redeemable preference shares with the earliest and latest dates the company has power to redeem; whether redemption is compulsory or not; whether a premium is payable on redemption and if so, how much;
(*b*) The number, description and amount of any shares for which any person has an option to subscribe; the period during which the option may be exercised and the price thereby payable.

10. Reserves and provisions

Provisions for depreciation are shown with the fixed assets to which they refer. Other provisions are defined as amounts retained to provide for known liabilities, the amount of which cannot be determined with substantial accuracy. Any other amount retained is a reserve. The aggregate amounts of reserves and provisions are to be shown separately.

Unless accounted for in the profit and loss account, the movements on reserve or provision accounts are to be stated, distinguishing the source of increases and the application of decreases.

11. Long-term loans

The total of loans payable partly or wholly five years after the balance sheet date must be shown, together with a note of repayment terms and rate of interest for each loan.

12. Taxation provisions

An amount set aside to prevent undue fluctuations in tax charges (*i.e.* a deferred tax account) is to be shown separately, and details of any application of it during the year stated.

13. *Comparative figures*

The corresponding amounts for the preceding financial year should be stated.

14. *Miscellaneous requirements*

To be shown on the face of the accounts or by note:

(*a*) Particulars of any charge on the assets of the company to secure the liabilities of any other person;

(*b*) The general nature, and amount if practicable, of any other contingent liability not provided for;

(*c*) The amount of:
   (*i*) contracts for capital expenditure authorised by the directors not otherwise provided for;
   (*ii*) authorised capital expenditure not contracted for.

(*d*) The basis on which foreign currencies have been converted into sterling.

19.4 The directors' report

Certain information supplementing the accounts is to be given in the directors' report, which is to be attached to the accounts laid before members of a company in general meeting. This comprises:

1. The state of the company's affairs;
2. The proposed amounts of dividends and transfers to reserve;
3. The principal activities of the company (or group);
4. The turnover, profit (or loss) of each class of business carried on. Companies which are neither holding, nor subsidiary companies, and with turnover of less than £1 million, are exempt;
5. The amount of turnover derived from exports. If total turnover is less than £1 million, disclosure need not be made;
6. The names of persons who were directors at any time during the financial year and the following details about them:

   (*a*) Their interest in shares or debentures of any company in the group, at the beginning and end of the year;
   (*b*) Details of any arrangement whereby the company

enables directors to acquire benefits by acquiring shares or debentures in the company or any other company;
(c) Material interests in contracts with the company.

7. An indication of the difference between market and book values of land, where these differ substantially;
8. The average number of persons employed by the company (or group) during the financial year and their total remuneration. Companies wholly owned by a company incorporated in Great Britain, or with less than 100 employees, are exempt;
9. The amount of political and charitable contributions, if the total exceeds £50;
10. Particulars of any other matters which are material for the appreciation of the state of the company's affairs, and which will not harm the company's business;
11. If items are shown in the directors' report instead of in the accounts, corresponding figures for the previous year are to be given.

20

Accounting Standards and the EEC Directives

The following statements of standard accounting practice and exposure drafts have been issued by the ASC:

SSAP 1	*Accounting for the results of associated companies*
SSAP 2	*Disclosure of accounting policies*
SSAP 3	*Earnings per share*
SSAP 4	*The accounting treatment of government grants*
SSAP 5	*Accounting for Value Added Tax*
SSAP 6	*Extraordinary items and prior year adjustments*
SSAP 8	*The treatment of taxation under the imputation system in the accounts of companies*
SSAP 9	*Stocks and work in progress*
SSAP 10	*Statements of sources and applications of funds*
SSAP 11	*Accounting for deferred taxation* (withdrawn)
SSAP 12	*Accounting for depreciation*
SSAP 13	*Accounting for research and development*
SSAP 14	*Group accounts*
SSAP 15	*Accounting for deferred taxation*
SSAP 16	*Current cost accounting*
SSAP 17	*Accounting for post balance sheet events*
SSAP 18	*Accounting for contingencies*
ED 21	*Accounting for foreign currency transactions*
ED 25	*Accounting for the results of associated companies*

SSAP 7 has been withdrawn. With the exception of ED 3, which is out of print, and ED 21, all other exposure drafts have been replaced by standards. ED 26 (on investment properties) and ED 27 (on foreign currency translation replacing ED 21) were expected by the end of 1980.

SSAPs 3, 4, 5 and 8 are discussed below. The remaining publications have been dealt with in the text, in the sections to which they refer.

20.1 SSAP 3 *Earnings per share*

The price-earnings (P/E) ratio is a very widely used indicator of the comparative value of shares, in terms of the number of years the earnings attributable to an ordinary share will take to repay the purchase price. It is computed by dividing the price of a share by the earnings per share. While the price of a share depends upon market conditions and, in the case of quoted companies, can be determined easily, earnings per share must be computed from the latest available accounts.

Because definitions of earnings can vary from one analyst to another, SSAP 3 was introduced to provide a standard definition and to require quoted companies[1] to publish the earnings per share prominently in their accounts. The standard does not apply to unquoted companies, as P/E ratios are not normally used by investors in such companies as a source of information.

The starting point for the definition of earnings per share (EPS) is the common-sense approach that EPS is the total earnings available for shareholders, divided by the total number of shares issued which are entitled to receive such earnings. The approach is modified in the following ways:

(*a*) *Earnings:* earnings are defined as profits after tax, minority interests and preference dividends (if any), but before extraordinary items. The latter are excluded because the figure of EPS cannot be computed consistently and be comparable between companies if it is distorted by extraordinary items.

(*b*) *Taxation:* the imputation system of corporation tax, in force in the UK since 1973 will, in certain circumstances, impose a tax charge on companies which varies with the dividend paid in any given year. It is important to make clear in the EPS calculation how dividend policy might alter the tax charge, and hence earnings. SSAP 3 requires that, when material, EPS calculated as though no dividend was to be paid (the 'nil' basis) should be disclosed, in addition to the usual calculation based on the actual tax charge (the 'net' basis).

---

[1] *i.e.* companies listed on a recognised stock exchange.

(c) *Share capital:* normally the number of shares issued during a year does not alter. But if there is a change, the figure of earnings per share will depend on which figure is used for shares in issue. EPS must be calculated in a consistent way and the nature of the change in the issued shares must be understood. If bonus shares (shares to current shareholders for which no cash has been exchanged) have been issued, the capital of the company has not changed and its earnings are unaffected. The EPS for the current year is based on the latest figure of share capital, but to be consistent the figure for the previous year should be recalculated using the current figure of issued shares.

If the share capital has been increased by the issue of shares for cash no adjustment to the previous year's figures is required, because the real capital of the business has changed and a direct comparison between the past year's EPS on the reduced capital base and the present year's increased capital is relevant. However, shares are often offered to existing shareholders at a more favourable price than that available to outsiders (a 'rights' issue). To the extent that a 'rights' issue increases the share capital at a discount on the market price, the element of discount should be treated as a bonus issue, and should be incorporated into the reworking of the EPS for the previous year. The EPS should be multiplied by the fraction

Theoretical *ex* rights price
_____
Actual *cum* rights price (on last day rights were available).

When new shares have been issued during the year, it is inconsistent to divide the earnings for the whole year by the share capital, which was only fully in existence for part of the year. In such cases (with the exception of bonus issues where only the previous year's figure of EPS is altered) the share capital used in the calculation of EPS at the end of the year should be a weighted average of shares in issue during the year.

SSAP 3 requires that the earnings per share, in pence, for the current and previous years be disclosed on the face of the profit and loss account, together with an indication, either on the face of the accounts or as a note, of which figures of earnings and share capital have been used in the calculation. In addition, where a company has outstanding shares which are to be issued in the future, or convertible loan stock which can be converted into shares, it is required that the figure for 'fully diluted' earnings per share be given. The earnings figure is the same as in the ordinary computation, but the share capital is that which would exist if all the new shares were actually issued or the loan stock converted to shares. The aim is to show what would happen to earnings if the share capital was to be 'diluted' by the issue of new shares. If the effect of dilution is immaterial (less than 5% of EPS), the figure need not be disclosed.

20.2 SSAP 4 *The accounting treatment of government grants*

From time to time it is government policy to stimulate industrial investment by paying cash grants for specified forms of expenditure by businesses. SSAP 4 attempts to produce a uniform method of accounting for such grants, in order to achieve consistency of practice in financial statements. There is no problem in accounting for revenue-based grants, but a variety of practices have been used in the past to deal with capital grants—grants paid against investment in fixed assets. Such grants reduce the cost of the asset to the business, and accounting theory requires that the benefit from the grant be spread over the same accounting periods as the benefit received from the asset. However, prior to the issue of SSAP 4, some companies used to take the entire grant as a credit to the profit and loss account in the year of receipt, while others credited grants to non-distributable reserves on the balance sheet. The former treatment has immediate effect on reported earnings; the latter has no effect.

To bring the treatment of grants in line with theory, SSAP 4 allows two methods to be used. Grants may either be deducted from the cost of the assets concerned, or credited to a deferred reserve account from which transfers to the profit and loss account are made over the life of the assets concerned. The methods produce identical results, but the second is more informative in that it shows the market cost of the assets held and the amount of aid received in the balance sheet, rather than the net figure.

20.3 SSAP 5 *Accounting for value added tax*

A common-sense, uncontroversial standard, SSAP 5 requires that where VAT is recoverable, all accounting figures should be shown net of VAT. To the extent that VAT is irrecoverable, it should be treated as part of the cost of the goods or services on which it is levied. There will be no separate disclosure of irrecoverable VAT.

The requirement to show figures net of recoverable VAT is particularly important in the case of turnover. However, retail businesses sometimes prefer to disclose gross turnover and VAT therein in arriving at net turnover.

20.4 SSAP 8 *The treatment of taxation under the imputation system in the accounts of companies*

In 1973 the system of corporation tax was changed and SSAP 8 was issued to ensure that companies would deal with the new system correctly and in a uniform manner. The requirements are:

1. For the profit and loss account

(*a*) The make-up of the tax charge should be shown, distinguishing between the charge to UK corporation tax divided into the actual charge and any material transfer to deferred taxation, the tax on dividends received from other UK resident companies (known as franked investment income), irrecoverable advance corporation tax (ACT), and overseas tax relief;

(*b*) The total charge for overseas taxation should be shown, including that amount for which UK tax relief is received, but showing separately any relief lost due to payment or proposed payment of a dividend.

2. For the balance sheet

Dividends should be shown net of related ACT. The ACT should be added to current liabilities. Recoverable ACT (normally identical to the amount payable) is to be deducted from the deferred tax account, or shown separately as a deferred asset if no deferred tax account is maintained.

20.5 International accounting standards

The following international accounting standards have been issued:

IAS 1 *Disclosure of accounting policies*
IAS 2 *Valuation and presentation of inventories in the context of the historical cost system*
IAS 3 *Consolidated financial statements*
IAS 4 *Depreciation accounting*
IAS 5 *Information to be disclosed in financial statements*

IAS 7 *Statement of changes in financial position*
IAS 8 *Unusual and prior period items and changes in accounting policies*

IAS 11 *Accounting for construction contracts*
IAS 12 *Accounting for taxes on income*

These standards are similar to UK standards and are not separately discussed except for IAS 5.

20.6 IAS 5 *Information to be disclosed in financial statements*

This standard deals with the information which should be disclosed in published financial statements which contain a balance sheet, profit and loss account, notes and other statements forming part of the normal reporting package. It does not propose a rigid format for the layout of accounts.

Financial statements should show all material items in a clear and intelligible manner. Most of the information specifically required by the standard to be mentioned is already required by the UK companies acts and accounting standards. However, the following disclosures which are not required in the UK must be made:

(*a*) Contingent assets;
(*b*) Methods of providing for pensions;
(*c*) Associated company balances;
(*d*) Restrictions on the availability of cash;

(*e*) A distinction between trade receivables (trade debtors)
and prepayments;
(*f*) A distinction between trade payables (trade creditors)
and accruals.

20.7 Expected standard (1)—Leasing

Two topics of contemporary importance are high on the
agenda of the ASC and standards are expected shortly. Both
topics concern business developments which, being comparatively recent, have not produced well-established
accounting practices. The first of these is leasing. The
practice of leasing has become far more widespread since
the late 1960s than ever before. A lease is a specialised form
of finance where the business wishing to operate an asset
(the 'lessee') agrees to pay specified amounts to the business
which owns it (the 'lessor'). The asset remains the property
of the lessor until the end of the lease period when it may
be bought by the lessee at special terms or is disposed of.
Leasing varies from the ordinary hire of assets because the
lessee retains the use of the asset over a long period. Indeed,
whatever the legal position may be, the economic reality is
that the lessee is operating the asset with finance provided
by the lessor and there is no difference between a leased asset
and one bought outright (and financed, say, by a bank loan).

There is however a crucial accounting difference. Accounting practice has in the past looked to the legal position.
The lessor has treated assets leased out as fixed assets; the
lessee has charged lease payments as they fell due to profit
and loss account. Thus a lessee operating, say, a computer
would not show it as an asset with a corresponding liability
for future lease payments, but an otherwise identical
business which had bought the computer would have higher
fixed assets and higher borrowings (or lower cash) in its
balance sheet; consequently it would appear to be less
efficient because the return on assets employed would be
lower, and its higher borrowings would make it appear to be
more highly geared (see Chapter 22).

The UK profession has been slow to produce proposals
for accounting for leases. The American FAS 13, issued in
1976, is the major influence on UK thinking. This standard

requires lessees to treat those leases which are effectively purchases of the assets concerned as though they were indeed contracts to purchase. The asset is capitalised and depreciated over its useful life. A corresponding liability for future lease payments is set up, at the net present value of the future payments. The interest rate applied to find net present value is the rate 'implicit in the lease'. Part of each lease payment is treated as being payment of interest on the outstanding liability; the balance is debited against the liability. Thus instead of charging the full amount of lease payments against profits, the lessee charges depreciation and interest. In any one year the sum of these two charges may exceed or fall short of the lease payment but over the period of the life of the asset the total of depreciation and interest will equal total lease payments. This is shown in the example below.

Similarly the lessor is required to account for the lease transaction as though it were an outright sale, and to set up a deferred receivable which is the counterpart of the lessee's liability.

There are tests to show whether a lease should be treated as described above (a 'capital' lease) or should continue to be treated in the conventional way (an 'operating' lease). In essence the tests compare the value of the asset to the value the lessee will derive from the lease agreement. Where the lease payments (net of interest) are effectively enough to pay for the asset, or where the lease period is going to cover most of the expected life of the asset, or where the lessee may take advantage of bargain purchase terms at the end of the lease period, the lease will be deemed a capital lease and must be accounted for accordingly. The UK standard is likely to follow FAS 13 in these tests, with one special exemption for leasehold property which is far more commonly found in the UK than in the US. The rule will be that property subject to rent reviews would not constitute a capital lease because the risks and rewards of ownership would remain with the lessor.

Example—A capital lease in the lessee's accounts
A business leases a car for three years. The lease payments are £2,000 a year. The car would cost £5,000 to buy. Because

the lease payments are enough to pay the cost of the car, the lease is accounted for as a capital lease.

The rate of interest implicit in the lease is 9·7%, because this rate will produce a net present value of £5,000 on the total lease payments of £6,000 over three years. (Yearly interest is calculated on the opening balance, for the sake of convenience.)

	Lease liability £	Interest £	Net lease repayment £	Total lease payment £
Year 1	5,000	485	1,515	2,000
Year 2	3,485	338	1,662	2,000
Year 3	1,823	177	1,823	2,000
Total		1,000	5,000	6,000

Impact on profit and loss account

	Depreciation	Interest	Total Charge to profit and loss
Year 1	1,667	485	2,152
Year 2	1,667	338	2,005
Year 3	1,666	177	1,843
Total	5,000	1,000	6,000

Impact on balance sheet

	Net fixed assets	Lease Liability	Difference
Year 1	3,333	3,485	152
Year 2	1,666	1,823	157
Year 3	—	—	—

In year 1 £2,152 is charged as the cost of the lease, divided into depreciation and interest as shown above. £2,000 is actually paid, and the difference is reflected in the different balance sheet values of the car and the lease liability. This difference increases in year 2 by £5 but is removed in year 3 when the Profit and loss charge of £1,843 is made (compared to a payment of £2,000).

20.8 Expected standard (2)—Pension fund accounting

Pension funds provide a special problem in accounting. Typically a company pension fund will be valued from time to time by actuaries who will relate the future liabilities of the fund—the pensions to be paid to retiring employees, against the assets, which are the funds presently invested and the future contributions. Actuaries will take a very conservative view of future income and the valuations will, in periods of high inflation, tend to show that pension funds are underfunded. Companies may try to make up deficiencies immediately or aim to raise their contributions gradually. Under the HC convention, pension fund contributions tend to be charged against profits as they are made, and this has allowed companies to 'tuck away' contributions in years of good profits, and reduce them in leaner years, thus smoothing out the profit trend and disguising the reality.

In addition there tends to be very little disclosure in accounts concerning the pension fund assets and liabilities and the claims of the fund on the company's assets and future income. An accounting standard to provide some minimal disclosure requirements together with consistency in charging pension fund contributions against profits, is expected.

Such a standard will apply to all companies which provide a fund. It will not necessarily apply to the pension funds themselves since such funds are usually constituted under trust deeds and do not have to produce accounts except as provided by the deed.

20.9 The EEC and harmonisation of financial reporting

A principal aim of the European Economic Community ('EEC') is to break down the barriers to free trade caused by differing company laws, taxes and accounting procedures. In particular it is intended that financial reporting should be similar in all member states, with common accounting concepts, a narrow range of permissible bases from which companies can select appropriate accounting policies, and reporting rules that will allow company accounts to be easily understood wherever they may have been produced.

The EEC does not legislate directly; the EEC Commission produces directives on various matters which are approved by the Council of Ministers and then passed by the parliaments of the various member states. The important directives relating to financial accounting and reporting are the Fourth and Seventh.

20.10 The Fourth directive

The Fourth directive establishes a degree of harmonisation in the preparation, audit and presentation of the annual accounts of limited liability companies. Unlike accounting standards it will be embodied in the law of each member state. The directive relates to individual companies—the Seventh directive deals with groups.

Layout of accounts
Annual accounts are to give a true and fair view and to conform to the prescribed layouts. There are two balance sheet formats—vertical and horizontal, and four profit and loss account formats. These are vertical and horizontal forms of profit and loss accounts based either on type of expenditure (wages, purchases, expenses *etc.*) or by operation (cost of sales, selling expenses, general expenses *etc.*). The option of a vertical, operations type profit and loss conforms closely to current American practice and is likely to be the normal choice in the UK, together with the vertical balance sheet. The directive specifies all the possible headings that can be used in accounts, requiring some to be shown on the face of the accounts by all companies and others to be shown as notes (if desired) or not shown at all by smaller companies. The approach is quite different from traditional UK practice which has allowed much variety in the format of accounts. Examples of the vertical form balance sheet and the vertical, operations-type profit and loss account are given below. These are the minimum requirements, subject to national law. Every heading in the accounts has a letter or number assigned by the directive and these are shown in the examples.

A minimum disclosure balance sheet

C	**FIXED ASSETS**	✕	
	I Intangible assets	✕	
	II Tangible assets	✕	
	III Financial assets	——	✕
D	**CURRENT ASSETS**		
	I Stocks	✕	
	II Debtors	✕	
	III Investments	✕	
	IV Cash	✕	
		——	✕
F	**CREDITORS** (due within one year)		✕
G	**NET CURRENT ASSETS**		✕
H	**TOTAL ASSETS LESS CURRENT LIABILITIES**		✕
I	**CREDITORS** (due in more than one year)		✕
J	**PROVISIONS FOR LIABILITIES AND CHARGES**		✕
L	**CAPITAL AND RESERVES**		✕
	I Called-up capital	✕	
	II Share premium account	✕	
	III Revaluation reserve	✕	
	IV Reserves	✕	
	V Profit or loss brought forward	✕	
	VI Profit or loss for year	——	✕
			✕

If this format is used, the notes will contain additional detail for almost all headings. The precise detail will depend on national law. The definitions of current assets and liabilities exclude any item not due to be realised within a year; amounts that are partially due within a year and partially for longer must be split on the face of the balance sheet. Thus, HP creditors, for example, which under traditional UK practice tend to be classed as current liabilities must be analysed between payments due within the year and the remainder and shown under two separate headings. Financial assets (C III) will consist principally of shares and amounts due to or from subsidiaries and associates, together with long-term investments. Provisions for liabilities (J) comprise taxation and pension creditors, together with any other provisions not yet crystallised into specific liabilities. Other headings are as normally found in the UK, and as discussed in this book.

A minimum disclosure profit and loss account (in 'operating' format)

1	Net turnover		
2	Cost of sales		×
3	Gross profit or loss		×
4	Distribution costs		×
5	Administrative expenses		×
6	Other operating income		×
7	Income from participating interests		×
8	Income from other investments		×
9	Interest receivable and other income		×
10	Value adjustments for financial assets		×
11	Interest payable		×
12	Tax on profit or loss on ordinary activities		×
13	Profit or loss after tax		×
14	Extraordinary income	×	
15	Extraordinary charges	×	
16	Extraordinary profit or loss		×
17	Tax on extraordinary profit or loss		×
18	Other taxes		×
19	Profit or loss for the year		×

Items 7 and 8 refer to income from subsidiaries and associates (7) and other forms of investment income where the investments are classified as fixed assets (8). Any amounts included in items (7), (8), (9) or (11) that are derived from affiliated undertakings (subsidiaries or associates) must be disclosed separately.

Valuation rules

The directive requires that the historical cost convention be used, together with the going concern and prudence concepts (as defined by SSAP 2). Provision must be made for all liabilities and for depreciation, but unrealised profits, must not be taken up. (Unrealised profits must, if accounted for, be classed as undistributable and transferred to revaluation reserve.) Goodwill and other intangible assets must be written off within five years, but member states may allow longer periods. Current assets must be valued at the lower of cost and net realisable value.

Notes to accounts

A director's report must give a fair review of the year and of post balance sheet events. The accounts should include notes explaining valuation methods, the makeup of share capital, long-term and secured debt, financial commitments the analysis of turnover, directors emoluments, and the average number of employees by category. Details of companies in which a greater than 20% stake is held are required similar to those already required by the UK Companies Acts and by SSAP 14. These requirements do not in general exceed current UK practice.

Inflation Accounting

Inflation accounting is permitted if member states inform the EEC Commission that they require it. Revaluation surpluses may not be distributed until realised and historical cost figures must continue to be given.

20.11 The Seventh directive

The Seventh directive requires that consolidated accounts be prepared for groups of companies. The directive was not finalised in 1980 but is unlikely to differ significantly from IAS 3 or SSAP 14. The definition of a group may include the concept of an 'economic group', where management control is the key, as well as the normal legal concept of a group based on ownership of shares.

There may be a requirement for 'EEC consolidated accounts where a non-EEC company has subsidiaries in the EEC. This would be a new departure in financial reporting and would mainly affect US, Japanese, Swiss and Swedish multinational companies. However, exemption may be granted where fully consolidated accounts are prepared by the holding company in a suitable form.

The directive will follow the layout and presentation rules of the Fourth directive, and will prescribe the same rules for goodwill on consolidation as for purchased goodwill. Associated companies will be accounted for on the equity method (as required by ED 25). The directive is not expected to lead to any significant changes in current UK practice.

PART 6

The Interpretation, Scope and Limits of Financial Accounts

21

The Interpretation of Accounts

For many accountants, financial reporting is an end in itself, but for others the accounts of an enterprise are a means to an end. They are used to help make decisions relating to the enterprise, and the information that can be derived may be crucial. For example, shares may be bought or sold according to the impression of a company's prospects given in the accounts; a bank may advance a loan on the strength of the balance sheet position; the sums paid in a take-over will often be calculated according to the net assets disclosed in the accounts.

Merely reading the accounts will produce useful information, but a more systematic approach can yield better results. The art of interpretation lies in the analysis of the accounts and background of an enterprise, producing a perspective on the figures which is not available to the casual reader. Interpretation means recasting the accounts to obtain insights into the position and management of the company, and in particular comparing the results with those of other entities, preferably in similar circumstances. It is not possible to ascertain from one Annual Report if the results are 'good' or 'bad' without reference to a measure of what is good. Comparisons provide such a measure.

In order to compare financial results, the most useful approach is to compute certain ratios which, by converting absolute figures into relative figures, allow direct comparisons to be made. Thus, in examining profitability it is of little value to know that company X earned £5m and Y £10m. But, if we know that X employed capital of £50m and Y £150m, so that X has generated a return of 10% compared to Y's 6·7%, a conclusion as to which is the more efficient can be drawn. The *ratio* of profitability is more useful than the absolute figure.

Ratio analysis can answer many questions about relative performance, but it cannot go beyond the accounts themselves. Financial accounts do not answer the most important question: what will happen in the period to come? They are confined to reporting on the immediate past. Ratio analysis can pick out trends which aid an understanding of the nature of the enterprise—its vulnerability to shifts in economic conditions, its ability to maintain profit margins *etc.*—but only a general impression of the future can be obtained in this way.

It should be emphasised that the technique is valuable only in so far as it allows questions to be answered. There is no point in computing ratios if a mass of figures is to be produced which add nothing to the understanding. The analyst decides what he needs to know before examining the sources of information in search of the answer.

Interpretation is limited by the nature of accounting techniques. Flexibility in the selection of accounting policies has hampered analysis in the past. Accounting standards are beginning to correct this deficiency and the disclosure of policies, required by SSAP 2 enables ratios to be adjusted where policies differ, so that the comparisons are realistic. One major defect of conventional accounting—the use of the historic cost convention—which rendered comparisons almost impossible between businesses, should be removed by the introduction of current cost accounting.

The theme of the limits of conventional accounting is resumed in Chapter 24 which discusses 'The Corporate Report'. Its recommendations are an attempt to break out of these limits by extending the range of information provided in financial reports.

Chapter 22 deals with ratio analysis and Chapter 23 with funds flow statements, which are now widely used to examine the sources of finance, and the way in which funds have been invested over the past accounting period, using the information to build a picture of future financing requirements.

Although ratio analysis and funds flow statements are produced using the financial accounts, other sources of information are useful in interpretation. The accounts of other enterprises indicate general trends in the particular sector of the economy under review. Press reports and specialist publications will fill in background information and indicate future developments. Economic surveys by government and private bodies can explain the factors influencing the financial results. The chairman's statement in the annual report of a public company is often highly informative. Discriminating use of such sources can add flesh to the dry bones of figures and allow financial accounts to develop a mere classified list of numbers into an authentic representation of the workings of an enterprise.

22

Ratio Analysis

Ratio analysis is a three step process:

1. The analyst must decide what he needs to know, and must then formulate the precise questions which will provide the required information.
2. The data which will answer the questions must be prepared and ratios computed, where needed.
3. The ratios and other data must be compared with data from other times and/or other companies, and conclusions drawn.

The questions usually asked about an enterprise, which can be answered from information in financial accounts, concern:

Efficiency—How has the enterprise used its resources?
Solvency—How financially sound is the enterprise?
Gearing—How is the enterprise financed and how are the financial rewards shared?
Investment potential—How profitable will an investment in the enterprise be, and how has it grown in the past?

22.1 Measures of efficiency

1. Rate of return on capital employed
In a free market economy, a business enterprise is expected to earn profits and the measure of success is the rate of return on the capital investment. The concept of 'rate of return' is used not only in appraising past performance but in allocating funds to new investment projects. The problem is to decide which figure of profit and which measure of

capital are appropriate. There are several figures of profit presented in the typical profit and loss account, including operating profits, pre-tax profit after interest, post-tax profit before extraordinary items *etc.* Capital can comprise shareholders' funds, shareholders' funds plus long-term loans, the same plus bank overdrafts *etc.* However, the most useful ratio is usually,

$$\frac{\text{Operating profit (before interest and taxation)}}{\text{Capital employed (total assets less current liabilities)}}$$

Two problems, common in ratio analysis, can be illustrated from Ratio 1:

(a) *The basis of comparison:* profits comprise a flow of income and expenditure generated during a time period. Capital is measured at a point in time. The rate of return will vary according to when capital is measured—at the start, or the end, or as an average over the period. Furthermore, because capital itself grows as profits are earned, if an average is to be used it should, in theory, be weighted to allow for the increments of profit. However, for convenience either the opening or closing values of capital employed are usually selected, and provided that the figure chosen is used consistently there should be no significant distortions when comparing one ratio with another.

(b) *Comparing like with like:* as both profit and capital comprise several diverse elements, it is essential that complementary figures are used; thus, if profits before interest are taken, then all interest-bearing liabilities should be included as capital employed. If the return to shareholders is to be computed, then the profit available for distribution should be compared. The formula for this ratio, also known as the *return on investment* (*R.O.I.*)

$$\frac{\text{profit (after interest and tax)}}{\text{shareholders' funds (share capital plus reserves)}}$$

The return on investment is an important indicator of the ability of the business to earn a satisfactory return. If (say) the R.O.I. was 10% at a time when interest rates were 15% and inflation 18% (a situation experienced by many UK companies in the 1979–80 recession) then the business would be seen to be doing badly and shareholders would do well to consider either changing their investment or changing the management.

2. Net profit ratio (net margin)
The rate of return compares profit to the funds used to generate it. But profits are earned through trading and the profitability of trading has significance as an indicator of the efficiency of one enterprise compared to another, and of market conditions. The *gross profit ratio* should be used, where feasible, since it relates sales to the cost of goods sold. In contrast the *net profit ratio* includes overhead expenses which are not directly related to turnover and which therefore obscure the figures for trading profitability. But since published company accounts do not normally disclose gross profits, the net profit ratio is the closest approximation, and is computed by

$$\frac{\text{Operating profit (before interest and taxation)}}{\text{Turnover}}$$

3. Capital turnover ratio
A third basic measure of efficiency is the *capital turnover ratio*:

$$\frac{\text{Turnover}}{\text{Capital employed}}$$

This ratio is identical to ratio 1. divided by ratio 2. and provides nothing new in itself. However, it emphasises the second aspect of profitability, which is that a high rate of return requires either a high gross profit ratio or a high rate of turnover relative to capital employed. Both factors together determine the rate of return on capital, thus:

$$\frac{\text{Operating profit}}{\text{Turnover}} \times \frac{\text{Turnover}}{\text{Capital}} = \frac{\text{Operating profit}}{\text{Capital}}$$

4–6. Labour efficiency ratios
In addition, the efficiency of a business in using labour—or its ability to reward its employees more handsomely than competing enterprises—can be measured. Information in

the director's report provides the raw data for the following:

4. *Average pay per employee* $\dfrac{\text{Total remuneration}}{\text{Average number of employees}}$

5. *Sales per employee* $\dfrac{\text{Turnover}}{\text{Average number of employees}}$

6. *Profit per employee* $\dfrac{\text{Operating profit}}{\text{Average number of employees}}$

The ratio of sales per employee is the most useful of these as it indicates the relative productivity of the business. Comparisons between different businesses must be used with care (since, *e.g.* retailers will sell more per employee than manufacturers) but in evaluating the performance of firms in the same industry, the ratio of sales per employee is a good measure of which business is most productive (*i.e.* which produces the greatest output from a given labour force).

22.2 Measures of solvency

A business fails when it cannot pay its debts. The ratio of assets to liabilities indicates how easily debts can be paid, but some assets or liabilities are not, and do not need to be, quickly realisable. The time periods to consider are the present, the short-term (usually meaning within a year) and the medium or long-term.

7. *Quick assets ratio*
The 'quick ratio' compares current liabilities to those assets quickly realisable. Stocks and work in progress are usually left out on the grounds that they may not be realised, but finished goods could legitimately be included. This ratio, also known as the 'acid test' is:

$$\dfrac{\text{Quick assets (cash, marketable investments and debtors)}}{\text{Current liabilities}}$$

8. *Current assets/liabilities ratio*
In practice, current liabilities do not all need payment at once and a business can be expected to realise its stocks in

the near future at least at the value at which they are stated in the balance sheet. The usual test of solvency is therefore:

$$\frac{\text{Current assets}}{\text{Current liabilities}}$$

This ratio is an important indicator of the ability of a business to meet its debts. For this reason businesses sometimes 'window-dress' their accounts by trying to raise the ratio of current assets to liabilities—for example, by borrowing cash and treating the borrowing as a long-term liability. Bank overdrafts are sometimes shown as long-term liabilities, thus reducing the amount shown as current liabilities. In recent years, many businesses have encountered cash-flow problems and current ratios have fallen to lower levels than was once thought reasonable.

The Ratios 7.–8. measure assets against liabilities. Ratios 9.–11. analyse the relationship between trading and working capital and thus reveal factors contributing to solvency.

9. Stock/turnover ratio

$$\frac{\text{Stocks}}{\text{Turnover}}$$

This shows how quickly the stocks are being turned over and suggests how long it will take for existing stocks to be realised. A better ratio would be

$$\frac{\text{Stocks}}{\text{Actual cost of stocks sold}}$$

thus eliminating fluctuations in the ratio that might be caused by changes in selling prices or in the composition of the cost of goods sold (*e.g.* direct labour costs included in the make-up of the cost of sales might alter relative to the cost of stocks). However, it is not normal for the cost of stocks sold to be disclosed and the stock/turnover ratio must be used as an approximation.

10. Debtors/turnover ratio

$$\frac{\text{Debtors}}{\text{Turnover}}$$

This is a measure of the company's credit control and shows how much cash is tied up in debtors and is not therefore available for other pruposes. Stock turnover is a crude measure in that stocks may not vary directly (*e.g.* profit margins may alter) with turnover, but as debtors derive directly from sales it is appropriate to compare the two.

11. Creditors/purchases (turnover)
If a business is in cash difficulties, it may delay payment of suppliers. This will be indicated by

$$\frac{\text{Trade creditors}}{\text{Purchases}}$$

but in practice figures for purchases are not disclosed. However, where gross profits are known, and competitors have a shrewd idea of the normal profit margin, they may be able to estimate the purchases figure from the profit and loss account. Alternatively, turnover can be used and should give reasonable comparisons over time, although not between different businesses.

Note that these ratios measure a balance sheet item at the year end against a flow during the year. A better comparison is derived from using average stock, debtor and creditor levels during the year. Working estimates of these can be obtained by taking the arithmetical average of the opening and closing figures in the balance sheet. Such an approach assumes that stocks do not fluctuate unduly in the year. If stocks alter significantly during the year, and details are not available the stock/turnover ratio ceases to be useful.

Ratios 9.–11. are often expressed in months and computed by multiplying the ratio by 12. Thus, debtors of £40,000 and turnover of £120,000 give a debtors ratio of 0·33. Multiplication by 12 produces 4 months as the average period of credit given to debtors. This ratio may be of particular interest if the stated terms of credit are, say, 1 month. Is there a breakdown in credit control, or are the business's customers in difficulty? The analyst often finds that ratios raise more questions than they answer, but the questions will usually be relevant and should be pursued.

22.3 Measures of gearing

A business may be financed by risk capital—(shareholders' funds or owners' capital)—or by fixed return capital (preference shares, debentures or other loans). The relationship between them is of major importance, because profit attributable to risk capital is computed *after* deducting payments made or due to holders of fixed return capital. A good year's trading will not alter the fixed deductions, and the risk capital will do well. A poor year might leave nothing for risk capital after the fixed charges have been deducted

Example 1
Rock Ltd and Roll Ltd are identical businesses, except that Rock is wholly financed by £20,000 of ordinary share capital and Roll is financed by a £10,000 loan, bearing interest at 10%, and £10,000 ordinary share capital. The results for the years 1977, 1978 and 1979, during which the capital of the two businesses is unchanged, are:

1977	**Rock**	**Roll**
Operating profit	2,000	2,000
Less interest	—	1,000
Net profit	2,000	1,000
Return on share capital	10%	10%

1978		
Operating profit	5,000	5,000
Less interest	—	1,000
Net profit	5,000	4,000
Return on share capital	25%	40%

1979		
Operating profit	1,500	1,500
Less interest	—	1,000
Net profit	1,500	500
Return on share capital	$7\frac{1}{2}$%	5%

The example shows that the fluctuations of the shareholders' rate of return are greater for the more highly geared company (Roll), because of the smaller amount of shareholders' capital against which profits are compared, and because of the importance of the interest charge which has the first claim on profits.

An understanding of the gearing of a business is crucial to the analysis of future profits and risks. The ratios summarising gearing are of two types, income and capital.

12. Income gearing

The income ratio compares the shares of shareholders and others in the profits available. Thus, if there are debentures as well as shares in a company the income ratio is

$$\frac{\text{Interest}}{\text{Net profit before interest and taxation}}$$

13. Capital gearing

The capital ratio compares the values of shareholders' funds and borrowings. Sometimes the nominal values of issued shares and debentures are used, but such comparisons are meaningless; the value of a share or debenture is the price it would fetch in an open market, and to assess the importance of the financial structure market values must be used.

$$\frac{\text{Market value of debentures (and preference shares)}}{\text{Market value of equity shares}}$$

The above ratio is suitable for a quoted company. For an unquoted company the book amounts as shown in the balance sheet may have to be used, in the absence of more relevant values. If book amounts are used, reserves should be added to the issued share capital so that the comparison is between shareholders' interests and the interest of the holders of fixed interest securities. In general terms, the higher the ratio of gearing (12.), the greater the degree of risk attaching to equity shareholders. At one end of the scale is the possibility of receiving all of the increase in profits (since fixed capital receives a fixed payout even if profits rise); at the other end is the risk of making no profit at all if profits are less than is necessary to maintain the fixed payouts (whereas a firm with low gearing would allocate most of its profit to equity shareholders).

22.4 Measures of investment potential

14. Earnings per share

The computation of earnings per share was given in Chapter 20. This ratio shows how earnings have changed over time and provides the basis for the standard stock exchange comparison of price earnings ratios. Earnings per share is computed by

$$\frac{\text{Profits after tax and preference dividends, before extraordinary items}}{\text{Number of shares entitled to participate in dividends}}$$

15. Price/earnings ratio (P/E)

$$\frac{\text{Market price of a share}}{\text{Earnings per share}}$$

It may be instructive to compare the earnings per share with net assets per share and the latter with the price. When the market price is below the figure of net assets, the company is in effect valued in the market at less than the values of the assets it is using in the business, and a takeover with the object of selling off the assets (asset stripping) may result. One of the virtues of a free market economy is said to be that efficiency is promoted by the more efficient companies taking over, or squeezing out through competition, the less efficient. The ratios of earnings and assets help to distinguish the inefficient from the efficient.

The P/E ratio is the market's estimate of future growth: the faster the earnings of a company are expected to grow, the higher the ratio, because the price is paid in expectation of future earnings. There is no comparable ratio for unquoted companies and for unincorporated businesses, and analysis tends to be limited to assessing past trends. With quoted companies, the past is still the main guide to the future but company statements are much more forthcoming about prospects, and in any case the P/E ratio provides the views of other people, who may have made a study of the company or the industry in which it operates. If other investors' opinions are desired, the P/E ratio, calculated on the latest market price of the shares, provides this in an encapsulated form.

16. Growth ratios

In addition, the investment potential may be expressed through the expected growth of the business. In the absence of profit forecasts, the analyst must use background information on the industry supplemented with an understanding of past performance. The rates of growth in such indicators as sales and profits will be useful, particularly if available for several years, thus pinpointing fluctuations previously experienced which might recur. Growth rates are computed thus:

$$\frac{\text{Present year} - \text{last year}}{\text{Last year}} \times 100$$

General example

The following ratios illustrate the mechanics of computation. They are drawn from the example of the current cost accounts of Z Ltd. in chapter 14.

Ratio		£000	Notes Item in accounts
1. Rate of return	6·6%	2,080	CC profit before interest
		13,528	Capital employed (see note 3 p. 178)
2. Profit/turnover	3·25%	2,080	
		64,000	
3. Turnover/capital	2·03	64,000	
		31,528	
Nos. 4–6 are not given			
7. Quick ratio	1·35	13,500	Cash and debtors
		10,000	Current liabilities
8. Current ratio	2·17	21,720	Current assets (includes stock at current cost)
		10,000	Current liabilities
9. Stock/turnover	1·54 mths	8,220 × 12	
		64,000	
10. Debtors/turnover	1·97 mths	10,500 × 12	
		64,000	

Ratio			£000	Notes Item in accounts
11. Creditors/turnover	1·12 mths		$6,000 \times 12$	
			64,000	
12. Income gearing	48%		1,000	Interest (before gearing adjustment)
			2,080	
13. Capital gearing	35%		8,000	Loan and stock overdraft
			23,528	Shareholders' Funds
14. Earnings per share	18·4p		1,290	CC profit after tax
			7,000	Average share capital in year (shares are assumed £1 each)

23

Funds Flow Accounting

23.1 The need for funds flow statements

A balance sheet shows the assets and liabilities of a business at a point in time. The profit and loss account explains why the total of net assets has changed. What is not shown is how the composition of assets and liabilities has changed during the year, and the extent to which the changes are created by the inflow of profits or by other factors. It became apparent in the late 1960s that many users of accounts were confused by the distinction between profits and cash, and it was widely believed that a profitable company must be building cash balances. This was sadly shown to be untrue in the case of many companies which did not pay sufficient attention to the finance of their businesses and concentrated on book profits without ensuring adequate finance to support the profit-making activities. Inevitably they became insolvent and were wound up. One distinction between profits and cash that was not recognised was the consequence of investing in fixed assets. Only part of the capital cost (depreciation) is treated as an expense in the accounts, but full payment must be made when the assets are acquired. A profitable company can face a crisis if it does not have the cash to re-equip.

The funds flow statement is a way of classifying the cash movements that have taken place in the past year and thus shows the sources of past finance and suggests the relative importance of those sources for future needs. It does not normally show anything not already contained in the accounts, but presents certain information in a more useful form than the normal balance sheet format.

23.2 The preparation of a funds flow statement

The preparation of a funds flow statement requires two steps:

(*a*) The calculation and listing of the movements on each item in the balance sheet; and

(*b*) The presentation of this information in a manner helpful to users of the accounts.

Step (*b*) is often disregarded by students, for whom the paramount need seems to be to list all the balance sheet movements and show that they sum to zero as a proof of their arithmetical ability. However, it requires little skill to subtract one year's figure from the next. If the funds flow statement merely reproduces these differences, it is valueless. It should inform the reader and draw attention to matters that might otherwise have been missed.

The purpose of the suggested layout in SSAP 10 is to highlight the way in which the business has been able to finance its needs from its own funds and from funds created by its trading operations during the year, in contrast to its need to borrow from external sources or to raise more capital from its owners. However, a different layout may be felt by some accountants to be a clearer presentation of the same financing position, and others may prefer to use the funds statement to highlight other features of the operations of the business. SSAP 10 does not specify a layout. A specimen is provided in an appendix to the statement, which it is hoped will be of general use, but it is in no way binding. The essential requirement is that the funds statement provide a true and fair view.

In Example 2 (see page 296) the layout suggested in SSAP 10 is followed, but the reader is recommended to compare this with the funds statements reproduced at the end of this chapter.

23.3 The classification of sources and applications

The first step is to calculate the movement on each item and to classify each as a source or an application of funds. A source of funds is any item which has provided cash. Thus, if the trade debtors figure has fallen, on balance the business must have received cash from those debtors who have reduced their debts. If trade debtors have risen, it is likely, on balance, that sales have taken place which have not been paid for. This is effectively a form of finance provided by the business—it has incurred the costs of producing the goods sold but has not received payment. Thus, an increase in debtors is an application (sometimes called a 'use'), of funds.

Conversely, if creditors have risen in value over the year, the business is increasing its borrowings. At all times creditors represent a source of finance: an increase in the amount owing to creditors is therefore a source of funds in the year. A decrease will be an application of funds since it represents a repayment of debts.

Any asset which has risen in value on the balance sheet between one date and the next is deemed to have been acquired by the business in exchange for cash (an application). If an asset has been reduced, the business is deemed to have received the amount of the reduction in cash (a source). If a liability is reduced, it is assumed that cash has been applied, and if a liability is increased the business is assumed to have received cash from that source.

The major source of funds will normally be profit. All profits are assumed to be sources of funds. If the transactions which have earned the profits are credit transactions, then the profit is still a source of funds, but as debtors will have increased, that will provide a corresponding application of funds.

The same principles apply to cash and overdrafts. If the business builds up its cash balance, it is using its available funds to do so and this is an application of funds. A reduction in an overdraft is also an application of funds (the bank is being paid off by cash obtained from some other source) and vice versa. There are two special points to be noted, which often cause confusion:

(a) *Non-cash items:* the purpose of a funds statement is to show those transactions which either give rise to an immediate movement of funds or which directly alter assets or liabilities (and are therefore deemed to be equivalent to a movement of funds, *e.g.* sales on credit). However, there will usually be some items in the accounts which do not correspond to movements of cash. These include depreciation, other provisions charged to special accounts, such as warranty provisions, deferred tax and the amortisation of research and development expenditure. These items affect the profit figure reported in the accounts, but the liabilities set up in the accounts represent internal adjustments and not the creation of external liabilities. They are not therefore true sources or applications of funds. Such items, usually called 'items not involving the use of funds' are, in the funds statement, added back to the net profit figure, if charges, or subtracted, if credits.

(b) *Tax and dividend payments:* these two items are selected by SSAP 10 for special treatment. It is recommended that the profit should be shown in the funds statement before deducting tax or dividend charges for the year. The tax and/or dividends actually paid during the year should be shown as an application of funds. Because it is the amount paid which is shown in the statement, the movements in the tax or dividend creditors are not shown. This is illustrated in the following example.

Example 1

In Year 1 a business earns £20,000 profit and its cash balance rises by that amount. £10,000 is deducted for tax. In Year 2 £25,000 profit is made and £12,000 then deducted for tax. The £10,000 tax from Year 1 is paid during Year 2.

Following the SSAP 10 presentation, the funds statement in Year 2 will show profit before tax of £25,000 and tax paid of £10,000, giving a net source of funds of £15,000. This will equal the increase in the cash balance for the year. The increase of £2,000 in the tax creditor is ignored because the source of funds—profit—is taken before tax.

Some accountants would prefer to put the figure of profit after tax into the funds statement, ignore the tax payment and show the change in the tax creditor. SSAP 10 allows this alternative treatment, but requires that profit before dividends be shown; consequently, the dividends paid in the year must be shown, with the change in creditors for dividends ignored. The reason may be that dividends (and perhaps tax) are regarded as payments within the discretion of management, so that the actual payments in the year are more relevant in understanding the financing of the business than a consideration of the amounts accrued.

23.4 General illustration

Example 2

The Balance Sheets of the Atlantic Tunnel Company Ltd for the years ending 31 December 1977 and 1978 are as follows:

	1978 £	1977 £
Assets employed		
Fixed assets at cost	40,000	30,000
Depreciation	16,000	12,000
	24,000	18,000
Current assets		
Stocks	25,000	15,000
Debtors	20,000	10,000
Cash	1,000	10,000
	46,000	35,000
Current liabilities		
Creditors	10,000	15,000
Taxation	14,000	10,000
Dividend	10,000	5,000
	34,000	30,000
Net current assets	12,000	5,000
Financed by	36,000	23,000
Share capital	20,000	10,000
Retained profits	16,000	13,000
	36,000	23,000

Pre-tax profits for 1978 were £27,000.

Notes: The taxation and dividend outstanding in 1977 were paid during 1978. No fixed assets were disposed of during 1978.

Procedure: The differences between items in one year's balance sheet and the next are listed.

The Atlantic Tunnel Company Ltd
Sources and applications of funds—worksheet

Item	1977 £	1978 £	Change £	Source £	Application £
Fixed Assets	30,000	40,000	10,000		10,000
Depreciation	12,000	16,000	4,000	4,000	
Stocks	15,000	25,000	10,000		10,000
Debtors	10,000	20,000	10,000		10,000
Cash	10,000	1,000	9,000	9,000	
Creditors	15,000	10,000	5,000		5,000
Taxation	10,000	14,000	see note		10,000
Dividend	5,000	10,000	see note		5,000
Share capital	10,000	20,000	10,000	10,000	
Profit (before tax or dividend)	—	27,000	27,000	27,000	
				50,000	50,000

Note: Profit has been taken before tax or dividend. The tax and dividend creditors are therefore ignored, and the amounts actually paid are inserted as applications. The total of sources equals the total of applications, proving the arithmetical accuracy of the calculations.

Example 2: Solution

The Atlantic Tunnel Company Ltd
*Statement of sources and applications
of funds for the year ending 31 December 1978*

	£
Sources of funds	
Profit before tax	27,000
Adjustment for item not involving the use of funds—depreciation	4,000
Total generated from operations	31,000
Funds from other sources:	
Issue of shares	10,000
	41,000

Application of funds		
Dividend paid	5,000	
Tax paid	10,000	
Purchase of fixed assets	10,000	
		25,000
		16,000
Increase/decrease in working capital		
Increase in stocks	10,000	
Increase in debtors	10,000	
Decrease in creditors	5,000	
		25,000
Movement in net liquid funds		
Decrease in cash		(9,000)
		16,000

The layout used is designed to bring out the difference between funds generated internally—profits—and long-term external sources, such as new issues of shares, and to distinguish between long-term applications—investment in fixed assets, tax or dividend payments—and short-term changes in working capital (net current assets). In particular, SSAP 10 recommends showing the change in net liquid funds separately from other changes in working capital. For this purpose, net liquid funds means cash-in-hand and cash equivalents (*i.e.* investments held as current assets) less overdrafts and other borrowings repayable within one year.

23.5 The interpretation of funds flow statements

The uses of funds flow statements can be illustrated with an example from the Atlantic Tunnel Company. In 1978 the company has managed to generate internally most of the funds required but has also needed to raise a substantial sum through an increase in share capital. The tax and dividend payments have bitten deeply into the profits, and the share issue was necessary to finance the purchase of fixed assets. Working capital has increased significantly, and while stocks and debtors have risen, creditors have been reduced. The company has run down its cash balances to finance these operations.

Some conclusions can be drawn from this sketchy analysis. If the company tries to expand its fixed assets and working capital at a similar rate in the future it will run into serious financing problems. An overdraft may be required, the interest on which would reduce future net profits. Share capital has been increased this year, but it may not be possible to increase it again in the future, particularly if profits are cut by interest payments. Meanwhile the dividend proposed for 1978 is double that of 1977. The company is committing itself to a payment which at present it cannot meet from existing funds. Perhaps it should think again about the dividend; there may also be scope for financing future activities by a higher level of creditors.

It should be noted that these comments are based on a study of the funds flow statement and the balance sheet; the funds flow by itself is of little use. The art of interpretation lies in relating the movements to the actual position reached and in evaluating future needs for resources against the resources available now. The funds flow statement does not predict the future, of course, although companies may eventually issue their estimates of future financing needs and resources. This would greatly assist users of accounts who at present can only guess at the future with the aid of information about the immediate past.

23.6 Further points

(a) *Group funds flow statements:* there is no difference in principle between a simple funds flow statement and one produced for a large group of companies. The consolidated accounts are used as the source of figures and the only additional items will be minority interests, associates *etc*. The deductions made in the consolidated profit and loss account for the share of minorities and for profits retained in associates should be treated as non-cash items, and added back. Goodwill acquired during the year of acquisition of a subsidiary is equivalent to an increase in fixed assets.

(b) *The disposal of assets:* when fixed assets or investments are disposed of, it is customary to show the book value as the source of funds, rather than the proceeds of the disposal. Should the proceeds differ from the book value, the difference will already have been dealt with through the profit and loss account. If the intent is to keep the figures in the funds statement virtually unchanged from the accounts, this is the right procedure. But, and this is surely a more useful presentation, if it is desired to show the proceeds as the source of funds, the profit or loss on disposal will have to be respectively subtracted from, or added to the profit figure, which will cease to be identical to that in the profit and loss account. SSAP 10 does not offer a ruling on this point.

(c) *Extraordinary items*: the profit figure is struck after any extraordinary items, so that they can be ignored in the funds statement if desired. But the statement will be of greater use if the trading profit and extraordinary items are shown separately as the constituents of the profit before tax. As with the disposal of assets, presentation remains a matter of choice.

23.7 SSAP 10 *Statements of sources and applications of funds*

The statement provides a very short section explaining the necessity for funds statements: 'The funds statement is in no way a replacement for the profit and loss account and balance sheet, although the information which it contains is a selection, reclassification and summarisation of the information contained in those two statements. The objective . . . is to show the manner in which the operations of a company have been financed and in which its financial resources have been used.'

The statement calls for a minimum of 'netting off', as this can mask the significance of individual figures; for example, it is potentially misleading to net off the purchase and sale of a building if the building itself is a material item. It is more revealing to show that the purchase was financed by the sale, and this is done by showing the two figures separately.

When a subsidiary is acquired, or a business taken over during the year, the statement allows alternative forms of presentation. One is simply to show the changes between one year's balance sheet and the next in the usual way; the alternative is to show the acquisition as a single item, as though it were the purchase of an investment, and to extract the net assets acquired from the closing balance sheet. In both cases it is recommended that the actual assets and liabilities obtained and the consideration for the acquisition be shown in a footnote, so that the effect of the purchase on the financial state of the group may be seen.

SSAP 10 recommends that certain items be shown in a specific way. For example, a funds statement could show net profit after tax or dividend, or net profit before such items with deductions for the amounts payable; a third treatment is to deduct any cash actually paid during the period, and to ignore creditors for tax and dividends. All three methods are dealing with the same transactions, but SSAP 10 requires that dividends be shown as to the amount *paid*, not *payable*; in an example in an appendix (which, unlike the statement itself, is not binding) it shows net profit before tax, and the tax paid, as separate items. Oddly enough, ED 13, which was the basis for SSAP 10, showed net profit after tax.

SSAP 10 also requires that the acquisition and disposal of fixed and other non-current assets, funds raised or expended on medium or long-term loan, changes in the share capital, and the change in the main components of working capital be shown as separate figures. Within the category of working capital, the movement on net liquid funds (defined as cash at bank and in hand, and cash equivalents such as investments held as current assets less bank overdrafts and other borrowings repayable within one year) is shown separately. The examples given as appendices to SSAP 10 make it clear what the ASC had in mind, and the layout recommended is that used in the example above.

Finally, the previous year's figures are to be shown in the statement of sources and applications of funds.

23.8 SSAP 10 in practice

SSAP 10 has aroused criticism. There are those who believe it should not have tried to lay down a standard format and others who prefer even more standardisation, to make statements more easily comparable. The layout shown on page 296, which follows the SSAP 10 recommendation, has not been universally adopted. Some companies have used the funds flow statement to bring in information not shown in the statutory accounts; others have altered the SSAP 10 layout to improve the presentation. Examples of these alternative approaches follow.

Exhibits 1 and 2 comply with the requirements of SSAP 10, while using a different presentation to that suggested. Courtaulds give a two-part statement. The first part is a value-added statement which shows how trading funds are generated and distributed, while the second part, '*Funds were required for . . . Funds were provided by*' is the main funds flow statement. The Corporate Report (see Chapter 24) recommends that value-added statements be presented with annual accounts. Courtaulds' synthesis of the value-added and the funds statement is an original layout, which

EXHIBIT 1

Courtaulds Limited
Report and Accounts for the year ending 31 March 1977
Source and Use of Funds

Year ended 31 March	£m	1977 £m	£m	1976 £m
Sales income		1,510·3		1,166·3
Less bought-in materials and services		906·5		673·0
Value added		603·8		493·3
Less payable in respect of:				
Wages, pensions and social security contributions	437·1		380·8	
Interest on borrowed money less income from investments	21·8		10·0	
Taxation	19·9		15·2	
Minority shareholders	7·8		6·9	
Extraordinary items (credit in 1976)	8·1		(2·1)	
Dividends	18·5		16·8	
		513·2		427·6
Funds available from trading		90·6		65·7
Funds were required from				
Investment in factories and equipment		96·0		103·4
Increase in working capital (Note 1)		85·1		66·6
Acquisitions and other assets (net)		5·4		5·8
		186·5		175·8
Funds were provided by:				
Funds available from trading (note 2)		90·6		65·7
New borrowings		29·9		31·5
Issue of shares		—		3·1
Other receipts *etc.*		3·5		1·7
Reducing balances at bank and on deposit		62·5		73·8
		186·5		175·8

Notes
1. Increase in working capital comprises:

Stocks	61·3	75·2
Debtors	67·4	33·8
	128·7	109·0
Less: creditors, taxation and dividends	43·6	42·4
	85·1	66·6

2. Funds available from trading comprise:

Profit retained	26·6	9·5
Depreciation	64·0	56·2
	90·6	65·7

EXHIBIT 2

Scottish & Newcastle Breweries Limited
Annual Report and Accounts for the 53 weeks ended 2 May 1976
Group Funds Statement

	Group	
	1976	*1975*
	£000	£000
Net inflow of funds		
Profit before taxation	30,938	22,748
Deduct the following items to the extent that they involve an outflow of cash:		
Taxation	(4,536)	(8,619)
Dividends	(8,971)	(3,926)
Adjust for items which do not involve a cash movement:		
Depreciation of fixed and other assets	9,315	8,277
Associated companies	(974)	(725)
Other items	(454)	(656)
Proceeds of the rights issue net of expenses	20,985	—
	46,303	17,099
Net outflow of funds		
Increase in working capital balances excluding taxation and dividends, net of bank overdrafts	10,118	12,925
Additions to investments, less sales	135	2,485
Loans advanced to customers, less repayments	158	2,385
Fixed and other assets:		
Additions at cost	12,025	18,116
Less sales	(2,657)	(2,734)
Less Government grants	(612)	(1,072)
Redemption of debenture capital	2,952	619
Other items	400	123
	22,519	32,847
The surplus (deficit) of net inflow of funds over outflow is reflected in:		
Increase in cash	24,457	854
Less increase in borrowings	(673)	(16,602)
	23,784	(15,748)

puts each into perspective and broadens the narrower approach of SSAP 10.

Scottish & Newcastle Breweries have presented a funds statement which is more logically related to the way a company finances its activities than that suggested by SSAP 10. Tax and dividend payments are deducted directly from trading profits. Other sources are then added to show the net inflow of funds. The additions to working capital are shown to be as significant an outflow of funds as the additions to fixed assets. The change in cash and in borrowings are the balancing items between the inflow and outflow of funds.

The exhibits illustrate aspects of the criticism of SSAP 10. Should the funds statement merely summarise the balance sheet movements, as SSAP 10 suggests? Should it be the source of information not at present contained in the accounts (Exhibit 1)? Or should it focus on the essential features of the financial position as in Exhibit 2?

The wording of SSAP 10, 'the funds statement will provide a link between the balance sheet at the beginning of the period, the profit and loss account for the period and the balance sheet at the end of the period', provides for no more than a funds statement which subtracts one balance sheet figure from another. Yet if different information is given, the statement will not be easily reconciled to the rest of the accounts and the reader may become confused as to which figures are correct. It could be argued that if important information is given in the funds statement, it ought to appear in the accounts as part of, or a note to, the profit and loss account or the balance sheet.

In addition to the major differences of opinion about the role of published funds statements, there are some minor problems. Although a minimum of netting off was called for, (though only in the explanatory note) this practice remains common. The question of whether the ASC prefer profit to be shown before or after tax is not completely clear. There is no guidance given as to whether disposals should be at book value (with profits or losses absorbed in the general profit and loss figure), or whether such disposals should be shown at the amount actually realised. Although SSAP 10 wants group accounts to be used where appropriate (rather than the balance sheet of the parent company) it does not suggest how minority interests are to be treated.

Time will provide generally accepted solutions. The student is advised to base answers on the SSAP 10 layout but to be aware of the alternatives and the criticisms. The practitioner is, of course, free to choose the layout he prefers; but he should remember that a funds statement is meant as an aid to interpretation of accounts and not as an exercise in erudite accounting technique.

24

The Uses and Limitations of Accounts

This chapter brings together some of the themes of the book. It discusses the uses of financial accounts, with reference to the various groups of users distinguished in The Corporate Report; it brings out the limitations of accounts prepared according to existing practices and legal requirements, and suggests the path that future developments in financial reporting might take.

24.1 The Corporate Report

The working party, set up by the ASC in October 1974 under the chairmanship of Derek Boothman, took a wide view of their subject—'the scope and aims of published financial statements'. At the heart of their recommendations in The Corporate Report lies a general assumption: that the fundamental objective of corporate reports is 'to communicate economic measurements of and information about the resources and performance of the reporting entity useful to those having reasonable rights to such information'.

This judgement is significant. For many years it has been thought that financial reports should be produced solely for the benefit of the owners of a business. The respect for private property, which is so important a feature of Western societies, has always tended to keep public disclosure of financial reports down to a minimum. As an example, partnerships do not have to publish any information about their activities and virtually never choose to do so. Among professional accountancy practices very few have made public their accounts.

The view in The Corporate Report was in tune with

modern thought, which tends to reject traditional notions of privacy. It is argued that large organisations have so important an impact upon a country's economy that everybody in the country has a right to know what such organisations are doing, and that the information necessary to explain activities fully should be provided in annual reports. There exists a counter-argument, that such information would only serve to satisfy idle curiosity and that the pressures for disclosure placed upon companies and other large entities are becoming intolerable. In time a balance will no doubt be reached between these views but at present the trend is in favour of the attitude typified in the Report.

The theme of disclosure to those with reasonable rights is developed by The Corporate Report in a similar way to that used in the Sandilands Report. The needs of the various types of users of financial accounts are considered in order to clarify the defects in existing accounts. The user groups and their requirements are summarised below.

24.2 User groups and accounting requirements

1. The equity investor group: the group comprises shareholders (or owners) of a business, who have an interest in the profits of the business and who can be presumed to wish to preserve the capital which is invested in the business. The group will therefore need to know how the business has performed in the previous accounting periods and what is likely to happen in the future. In order that they can appraise the value of their investment, the business must provide a balance sheet capable of showing such a valuation. In addition, equity investors need to know whether or not the business can meet its future commitments from existing resources and whether they will be called upon to provide additional capital.

2. The loan creditor group: this group comprises all those who have lent a fixed sum to a business and who are entitled to repayment, with or without interest, at some later date. The group need to know whether the business can repay the debts at the due time, whether there is any danger of the business defaulting on the debt and repaying only part or none of it, and whether the business will earn sufficient profits to pay interest due in the future.

3. Employees: a comparatively recent addition to the list of those entitled to request information about the activities of a business is the group comprising its existing, past and potential employees. It is now widely accepted that employees have a right to know of plans that may affect their pay, employment and working conditions, and that employees have a legitimate interest in the financial health of their employers. Many large limited companies have begun to issue special reports to their employees which contain in simplified form the information available in the published accounts. Frequently these employee reports are easier to read, more striking in appearance and more informative than the standard accounts issued to shareholders.

4. The analyst adviser group: investment analysts, merchant bankers, bank managers and other professional advisers make use of financial accounts to advise business managers or other interested parties. Financial accounts will be required before any assessment of a business can be carried out and are a major source of information about a business to outsiders.

5. The business contact group: prospective creditors or customers of a business may need to know more about it before proceeding and competitors will usually find the financial statistics and ratios of great interest. One of the principle reasons for the legal requirement that limited companies should deposit their accounts with the Registrar of Companies was the realisation that traders would be reluctant to deal with a limited company unless they had some assurance that the company could meet its obligations.

6. The Government: the state has two areas of interest in published financial accounts. It needs information on particular businesses or industries where it may feel impelled in the national interest to give economic assistance or to intervene with power to restructure or nationalise; and statistics are needed from all forms of enterprise to assist in the formulation of economic policy. The Companies Act 1967 contained provisions which were designed to assist in the collection of statistics which the Government deemed necessary, *e.g.* the disclosure of export turnover. Future Companies Acts may call for still wider disclosure, although it is possible that companies will be able to issue certain information to the Government alone, rather than publishing it in a report which would be issued to the public.

7. The public: the traditional justification for the right of the public to see company reports—the privilege of limited liability—was discussed in Chapter 3. The modern justification, based on the economic power and influence of business organisations has been mentioned in this chapter. Although the public appear to have an indisputable interest in the activities of business organisations, it is not clear what sort of information would be useful, since unlike all the other groups the public has no specific interest; rather, its concern is a general one with anything that might affect it. It is reasonable to assume that if accounts can meet the requirements of the other groups of users the public will also be satisfied.

24.3 The modern critique of financial accounts

Using the requirements of the various user groups as the point of reference, it is easy to see that existing financial accounts can only partially satisfy these requirements. They summarise past performance and the present financial state, leaving the reader to draw his own conclusions about the future. Information about money transactions is the only kind of information made available, apart from certain specific requirements of the Companies Acts concerning number of employees, activities *etc*. It is true that a number of leading companies provide far more information about their activities, products and prospects in published reports than the legal minimum requires. However, there is no accepted practice for the provision of additional information and hence no consistency of disclosure. The majority of companies provide only the minimum, and of course, unincorporated businesses need provide no published information at all. Much of the proposals for reform are directed at these last groups.

The criticism of present-day practices can be most easily thought of as having two main lines:

(*a*) Dissatisfaction with existing accounting practices;
(*b*) A requirement for entirely new disclosure practices.

The dissatisfaction with existing practices has been the principal driving force for reform in recent years. The work of the ASC and the IASC is designed to meet the criticisms of conventional accounting by improving balance sheets and profit and loss accounts. The most important of these criticisms has probably been that associated with inflation. But after many years of discussion, it has been the achievement of the profession in the 1970s to create the standards and proposed standards which should in time become the basis of accepted methods of accounting for inflation.

Other problems have included the wide choice of accounting policies available to deal with the same transaction, which at one time allowed businessmen and their accountants virtually to fix their own profit in any year; the difficulty of knowing what was to be regarded as true and fair; and the virtual impossibility for outsiders to find out which accounting policies a business was using, which made comparisons between businesses vexing and futile. Accounting standards have begun to narrow the choice of policies, and to insist on disclosure of the policies chosen. Several of the standards apply to all accounts which are meant to be true and fair, and are thus not confined to limited companies.

Although accounting standards are published by the ASC on behalf of the UK accountancy profession, and by the IASC on behalf of the profession in over thirty countries, they should not be regarded as beyond criticism. Much discussion goes on at the exposure draft stage and, even when produced as a standard, the recommended accounting practice is not always found acceptable. It follows that the student should not only understand the reasons behind standards, but must also be aware of the criticisms attaching to each one. The Explanatory Foreword to accounting standards issued by the ASC states that 'Significant departures in financial accounts from applicable standards would be disclosed and explained. . . . Where members (of the various professional bodies) act as auditors or reporting accountants the onus will be on them not only to ensure disclosure of significant departures, but also, to the extent that their concurrence is stated or implied, to justify them'.

In other words, accountants may choose to use a policy other than that in the relevant SSAP, but they must be prepared to justify their choice. Indeed, if they believe that their preferred method gives a true and fair view and that the method required in the SSAP does not, then they *must* use their preferred method and state that they have done so, and why. Accountants who have been taught what the standards contain but not why, and who do not understand the basic theory of accounting will be unable to decide whether or not the policy in a standard is suitable for a particular case, and even if they have an intuitive feeling that the standard is unsuitable, will find it hard to justify their feeling.

The second line of criticism of financial accounting finds existing financial and other information inadequate to meet user needs. Broadly speaking, users can be seen to want information relating to the future of the business—its profits, liquidity and prospects—and disclosure of activities in various specialist fields, such as dealings with employees or the state. The suggestion of The Corporate Report was that six additional statements be included with existing financial accounts. These statements are:

1. A statement of value added, showing how the benefits are shared between employees, the providers of capital, the state and reinvestment;
2. An employment report, showing the size and make-up of the work-force, the work contribution of employees and the benefits earned by them;
3. A statement of money exchanges with government;
4. A statement of the transactions in foreign currency;
5. A statement of future prospects, showing the ability of the reporting entity to fulfil its obligations;
6. A statement of corporate objectives, revealing the priority given by management to competing demands.

The first point to be emphasised is that the working party decided that the correct response to criticisms of inadequate disclosure was greater disclosure. This was not the only solution possible. An alternative is to allow representatives of user groups access to detailed information, by way of reassurance that their own interests are looked after, without publishing that information. The principle has already been established in the field of auditing where the auditors are given full access to the books of their client company on the understanding that they will not disclose information to shareholders (except in very special circumstances). However, it is now felt that it is the *available* information which is inadequate, and that only the disclosure of more information would suffice.

The statements provide an important contrast to traditional accounts. They are not specifically geared to shareholders but take a broader view of the business. Three of the six statements are non-quantitative, that is, they do not involve figures but require written information. The general emphasis is on present and future, rather than past and present.

The value-added statement is a representation of the profit and loss account in which the cost of materials (and other direct expenses) acquired from outside the business is deducted from turnover, to show the net proceeds retained for the benefit of those working in or financing the business— the value added by the business to the raw materials. The first half of the Source and Use of Funds statement of Courtaulds Limited on page 301 is a good example of a value-added statement. This form of statement is of use to employees and to analysts, the latter because it is a useful measure of productivity and efficiency.

Of greater interest to the work-force and others concerned with the business's ability to operate successfully into the future is the *employment report*. This should contain such information as pay rates, employment prospects, safety records, training programmes, the effect of stoppages, disputes *etc*.

The *statement of money exchanges with government*, which includes taxes of all kinds, rates grants and levies, will emphasise the interdependence of business and state and may provide helpful information to government advisers although its uses are perhaps less obvious than the other statements.

The *statement of transactions in foreign currency* will show the extent to which an entity contributes to the national balance of payments, and how vulnerable it is to changes in exchange rates or developments overseas.

The *statement of future prospects* is designed to be the first step in the sequence which will result in user groups obtaining what they really want—detailed information about the future. At present forecasting techniques rarely allow businesses to do more than make vague estimates. In any case there are potential legal snags if forecasts are made and acted upon by shareholders or others who then incur financial losses because the future results differ from the forecasts. Directors are understandably reluctant to expose themselves to possible legal actions alleging fraud or negligence and auditors will refuse to have anything to do with forecasts, other than check that the workings are consistent and correctly computed.

Recognising these problems, The Corporate Report suggests that the statement be confined to estimates of profits, employment and investment, together with explanations (if necessary) of why the previous years' forecasts differed from the outcome. By requiring a *statement of corporate objectives* it will be possible to see whether management has achieved what it intended and whether it is now planning to do so. Shareholders will thus be provided with a means of evaluating the performance of management, in addition to the achieved profits. In practice it is likely that these two statements will be public relations exercises in which management will try to say as little as possible. Unless and until forecasting techniques improve, it would be optimistic to expect anything else.

24.4 Extensions to financial accounting

The proposal for an employment report, a statement of future prospects and a statement of corporate objectives widens the scope of traditional accounting. To complete the overall review of financial accounting in this chapter, two further suggestions of The Corporate Report are considered. They concern social accounting and human assets accounting. These encompass ideas which were developed in the 1960s and 1970s, mostly in the USA, and which seek to broaden accounting and enable it to report on all of the activities of an enterprise and not just on the monetary transactions. The suggestion of The Corporate Report was that research into these areas was desirable and, because understanding of the concepts involved is still limited, that any disclosure in published accounts relating to either of the areas be entirely at the discretion of the management of the reporting entity.

Social accounting concerns the relations between an individual enterprise and society. Entities use the resources of society: labour, land, raw materials, social capital such as roads and harbours; they pay taxes for their share of what is used, and may also either use or provide resources which are not the subject of economic transactions. For example, factories may pollute their local environment with smoke or waste products, which legislation cannot always prevent. Social accounting would require that the annual reports of enterprises should include information showing their impact on society, its amenities and environment. The expenditure incurred in complying with social legislation such as anti-pollution laws would be stated, together with voluntary expenditure in these fields.

The major drawback to social accounting is that no measurement procedures exist for appraising the 'impact of an enterprise on society'. Many of the arguments in favour of the idea were developed during the recent period of increased public concern about the environment, but it is unclear what the information would be used for.

There is a tendency in public thought to confuse dealing with a problem with obtaining information about it. Merely knowing what an enterprise is doing will not of itself solve the problem, although it may be a necessary step before action can be taken. It is reasonable for accountants to ask how social accounting will be used before devising the new techniques which will be needed to bring it about.

Human asset accounting is perhaps more advanced than social accounting, in that measurement techniques have been developed and applied by certain enterprises. The concept views the labour of an enterprise as an asset, as useful to it as plant or cash. The value of the human assets change from year to year as the quality of the work-force changes, and if that value can be measured then information relevant to the future prospects of the enterprise may be deduced. One way of valuing the human assets employed in an enterprise is to multiply the remuneration of each employee by a given factor, but the method is not used in this country and considerably more research will be required before financial accounting can embrace human assets measurement.

An additional problem with the concept is that employees and their unions may resent being valued as if they were 'owned' by their employer, although management should be able to overcome such resistance by a programme of education.

In addition The Corporate Report criticised the historical cost convention (using an argument virtually identical to that employed in the Sandilands Report). Historic cost is rejected as giving misleading information and a form of current value accounting is recommended showing the true value of assets and a fairer measure of performance. These proposals are in substance those of SSAP 16.

It is unfortunate that the Sandilands Report was published so soon after The Corporate Report for the interest that had been aroused by publication of the latter was at once switched away toward inflation accounting. However, The Corporate Report is a discussion paper intended to influence longer-term thinking and to stimulate research, rather than to be implemented rapidly. The response has been strongly favourable, and a Department of Trade paper[1] has endorsed part of its findings.

Conclusion

What is thought of as 'financial' accounting has become a broader discipline within the last thirty years. Much of the content of a typical set of company accounts today is outside the scope of traditional accounting which considered a profit and loss account and balance sheet, sent to the shareholders only, as the only output necessary. Today much of the director's report and some of the notes to the accounts

[1] See *Accountancy* August 1976.

provide important information which is not directly related to the accounts. The recommendations of The Corporate Report continue this trend. Purely financial information is only a part of the full 'information package' which limited companies are increasingly presenting, and which may come to be produced by other forms of enterprise in the future. However, the heart of a financial report will remain the profit and loss account and balance sheet, and the primary task of financial accountants will continue to be to produce and present the figures which will provide a true and fair view.

Appendix

Appendix:

Recent Examination Questions

1. (Chapters 1–4)

'The valuation of assets is a subjective process and the measurement of profit can therefore be no more than approximate.' Discuss this statement and in particular explain why the valuation of assets affects the measurement of profit.

Or

'Examine the problems which the calculation of periodic profit present for the accountant. What assumptions are made by the accountant in order to help achieve this objective?'

(*Institute of Chartered Secretaries and Administrators Financial Accounting II* [*company*], *May 1977*)

2. (Chapters 1–5)

Roy Brockway carries on business as a farmer, and during the current year produced on his farm 12,000 bushels of rye, 8,000 bushels of barley and 6,000 bushels of beans. The total expenses incurred in operating the farm during the year were £28,570 including depreciation of buildings and equipment.

During the year Brockway sold three-quarters of each of his crops at the following prices Rye £1·10 per bushel, Barley £2 per bushel, Beans £3 per bushel. He estimates that the cost of selling and delivering the crops, which is included in his operating expenses amounted to 20 pence per bushel. At the end of the current year the market price per bushel of each of the commodities was as follows: Rye £1·15 per bushel; Barley £1·80 per bushel and Beans £3·20 per bushel.

You are required to:

1. Prepare an income statement for Brockway in the current year, and explain the concept of realisation employed in your measurement of income, and in particular the basis you used in assigning a valuation to the commodities on hand at the end of the year.

2. What is the essential difference between the problem of measuring income for Brockway, and measuring income for a manufacturer of farm machinery.

(*Certified Diploma in Accounting and Finance, Accounting and Taxation, December 1976*)

3. (Chapter 5)

A manufacturing company has a turnover of £6 million and pre-tax trading profits of £1 million before taking account of the following items:

1. Costs of £750,000 incurred in terminating production at one of the company's factories.
2. Provision for an abnormally large bad debt of £500,000 arising on a trading contract.
3. Currency exchange surplus amounting to £7,500 arising on remittances from an overseas depot.
4. Profits of £150,000 on sale of plant and machinery written off in a previous year when production of the particular product ceased.
5. An extra £100,000 contribution by the company to the employees pension fund.

You are required to indicate whether these items should be treated as exceptional, extraordinary or normal trading transactions within the constraints of SSAP 6, giving your reasons.

(*Institute of Chartered Accountants in England and Wales, Professional Examination 2, July 1977—Financial Accounting 2*)

4. (Chapter 7)

Wellbuild Ltd commenced business on the 1 June 1975 as building contractors. The following details relate to the three uncompleted contracts in the company's books on 31 May 1976.

Contact name:	Rosebank £	Millfield £	St. George £
Cost of work to 31 May 1976, all certified (*see note*)	30,470	27,280	13,640
Value of work to 31 May 1976 as certified by contractees' architects	38,500	22,000	14,300
Progress payments invoiced to 31 May 1976	33,000	17,600	11,000
Progress payments received by 31 May 1976	27,500	17,600	11,000
Estimate of:			
Final cost including future costs of rectification and guarantee work	33,000	38,500	66,000
Final contract price	41,800	30,800	88,000

Note: The cost of work to 31 May 1976 has been determined after crediting unused materials and the written down value of Plant in use,

You are required:

(a) To prepare a statement for the board of directors showing your calculations for each contract of the valuation of work in progress at 31 May 1976 and of the profit (loss) included therein.
(b) To show as an extract therefrom, the information which should appear in the Balance Sheet for work in progress.

(*Association of Certified Accountants, Professional Examination 2, Section 2, June 1976—Accounting 4*)

5. (Chapter 8)

The Wheelbase Company is a road haulage company with a group of light vehicles. From a survey carried out during the last four years, the following figures are typical of the appraised value and average miles driven per year per vehicle.

Year	Miles Driven	Appraised Value (% of cost)
1	15,000	70
2	40,000	50
3	30,000	35
4	15,000	24

On the basis of this information prepare a depreciation schedule showing the annual depreciation charge for each year during the four year service life of a vehicle as calculated by the straight line method, and also by the usage method.

Assume that the vehicle cost £10,000 and has an expected scrap value of £2,400 and discuss the effect of the differing results on the annual net income figure.

(*Certified Diploma in Accounting and Finance, June 1977—Accounting and Taxation*)

6. (Chapter 8)

The board of directors of Chambers Ltd, believes that it is good accounting practice when determining the results of operations to provide for depreciation. Because depreciation does not affect the cash position of the company, the board believes that it can be disregarded in determining the amount of net income available for dividend distribution.

You are required to discuss what conditions could develop if the company follows this policy.

(*Certified Diploma in Accounting and Finance, December 1976—Accounting and Taxation*)

7. (Chapter 9)

You are required to define and discuss the nature of goodwill from an accounting point of view.

(*Association of Certified Accountants, Professional Examination Section 2, December 1976—Accounting 4*)

8. (Chapter 10)

(*a*) The difference between book income and taxable income is a result of the different manner in which certain items are treated for tax purposes. SSAP 11 defines these differences for us.

In relation to accounting for deferred taxation, explain in your own words the following terms:

   (i) Permanent differences
   (ii) Timing differences
   (iii) Originating timing differences
   (iv) Reversing timing differences

(*b*) Give three examples of items which give rise to permanent differences.
(*c*) Give three examples of items which give rise to timing differences.
(*d*) A company commenced trading on 1 April 1974. The tax computation for the year to 31 March 1975 was as follows:

	£
Trading profit, before tax	50,000
Add: UK entertainment (absolute disallowable)	5,000
Depreciation	15,000
Increase in general bad debt reserve	10,000
	80,000
Less: Capital allowances	(40,000)
Profit chargeable to corporation tax	£40,000

You are required to:
  (i) Compute the tax charge for the year (corporation tax rate 52%).

(ii) Show how this would be presented in the company's financial statements.

(iii) If the tax rate for the financial year 1975 (*i.e.* 1 April 1975 to 31 March 1976) is reduced to 50%, what adjustments, if any, would be made to the tax charge, assuming the liability method is used?

(*Association of Certified Accountants, Professional Examination Section 1, June 1976—Accounting 3*)

9. (Chapter 12)

What are the shortcomings of the historical cost convention in the preparation of accounts in inflationary times? How do the proposals contained in the Accounting Standard Committee's Exposure Draft '*Current Cost Accounting*' seek to remedy these defects?

(*Certified Diploma in Accounting and Finance, June 1977—Accounting and Taxation*)

10. (Chapters 12–13)

Professor R. S. Gynther in his book *Accounting for Price-Level Changes Theory and Practice* writes:

'It seems that those who look upon a company from outside its four walls will want its profit determined with the aid of one general index . . . their prime interest is that of the shareholders . . . it seems too that those who look upon a company as from within will want its profit determined with the aid of specific indexes (or specific prices, if available) . . . their prime interest is that of the company itself.'

You are required to comment on this quotation within a discussion of the relative cases for the use of Current Purchasing Power accounting (as advocated in provisional SSAP 7) and the use of current cost accounting, for the adjustment of company accounts to reflect the impact of inflation.

(*Association of Certified Accountants, Professional Examination Section 2, June 1976—Accounting 4*)

11. (Chapters 7, 14)

Bright Ltd, Clear Ltd and Dawn Ltd each had in stock 750 units on 1 April 1975. Bright and Clear valued their stocks on a LIFO basis at £2 per unit. Dawn valued its stocks on a FIFO basis at £5 per unit, the

price current in the period January to March 1975. During the year to
31 March 1976 purchases and sales are made as follows:

		30 June	Quarter to 30 Sept.	31 Dec.	31 Mar.
Bright					
purchases	quantity (q)	1,000	1,000	1,000	1,000
	price per unit (p)	£5	£6	£7	£8
sales	q	1,000	1,000	1,000	1,000
	p	£6	£7	£9	£10
Clear					
purchases	q	500	750	1,250	1,000
	p	£5	£6	£7	£8
sales	q	1,000	1,000	1,000	1,000
	p	£6	£7	£9	£10
Dawn					
purchases	q	500	1,000	1,500	1,000
	p	£5	£6	£7	£8
sales	q	1,000	1,000	1,000	1,000
	p	£6	£7	£9	£10

You are required to:

(a) (i) prepare trading accounts for Bright, Clear and Dawn for the year
ended 31 March 1976 using their customary basis of valuation,

(ii) calculate the effect of using a current cost basis,

(iii) discuss the advantages and disadvantages of each basis, and

(b) Discuss briefly two accounting problems that have arisen in connection with the implementation of SSAP 9 'Stocks and work in
progress'.

(*Institute of Chartered Accountants in England and Wales, Professional
Examination 2, December 1976—Financial Accounting 2*)

12. (Chapter 14)

The Sandilands Report recommended a system of accounting for
inflation entitled 'Current Cost Accounting'.

(a) In its accounts for the current financial year CCA Ltd had opening
stock valued at £2,500 and closing stock valued at £3,520. Purchases
and sales were £20,000 and £40,000 respectively. Appropriate stock
index numbers were 100 at the beginning of the year and 110 at the
end of the year. The average index for the year was 105.

You are required to state:

(i) following current cost accounting principles, the gross profit
both on the historic cost and the current cost basis; and

(ii) what double-entry adjustment is recommended in the historic
revenue account to adjust it to current cost.

(b) The following entry appeared in the company's balance sheet at the end of the current financial year ended 31 March 1977 for furniture and fittings.

Historic Cost	Accumulated Depreciation Based on Historic Cost	Net Book Value
£1,040	£680	£360

The furniture and fittings were acquired:

During year ended March 1973 at a cost of £600	Accumulated depreciation to 31 March 1977	£480
During year ended March 1976 at a cost of £440	Accumulated depreciation to 31 March 1977	£200

Depreciation charged in the current year profit and loss account on furniture and fittings was £280 (£180 on 1973 purchases and £100 on 1976 purchases).

Relevant specific price indexes were 150 for 1973, 200 for 1976 and 225 at 31 March 1977. You are required:

(i) To calculate and state the depreciation charge for furniture and fittings based on current cost accounting principles, to be entered in the 1977 profit and loss account;

(ii) To show the entry for the asset, furniture and fittings in the current cost accounting balance sheet as at 31 March 1977; and

(iii) To state the amount credited to Fixed assets (furniture and fittings) revaluation reserve in that balance sheet.

(*Association of Certified Accountants, Professional Examination Section 2, June 1977—Accounting 4*)

13. (Chapter 16)

The following is the summary of the balance sheet capitals of Roberts Ltd, Grove Ltd, and Dillwyn Ltd, as at 30 September 1976:

	Roberts Ltd £	Grove Ltd £	Dillwyn Ltd £
Issued share capital in ordinary shares of £1 each, fully paid	40,000	32,000	20,000
Profit and loss account	104,700	40,020	51,880
	£144,700	£72,020	£71,880

Roberts Ltd purchased 20,000 shares in Grove Ltd on 30 September 1967, at a cost of £32,000; Grove Ltd profit and loss account had a credit balance of £29,312 at that time.

Grove Ltd purchased 18,000 shares in Dillwyn Ltd on 31 March 1968 at a cost of £30,000 when there was a debit balance of £8,000 on the latter's profit and loss account.

There has been no variation in the share capitals of the subsidiaries since these acquisitions.

You are required to prepare a summary consolidated balance sheet of the group as at 30 September 1976, inserting therein a balancing figure representing the net assets. As a note to the consolidated balance sheet, show a reconciliation of this figure of group net assets with the net assets of the individual companies.

(*Association of Certified Accountants, Professional Examination Section 2, December 1976—Accounting 4*)

14. (Chapter 16)

Summarised balance sheets of Frank Ltd, George Ltd and Harry Ltd at 31 December 1975 are shown below.

	Frank Ltd £	George Ltd £	Harry Ltd £
Issued share capital (£1 ordinary shares)	50,000	100,000	15,000
Revenue reserves	73,200	46,000	12,600
Debentures	50,000	80,000	15,000
Current liabilities	96,800	64,000	27,400
	£270,000	£290,000	£70,000
75,000 shares in George Ltd at cost	130,000	—	—
Sundry assets	140,000	290,000	70,000
	£270,000	£290,000	£70,000

Frank Ltd purchased its shares in George Ltd on 31 December 1973 when the revenue reserves of George Ltd were £60,000. Since that time George Ltd has not declared any dividends.

On 31 December, 1975 the following transactions took place:

(*a*) Frank Ltd acquired two-thirds of the share capital of Harry Ltd by purchasing 10,000 shares in that company at £2 per share. The purchase price was entirely satisfied by the issue of 15,000 new ordinary shares in Frank Ltd to former shareholders in Harry Ltd.

(*b*) Frank Ltd made a loan of £12,000 to George Ltd.

(*c*) George Ltd acquired all the debentures of Harry Ltd for £15,000 cash from the existing debenture holders.

None of the three transactions above have yet been entered in the accounts of the companies concerned.

Included in the current assets of George Ltd at 31 December, 1975 were goods which were purchased from Frank Ltd for £6,300. These goods had cost Frank Ltd £4,200.

Required:
The consolidated balance sheet of the group at 31 December 1975.

(*Institute of Bankers, Banking Diploma Examination Part 2, September 1976—Accountancy*)

15. (Chapter 16)

Greater Combinations Ltd, and its subsidiary Cooperative Ltd, have produced the following summarised balance sheets as on 30 November 1975 and profit and loss accounts for the year ended on that date.

Summarised Balance Sheets as on 30 November 1975

	Greater Combinations	Cooperative
	£'000	£'000
Issued share capital ordinary shares of £1	500	100
Reserves and unappropriated profits	800	260
Deferred taxation	100	90
	1,400	450
Fixed assets	600	100
Shares in subsidiary 75,000 shares of £1	25	—
Patents and trade marks	75	20
Net current assets	700	330
	1,400	450

Summarised Profit and Loss Accounts for year ended 30 November 1975

	Greater Combinations	Cooperative
	£'000	£'000
Trading profit	300	80
Taxation at 55%	165	44
	135	36
Proposed dividend	75	20
Retained	60	16

You have ascertained that:

1. The entire issued share capital of Cooperative Ltd was acquired on 1 August 1966 at £1 per share. At this date total reserves and unappropriated profits of Cooperative Ltd were equivalent to £0·80

per share. There have not been any changes in the issued share capital since that date.

2. On 31 May 1975 25,000 shares of Cooperative Ltd were sold at £3 per share.

3. The sale had been recorded in the books of Greater Combinations Ltd by crediting the receipt against the cost of purchase.

4. Trading and profit of Cooperative Ltd arise evenly throughout the year.

5. Greater Combinations Ltd sells to Cooperative Ltd on the normal trade terms of cost plus 25%, goods to the value of £100,000 per month. Stock held by Cooperative Ltd at the end of the year represents one month's purchases.

6. Both companies maintain the deferred taxation account under the deferral method.

7. Greater Combinations Ltd does not take credit in its own accounts for dividends until they have been received.

You are required to:

(a) Prepare a consolidated balance sheet at 30 November 1975 which complies with the best current practice in so far as the information provided will allow,

(b) Prepare a detailed analysis of the movements in the group 'reserves and unappropriated profits', and

(c) Write a *brief* note with numerical illustration comparing the alternatives available to reflect in the group accounts the trading between parent and subsidiary.

(*The Institute of Chartered Accountants in England and Wales, Professional Examination II, December 1975—Financial Accounting 2*)

16. (Chapters 17, 18)

On 1 February 1976 Abstract Ltd purchased 150,000 ordinary shares and 50,000 preference shares in Bran Ltd, and on 1 March 1976 purchased 45,000 ordinary shares in Corn Ltd. All three companies make up their accounts to 30 June in each year. The following figures were extracted from the companies' records for the year ended 30 June 1976:

	Abstract Ltd £	Bran Ltd £	Corn Ltd £
Sales	900,000	850,000	500,000
Purchases	497,990	482,580	221,100
Selling expenses	45,000	67,500	45,000
Overhead expenses	115,000	52,500	65,000
Interim dividends paid 1 January 1976 on ordinary shares	75,000	40,000	
on preference shares		4,500	
Stocks on hand as on 30 June 1975	49,650	100,280	34,500

Issued share capital			
Ordinary shares of £1 each	300,000	200,000	100,000
9% Preference shares of £1 each		100,000	
Revenue reserves as on 30 June 1975			
after deducting all dividends to			
that date	26,750	32,000	48,000

You also obtain the following additional information:

1. Profits of Bran Ltd and Corn Ltd accrued evenly throughout the year.
2. Stocks on hand at 30 June 1976 were: Abstract Ltd £87,640; Bran Ltd £92,860; and Corn Ltd £45,600.
3. Provision for corporation tax based on the profits for the year at 52% is to be made as follows:

Abstract Ltd	£150,000
Bran Ltd	£108,000
Corn Ltd	£86,400

4. Abstract Ltd proposes to pay a final dividend on ordinary shares of 25%; Bran Ltd a half-year's dividend on the preference shares and a final dividend on ordinary shares of 30%; and Corn Ltd a dividend on ordinary shares of 60%.

You are required to prepare a consolidated profit and loss account of Abstract Ltd and its subsidiary company, incorporating the results of its associated company for the year ended 30 June 1976, together with your consolidation schedules.

(The Institute of Chartered Accountants in England and Wales, Professional Examination I, November 1976—Financial Accounting I)

17. (Chapters 19–20)

Jay Walker Ltd was formed with an authorised capital of £1 million, divided into 800,000 ordinary shares of £1 each and 200,000 10% cumulative preference shares of £1 each. Issues of these shares have been made as follows:

Ordinary	180,000 at par
	320,000 at a premium of 25%
Preference	200,000 at par

On 31 March 1976, the ledger showed the remaining balances as:

	£'000
General Reserve	250
Dividend equalisation reserve	100
Goodwill	60
Freehold land and buildings at cost	625
Leasehold property at cost	100
Provision for amortisation—leasehold property	40
Profit and loss account—1 April 1975	150
Plant and machinery at cost	250

Provision for depreciation—plant and machinery	50
Fixtures and fittings at cost	120
Provision for depreciation—fixtures and fittings	30
Motor vehicles at cost	185
Provisions for depreciation—motor vehicles	65
10% debentures 1990/1995 secured on the freehold property	100
Creditors—trade	170
—expense	25
Bank overdraft	15
Current taxation	50
Gross profit on trading	1,150
Stock in trade (FIFO cost)	510
Debtors	499
Provision for doubtful debts	25
Cash	5
Administration expenses	250
Selling and distribution expenses	225
Financial, legal and professional expenses	26
Dividends paid—Ordinary	50
—Preference	20
Investments—quoted at cost	50
—unquoted at cost	25
Investment income—quoted	10
—unquoted	5
Pensions—ex Directors	15

Additional information
1. The following expenses have been included in

	£
(*a*) Gross profit for the year:	
Production director's salary	10,000
Production director's expenses	1,500
Factory manager's salary	5,000
Depreciation—factory plant	25,000
(*b*) Administration expenses:	
Chairman's salary	10,000
Managing director's salary	15,000
Finance director's salary	12,500
Other executive directors' salaries:	
1 at £2,000	2,000
1 at £3,500	3,500
3 at £4,000	12,000
Motor running expense	5,000
Amortisation—leasehold property	4,000
Depreciation—fixtures and fittings	6,000
Depreciation—motor vehicles	5,000

(c) Selling and distribution expenses:	£
Sales director's salary	10,000
Sales commissions	5,500
Provision for doubtful debts	5,000
Advertising expenses	25,000
Depreciation—motor vehicles	30,000
(d) Financial, legal and professional expenses:	
Debenture interest	10,000
Bank interest	1,000
Bank charges	100
Legal expenses (conveyancing of freehold property)	5,000
Surveyor's expenses (*re* freehold property purchased)	1,000
Auditors' fees	5,000
Auditors' expenses	1,000
Tax consultant's fees	2,900

2. Directors' fees for the year are agreed at £2,000.
3. The turnover for the year amounted to £4.5 million.
4. The freehold property including that purchased was revalued during the year by a firm of valuers and the directors have agreed that the new valuation of £851,000 should be reflected in the books.
5. The directors resolve to transfer £274,000 to General Reserve and £100,000 to Dividend Equalisation Reserve, and recommend that a final dividend of 10% be paid on the ordinary share capital, making 20% for the year.
6. Corporation tax at the rate of 45% on the profits of the year has been estimated at £250,000.
7. The market price of the quoted investments on 31 March 1976 was £48,000, and the directors have placed a valuation on the unquoted investments of £30,000.
8. There are contingent liabilities amounting to £5,000, in respect of discounted bills of exchange, and the company has entered into contracts for future capital expenditure amounting to £250,000.
9. The following fixed assets were purchased during the year:

Freehold land and buildings at cost	£100,000
Plant and machinery at cost	£50,000
Motor vehicles at cost	£25,000

10. There were no sales or retirals of fixed assets during the year.

Required:

From the information above, prepare, in a manner conforming with the requirements of the Companies Acts, 1948 and 1967,

(a) The Profit and loss Account of Jay Walker Ltd for the year ended 31 March 1976;

(b) A balance sheet as of that date.

(Association of Certified Accountants, Professional Examination Section 1, June 1976—Accounting 3)

18. (Chapters 19–20)

Hutch Ltd, a trading company, has an authorised share capital of £2,000,000 divided into 1,000,000 6% (net) non-redeemable preference shares of £1 each and 2,000,000 ordinary shares of 50p each.

A trial balance extracted from the books of the company as on 31 December 1976 showed the following position:

	£'000	£'000
Preference share capital		1,000
Ordinary share capital (fully paid)		850
Profit and loss account as on 31 December 1975		126
Corporation tax		198
Creditors		642
Debtors	2,450	
Stock on hand as on 31 December 1976	860	
Freehold land and buildings	1,540	
Fixtures and fittings	110	
Trading profit for year (from turnover of £27·5m)		2,725
Preference dividends paid	60	
Interim ordinary dividend paid	85	
Advance corporation tax	78	
Bank balance	358	
	5,541	5,541

The following information is also relevant:

1. The trading profit has been arrived at after charging:

   (i) directors' salaries of £130,000 (including chairman £45,000);
   (ii) £50,000 deferred advertising costs from 1975. The directors have decided to alter the former policy of writing off advertising costs on new lines over a period of years and now charge the full amount in the year in which it is incurred;
   (iii) audit fees of £29,000;
   (iv) £100,000 goodwill written off, being an amount paid many years ago for a marketing licence no longer used.

2. There have been no changes during the year in fixtures and fittings, which had originally cost £260,000. Freehold land and buildings had cost £1,540,000, including an extension built in the year at a cost of £290,000.

3. Provisions are to be made for:

   (i) doubtful debts at 2% of outstanding debts;
   (ii) depreciation on fixtures and fittings at 20% on cost;
   (iii) corporation tax, on the profit for the year, of £1,450,000, based on a rate of 52% and due 1 January 1978;

(iv) a proposal by the directors to pay a final ordinary dividend of 10p per share.

You are required to prepare a balance sheet as on 31 December 1976 and a profit and loss account for the year ended on that date, together with notes thereon, in a form suitable for presentation to members.

Corresponding figures are not required and the information given may be taken as if it included all that is necessary to satisfy the requirements of the Companies Acts 1948 to 1967.

(*The Institute of Chartered Accountants in England and Wales, Professional Examination 1, May 1977—Financial Accounting 1*)

19. (Chapter 20)

SSAP 3 (as revised 1974) sets out a basic definition of 'earnings per share' attributable to a group of companies in which there are minority interests, ordinary and preference shares, and in whose profit and loss account extraordinary items occur.

You are required to:

(*a*) Set out the definition, either as in the SSAP or in your own comparable words.
(*b*) Calculate from the following information for the year ended 31 December 1975:
  1. The basic earnings per share.
  2. The fully diluted earnings per share.

Your calculations must be presented.
The capital of High-Gear Ltd is as follows:
  £500,000 in 7% (formerly 10%) preference shares of £1 each.
  £1,000,000 in ordinary shares of 25 pence each.
  £1,250,000 in 8% convertible unsecured loan stock carrying conversion rights into ordinary shares as follows:
    On 31 December 1976—124 shares for each £100 nominal loan stock.
  or On 31 December 1977—118 shares for each £100 nominal loan stock.
  or On 31 December 1978—110 shares for each £100 nominal loan stock.

The profit and loss account for the year ended 31 December 1975 showed:

Profit after all expenses, but before loan interest and Corporation tax—£1,100,000.

Corporation tax is to be taken as 45% of the profits shown in the accounts after all expenses and after loan interest.

(*Association of Certified Accountants, Professional Examination Section 2, June 1976—Accounting 4*)

20. (Chapter 21, 22)

The financial director of Peak Canning Co. Ltd has recently examined the financial statements for 1973 to 1975, and concluded that the present level of sales cannot be continued without an increase in borrowing. He has requested you to make an analysis of the firm's financial position in the light of the industrial averages and to advise him of the firm's strengths and weaknesses.

Peak Canning Co. Ltd
Balance Sheets as at 31 December

	1973		1974		1975
Fixed assets					
Land and buildings		£61,200		£163,200	£153,000
Machinery		188,700		147,900	127,500
Other fixed assets		35,700		10,200	7,600
		285,600		321,300	288,100
Current assets					
Stock	382,500		637,500		1,032,800
Debtors	306,000		346,800		484,500
Cash	76,500		35,700		25,500
		765,000		1,020,000	1,542,800
		£1,050,600		£1,341,300	£1,830,900
Ordinary share capital		459,000		459,000	459,000
Undistributed profits		351,900		438,600	489,600
		810,900		897,600	948,600
Long-term loan (mortgage)		56,100		51,000	45,900
Current liabilities					
Accruals	61,200		71,400		96,900
Creditors	122,400		193,800		382,500
Bank overdraft	—		127,500		357,000
		183,600		392,700	836,400
		£1,050,600		£1,341,300	£1,830,900

Income Statement for the year ending 31 December

	1973		1974		1975
Net sales		£3,315,000		£3,442,500	£3,570,000
Less cost of goods sold		,652,000		2,754,000	2,856,000
Gross operating profit		663,000		688,500	714,000
General administrative and selling expenses	255,000		280,500		306,000
Depreciation	102,000		127,500		153,000
Miscellaneous expenses	51,000		107,100		153,000
		408,000		515,100	612,000
Net income before tax		255,000		173,400	102,000
Corporation tax (50%)		127,500		86,700	51,000
Net income after tax		£127,500		£86,700	£51,000

Canning industry ratios (1975)†

Quick ratio	1·0	Total asset turnover*	2·6 ×
Current ratio	2·7	Return on total assets	19·0%
Stock turnover*	7·0 ×	Return on net worth	36·0%
Average collection period	32 days	Debt ratio	50·0%
Fixed asset turnover*	13·0	Profit margin on sales	7·0%

* Based on year end balance sheet figures.
† Industry average ratios have been constant for the past three years.

You are required to:

(a) Calculate the key financial ratios for Peak and compare with the industrial averages;

(b) State the strengths and weaknesses revealed by the ratio analysis.

(*Certified Diploma in Accounting and Finance, December 1976— Accounting and Taxation*)

21. (Chapters 21, 22)

The following is an extract from *Accountancy*, March 1977, p. 50:

'Take profit before tax divided by current liabilities; current assets as a proportion of total liabilities; current liabilities as a proportion of total tangible assets; take into account the no-credit interval; mix them in the right proportions and you can tell whether a company will go bust.'

The no-credit interval is defined as (current assets—current liabilities) ÷ (operating costs excluding depreciation).

The following are the summarised accounts of Go-go Products Ltd and Numerous Inventions Ltd for the years ended 30 April 1977 and 1976.

	Go-go Products		Numerous Inventions	
	1977	*1976*	*1977*	*1976*
	£	*£*	*£*	*£*
Turnover	30,067	25,417	9,734	8,044
Costs: depreciation	311	284	331	195
other	28,356	24,198	8,313	6,571
Profit before tax	1,400	935	1,090	1,278
	30,067	25,417	9,734	8,044
Intangible assets	918	937	—	—
Fixed assets	4,644	5,228	1,950	1,530
Stock	6,243	6,773	986	1,257
Debtors	4,042	4,580	3,234	2,236
Bank	516	184	2,578	1,366
	16,363	17,702	8,748	6,389
Creditors	5,261	5,144	1,297	972
Current taxation	312	379	483	321
Short-term borrowing	2,357	4,447	2,577	1,174
Long-term loans	1,409	1,168	55	38
Capital and reserves	7,024	6,564	4,336	3,884
	16,363	17,702	8,748	6,389

You are required to:

(a) Calculate three of the stated factors for the two companies and two others you consider relevant to their going-concern status;

(b) Compare the two companies stating clearly which of your calculated ratios have moved in an unfavourable direction;

(c) Describe and discuss the limitations of ratio analysis as a predictor of failure.

(*Institute of Chartered Accountants in England and Wales, Professional Examination 2, July 1977—Financial Accounting 2*)

22. (Chapter 23)

The following accounts of a company have been prepared for the year ended 30 September 1976:

Balance sheet	1976		1975	
	£m	£m	£m	£m
Share capital		273·3		266·5
Share premium		71·9		45·6
Reserves		412·3		350·6
Deferred tax		132·9		116·6
Long-term indebtedness		478·8		360·0
		1,369·2		1,139·3
Represented by				
Property, plant and equipment		782·9		695·7
Preproduction expenditure		53·5		40·8
Exploration and development		4·8		10·0
Associated companies		101·8		86·1
Current assets				
Stock	314·6		243·2	
Debtors	247·5		221·0	
Bank	301·2		259·1	
	863·3		723·3	
Deduct current liabilities				
Creditors	261·0		240·0	
Short-term indebtedness	94·8		72·8	
Tax	68·2		93·0	
Dividend	13·1		9·9	
	437·1		416·6	
		426·2		306·7
		1,369·2		1,139·3

Profit and loss account

Sales revenue		1,184·0	
		___	
Operating profit		92·8	
Share of profit of associated companies		6·0	
Interest receivable		26·4	
		___	
		125·2	
Deduct interest payable		37·9	
		___	
Profit before tax		87·3	
Tax on profit for the year			
(incl. £16.3 for deferred tax)		48·7	
		___	
Net profit after tax before			
extraordinary items		38·6	
Extraordinary items		22·3	
		___	
Net profit after tax and			
extraordinary items		60·9	
Dividends paid and proposed			
Preference	0·4		(0·4)
Ordinary			
Interim paid	6·3		(4·1)
Final proposed	6·6		(5·6)
	___		
		13·3	
		___	
Retained			
By company	46·0		
By associates	1·6		
	___		
		47·6	
		═══	

During the year 27,200,000 ordinary shares of 25p each were issued at
a premium of £1 per share under a rights issue made to ordinary shareholders. The expenses of the issue, amounting to £900,000 were charged
against the share premium account.

The investment in associated companies was revalued during the
year, providing a surplus over book value of £14·1 million. There was no
additional investment.

Operating profit is after charging depreciation on property, plant
and equipment of £77·1 million, preproduction expenditure of £8·6
million and exploration and development cost of £22·2 million.

You are required to:

(a) Prepare a statement of source and application of funds for the year
ended 30 September 1976 in a form consistent with best practice as
far as the given information permits;

(b) Briefly discuss the reasons for an accounting standard on this topic.

(*Institute of Chartered Accountants in England and Wales, Professional
Examination 2, December 1976—Financial Accounting 2*)

23. (Chapter 23)

The balance sheet of Plan Ahead Ltd as at 31 March 1976, together with its projected balance sheet as at 31 March 1977, and profit and loss account for the year ending on that date, is as follows:

Plan Ahead Limited
Balance Sheets

	31 March 1976 £'000	£'000	31 March 1977 £'000	£'000
Ordinary share capital in £1 shares fully paid		200		250
Capital reserve—share premium A/c		—		25
Revenue reserves—				
General reserve	30		40	
Profit and loss A/c	40		68	
		70		108
		£270		£383
Represented by:				
Fixed assets				
Freehold premises—cost		60		90
Plant and Machinery at cost *less* depreciation		48		125
		108		215
Current assets				
Stock	140		170	
Debtors	100		120	
Cash	1		2	
	241		292	
Less: Current liabilities				
Trade creditors	40		64	
Accrued expenses	1		2	
Corporation tax	16		26	
Proposed dividends	16		20	
Bank overdraft	6		12	
	79	162	124	168
		£270		£383

Budgeted Profit and Loss A/c (extract) for the year ending 31 March 1977

£'000

Trading profit for the year *after* charging all expenses
including depreciation of plant and machinery (£28,000),
but before taxation   84
Less: corporation tax   26
                                                                  ——
Profit after taxation   58
Add: balance of profit unappropriated last year b/f   40
                                                                  ——
                                                                   98

Appropriations	£'000	
Proposed dividend to ordinary shareholders	20	
Transfer to general reserve	10	
	—	30

Profit unappropriated c/f   £68
                                                                  ===

Note: No disposals of Fixed Assets were anticipated for the year ending
31 March 1977.

You are required to produce as part of the planning information, a
Source and Application of Funds Statement for the year ending 31
March 1977. You should bear in mind the objectives of SSAP 10 and
choose a presentation format which will demonstrate clearly the
manner in which the operations of the business will be financed and the
utilisation of its financial resources. You should highlight the excess
or deficiency of internally generated funds over the disposition thereof
and end your statement with the variation in the company's liquid
resources.

(*Association of Certified Accountants, Professional Examination Section
2, December 1976—Accounting 4*)

24. (Chapter 24)

The following information has been extracted from the annual report of a public quoted company.

	£'000
Dividends to stockholders	59
Depreciation	182
Employees pay, pension and national insurance	816
Exchange gain on net current assets of overseas subsidiaries	29
Extraordinary items, net loss	1
Government corporate taxes, less grants	125
Interest paid on borrowings	73
Materials and services used	1,842
Minority shareholders in subsidiaries	24
Profit retained	112
Profit sharing bonus to employees	17
Royalties received and other trading income	30
Sales	3,129
Share of profits of principal associated companies and investment income	63

You are required to prepare a value-added statement and discuss briefly its purpose.

(*Institute of Chartered Accountants in England and Wales, Professional Examination, 2 July 1977—Financial Accounting 2*)

25. (Chapters 3, 24)

'To businessmen, accountants, and knowledgeable users, balance sheets are worthless, in the sense of conveying useful information.'

State what you regard to be the objectives of balance sheets and discuss the extent to which you agree with the above statement. Examples may be introduced in the discussion where considered appropriate.

(*Association of Certified Accountants, Professional Examination Section 1, June 1976—Accounting 3*)

INDEX

Index

MANAGEMENT ACCOUNTING

Brian Murphy

The role of the management accountant is to present management with the best possible financial information upon which they can base their decisions, and to establish control systems to ensure that the best use is being made of the concern's resources.

This book describes the main systems and techniques which are at present available to the management accountant. Topics covered include historical and standard costing, budgetary control, financial planning and marginal costing. Working examples are included throughout and a number of practical exercises are given in each chapter.

The author is Principal Lecturer in management accounting at Huddersfield Polytechnic.

TEACH YOURSELF BOOKS

MANAGEMENT SCIENCE

DENNIS WHITMORE

A major business objective today is to improve productivity, that is, to make better use of available resources, such as labour, materials and capital. However, the increasing specialisation of modern commerce and industry has meant that the contemporary manager often has to deal with a wide range of specialist functions in order to solve the problems with which he is faced.

This book is a compendium of the techniques available to help the manager both to recognize problems and formulate the most effective way of solving them. These techniques provide a tool kit of possible solutions from which the most appropriate method can be selected.

The fifteen chapters are grouped into two basic divisions, the first covering the fundamental concepts, such as problem solving and the science of control, and the second presenting a detailed analysis of the techniques, such as work study, ergonomics and operational research.

This is a book for all students whose studies include productivity or management sciences and for all personnel in line or function management.

Dennis Whitmore is a consultant in Management Sciences.

TEACH YOURSELF BOOKS

COST ACCOUNTING

A. J. TUBB

The role of costing and cost accounting has become increasingly important in recent years and is now one of the most vital parts of any business.

This book, based on a decade of lecturing to students of the professional accounting bodies, explains and illustrates the basic techniques of cost accounting and, by demonstrating the role of cost accounting in management, sets the whole subject in its proper perspective within the organisation. Throughout, questions taken from the examinations set by the various professional bodies enable the student to test his understanding and his progress.

This book is primarily intended for students of cost accounting at the foundation stage and for those on business and management courses where the study of cost accounting plays a very important part. However, it is also an excellent and comprehensive introduction for all those in any way involved in the development or use of cost accounting systems at work.

A. J. Tubb is Senior Lecturer in Finance and Accounts at Ealing Technical College.

TEACH YOURSELF BOOKS